Sir Ian Botham OBE is a former England Test cricketer and Test team captain whose playing career lasted from 1976 to 1993, and he still holds the record for the highest number of Test wickets taken by any England bowler. Widely known by the nicknames 'Beefy' and 'Guy the Gorilla', Botham was knighted in 2007 and is the author of two autobiographies, most recently *Head On*, as well as *Botham's Book of the Ashes*. He is now a writer and cricket commentator and is regularly involved in charity work.

Dean Wilson is the cricket correspondent for the *Daily Mirror*. He spends his days following the England cricket team around the globe and his nights trying to follow Beefy. He moved into sports journalism first with rugby union at Sky Sports and then with Hayters sports news agency. He covered the Athens Olympics and the British and Irish Lions rugby tour to New Zealand. He lives in London with his wife, Kate.

MY SPORTING
HEROES
BOTHAM

HIS 50 GREATEST FROM BRITAIN AND IRELAND

SIR IAN BOTHAM

MAINSTREAM
PUBLISHING

EDINBURGH AND LONDON

To every young sportsman and woman with a passion
to make sport their life – this is the fun you can have.
It is better than working.

This edition, 2010

First published in Great Britain in 2009 by
MAINSTREAM PUBLISHING COMPANY
(EDINBURGH) LTD
7 Albany Street
Edinburgh EH1 3UG

ISBN 9781845965983

A catalogue record for this book is available
from the British Library

Typeset in Florencesans and Palatino

Printed in Great Britain by
CPI Cox and Wyman, Reading RG1 8EX

CONTENTS

INTRODUCTION

It takes a lot to reach the top in any walk of life and sport is no different. There are all sorts of champions out there in wildly different sports, but the characteristics that go into making a world-beater rarely change from one sport to the next.

Be it the bravery to take on the world's fastest and meanest bowlers or the dedication to get up and train at some ungodly hour six days a week just to row for 2,000 metres once every four years, the qualities are there in most top-class sportsmen. Nearly every person in this book has got the same traits of determination, skill and passion and it has been tough to try and suggest which category best suits some of them when the bare truth is they could fit into any one of the categories. What I have tried to do is suggest which traits I think are stronger in them and of course that is all open to debate.

Throughout my sporting life I have been very lucky to play with and associate with some of the biggest and most successful names in British and Irish sport and as a result have met some remarkable people. Some have impressed me with their deeds on the field alone, whilst others have gone up in my estimation as I've come to know them over a period of time, and so in this selection of my top 50 heroes, both angles have been taken into account.

It is a very personal list and by no means a definitive guide to the sporting successes of Great Britain and Ireland over the past

MY SPORTING HEROES

50 years, but I do hope many of you will agree with some of my selections and if you don't, perhaps it will spark some debate as to who you would rate higher in a given sport.

That is the beauty of sport, where arbitrary success such as winning a game of football might come second to the outrageous skills of a George Best or Paul Gascoigne because sport involves matters of the heart as well as the head.

It has been a real pleasure to think long and hard about which sportsmen or woman would make it into this list and the longer I've deliberated the more proud I am of what our region has given to the sporting world. We have provided so many world champions in so many sports that it would take a set of encyclopaedias just to list them and that is a heritage to celebrate.

Whether you are rugby fan, a cricket fan or a motor sport fan there has been and there will be someone for you to cheer and that will never end thanks to the talented people all around us.

I hope you enjoy reading this book and not just my thoughts on these sporting heroes but also in many cases their own theories on what it took to get them where they are. They are all not too different from each other really, but they are all certainly special in their own right.

Enjoy the book.

SIR ALEX FERGUSON
LEADERSHIP

I have so much admiration for Alex Ferguson. For nearly 25 years he has guided Manchester United from trophy to trophy without stopping for breath – a feat that leaves me a little tired just thinking about it!

His move into management at a young age was a bold statement of intent, but to then work his way to United and survive while commanding the respect that he has done over the years as the manager of the biggest club in the world is remarkable.

He had ability as a player, but it is fair to say he wasn't the greatest footballing talent to play the game. He knocked in his fair share of goals as a striker in the Scottish league for Dunfermline and Rangers amongst others, but when he retired from playing in 1974, his true calling in football was just about to get under way.

He cut his teeth as a manager at East Stirlingshire and then St Mirren, where he had a taste of second-tier success as first division champions in 1977. It was his move to Aberdeen though that caught the attention as he guided them to the Scottish Premier League title in 1980 to end the dominance of Rangers and Celtic. It turned out to be just the first of three league titles as well as four Scottish Cups that he won there, but I can remember the real news being when they triumphed in the European Cup Winners'

MY SPORTING HEROES

Cup and that was when I really noticed who 'Fergie' was and what he was doing. So when he took over at Manchester United in 1986 having shunned one or two other English clubs, I thought this could be a career worth paying attention to, and so it has proved.

For him to have stayed at the helm of that ship in this day and age when demand for instant success has managers moving through clubs quicker than an Andrew Flintoff bouncer is a testament to his skill as a leader and decision maker.

The requirements of the chairmen, the fans and the media in football is intolerable and it often surprises me how anyone can work in such a high-pressure environment when so many chips are stacked against you, but that is the beauty of top-flight sport and it is what gets the blood pumping as a player. Sir Alex Ferguson has still got that blood pumping at this stage in his life and that is great to see.

Occasionally we've talked about just how bizarre the current footballing world is and he is honest enough to acknowledge that if he were starting his Premier League career today at any club other than Manchester United and had the same start as he did back in the mid-'80s he probably wouldn't have lasted. He says it is madness how quickly managers these days are expected to deliver a title-winning team in the blink of an eye when it takes time to do things properly and I agree with him. Yes, he buys in talented players like Dimitar Berbatov and Cristiano Ronaldo, but they are being placed on top of some very sound foundations with an academy, backroom staff and club officials all sharing his ethos for success. It is why the rest of the Premier League clubs will always be chasing Manchester United, because it takes more than money to build success.

Fergie has taken his leadership of the team and the club to an astonishing level and that is what I admire most about him. He sets the standards, the work ethic and as a decision maker is not afraid to make the big calls. Whether you're a player or a manager you have to stand by the decisions you make and time and again Fergie has put the team above all else in letting the likes of Paul Ince, David Beckham and Jaap Stam leave the club when they still had more to give. Those decisions could have backfired, but he stood firm, continued to be successful and as a result retained and increased the amount of respect his players and those in the game have for him.

His office at Carrington, the Manchester United training ground, is built so that he can see every corner of the place and can monitor exactly what is going on, whether it is a session with the strikers in the academy or one with the defenders in the first team. Fergie sees it all, logs it all, and the players know it. He is truly the master of all he surveys in that part of the world and the results show just how good he is at doing just that.

His crowning glory as a manager surely came in 1999 when he collected an incredible three trophies in one season; the fact that he put himself in a position to do the same thing again ten years later tells you everything you need to know about his unquenchable thirst for success. However, to win the European Cup for the first time in his life I know ranks right up there as one of the things he is most proud of, and as an English sports fan, to see a home club pick up that trophy for the first time in 15 years was very satisfying.

I've been lucky enough to share his company a few times and his passion for the game comes out time and again. Football is his life and Manchester United is his heartbeat and without either of them I'm not too sure what he would do. There's time for a few other things like horse racing and a good glass of red wine, but none of them comes close to filling the true focus of his life which is football.

He shows his emotion at times on the sidelines, he gives no quarter to other managers during the 90 minutes and he'll give journalists what for in press conferences and interviews, but when all is said and done he does it because he cares, and when the game is over, usually with three points in his back pocket, then he can unwind and relax, until of course his mind turns to the next game.

Fergie and I went to dinner on the Tuesday night before the Ashes Test at Old Trafford in 2005 and it was about four days before the start of the Premier League season. On the way he had picked up the Manchester evening newspaper to have a look at what they were saying about his team's first game up against

Everton. He looked through the first four pages from the back of the paper and also from the front and couldn't see anything about Manchester United. So when he saw me he said: 'What have your boys done up here!? For the first time I can ever remember there is no football on the front or the back pages and the season is about to start!' I gave him a smile and said, 'After all these years you lot have finally realised that there is only one summer game that matters! Serves you right for starting the season in August.' He just laughed and said: 'Fair point, but it took you long enough to get there!'

He didn't mind though because he loves his sport and he loves sport played at its best, which is certainly what we saw in 2005, and I think he had some genuine respect for what the cricketers had done that summer.

The thing that sets him further apart from most managers is not only the length of time that he has been involved in the game, but his ability to overcome so many seismic changes in football and he has survived them all.

The game has changed hugely since he was a player, but through it all he has managed to adapt and to adjust so that he not only competes at the same high standards but he succeeds. Even on the one issue of the money that is now in the game, he has kept the football at the forefront of everything he does at the club. It doesn't matter how many baby Bentleys the players have in their driveways and it doesn't matter how many film premieres and Christmas lights they get asked to go to or switch on, if their football isn't up to scratch Fergie is not interested and that attitude should be instilled around the country, not just in football clubs.

His motivation for what he does is quite pure really; he is trying to make his club as strong as possible from top to bottom. Whether you're a 15 year old making your way or a 35 year old ready to bow out, Fergie instils the same passion in you and demands the same level of professionalism and that is something to hold dear.

His attention to detail is also a big reason why he is still at the top. About eight years ago he told me to watch out for a lad called Rooney. I said I'd never heard of him, and wanted to know who he played for. He said, 'There's this kid who is at Everton and has the full package. He's strong, yet incredibly skilful and one day he'll play for me.' That was that and I thought nothing of it until three years later when Rooney had taken the Premiership by storm and was a Manchester United player just as Fergie had promised. To have that clear vision of what your side needs and to go out and get it is something Fergie has done for years and for all the players that move through the transfer system each year he has got the knack of picking out some very special ones indeed.

His decision to bring Eric Cantona to Old Trafford must rank as one of the best sporting decisions in history, not only for the success it brought almost immediately but for the tone it set for Fergie's three dynasties. Most are lucky if they get one, but during his time at United he has put together three different teams that have risen to the challenge.

Some people like to paint a picture of Fergie as a tyrant and a bit of a control freak. Examples of him keeping his young lads in line when they might have wandered astray are par for the course with him, but would he have got the best out of Ryan Giggs, Paul Scholes or Ronaldo if he hadn't? Can you imagine what else George Best might have accomplished had Fergie been his boss at the time?

His man-management skills are second to none, and there isn't a footballer that has played under him who hasn't become better for the experience.

It was a testament to him and his leadership of players like Ronaldo that after a summer of will-he-won't-he leave United for Real Madrid that Ronaldo went on to pick up the World Footballer of the Year crown and said: 'It's true that the manager always has an important role to play. The coach was important for me because I learned a lot from him. His experience over so many years is of paramount importance – it's a privilege to have such a great club manager.'

And that could have been said by any footballer to have passed under Fergie's wing.

There are a variety of reasons why the people in this book have made it into my top 50, and for me Sir Alex Ferguson ticks all the boxes. His success is unarguable, his passion and commitment the right thing. The first team is where you're judged but it took a while to get them going.

What I've learnt over the years is that managing changes is the most difficult part of the job. You have to rely on your observation to know when to change. I've had some great players here who have got older and then you have to part with them. Guys like Steve Bruce, Peter Schmeichel and Denis Irwin all got older and that is an unfortunate part of the job, but you have to recognise that and you have to be prepared to make the changes, which I think we've done well over the years. You have to be decisive and maybe a little ruthless in deciding when to let a player go who has been a great servant to you. The longer I've been here the more confident I've been at doing that because I've had some success behind me.

I quite like big characters because they are the sort of people who want success all the time and that never interferes with the playing field. Players with egos have to have them massaged and you've got to be successful to massage them by keeping them at the forefront of the game. They want recognition and acclaim and they want to be talked about. The greatest players want to be told how wonderful they are, so it doesn't bother me one bit and I quite enjoy that. What you can't allow at any point is if that ego disrupts the dressing-room harmony or the team spirit of the players and that is when you have to make a decision about someone. The way you handle players is important and you have to be tough sometimes, but also fair, and if the player can see that then your relationship will work and you'll get the best out of them. In the main I've been very lucky with the players we've had at the club.

European football provides the extra kick I need that gets me going. Don't get me wrong, the league is important because England is built along tribal regional lines and when you take on another team from another area and you've got 20,000 plus fans screaming blue murder at you it is one of life's great challenges, but the extra incentive that comes with a big European night is special. There is nothing like it, especially travelling to some of the great European cities and stadiums. The smell, the build-up and the games are all different and we couldn't do without it now.

MY SPORTING HEROES

Sir Ian is a man I've long admired for his deeds as a cricketer and then as a charity fundraiser. His commitment to Leukaemia Research has been fantastic. It is not easy to commit yourself for a long period to charity work because it can be quite draining having to try and hit all those targets that you go for, but he has continued to do that and persevered with it, which tells you how special he is. I'm an admirer of sports people who've done well in whatever sport it might be and can keep their feet on the ground. Sir Ian is one of those who achieved on the field and remained the same off it.

ALLAN LAMB
BRAVERY

Where do I begin with A.J. Lamb? The maddest little bugger I ever shared a hotel room with, but also one of the finest batsmen I ever played cricket with too. And it was this hint of madness that made him such a tremendous cricketer that England were lucky to have.

Our England careers dovetailed perfectly and I'm glad we got to play together as much as we did, because life with 'Lamby' was always much more fun than without him.

His position in this book does stem a little from how well I got to know him as a bloke as well as a player; however, when I was thinking about the traits needed to be one of the very best sportsmen at the highest level Lamby came to mind for the purest of reasons. His bravery.

Lamby was as brave a batsman as you are ever likely to find. He would stand up to the quickest and most ferocious bowlers the world had to offer, and by world I mean the Caribbean, and he took them head on and triumphed.

His record against the might of the West Indies is what sets him apart from the other players of his generation and it is what I admired most about him as a sportsman. He was the bravest competitor against that bowling attack I had ever seen up close, but allied to that was his ability as a batsman to back up his bravery with talent. Together they made one hell of a cricketer.

Six times out of twenty-two matches he took hundreds off their pace attack when they were the calypso kings of cricket. Six times! I couldn't manage it at all during my career so I know just how tough a task it is to achieve.

Perhaps it is hard to imagine now what Lamby stood up to back in the 1980s and early 1990s when he had the likes of Malcolm Marshall, Joel Garner, Michael Holding, Patrick Patterson, Courtney Walsh, Ian Bishop and an emerging Curtly Ambrose to face up to. Now they just have Fidel Edwards in the raw pace bracket, so multiply him by four and you'll soon see how much hopping about Andrew Strauss and co would have to do. All day every day, from both ends on some of the fastest pitches the game has seen, batsmen from around the world had to stand up to the barrage of West Indian bowling brutality and it broke many a man – literally. I couldn't even begin to count how many broken fingers, jaws and arms the West Indian bowlers have been personally responsible for, but they almost always took a hat full of wickets nevertheless.

There was a rare breed of batsman around that time though who did stand up to the onslaught. Names such as Gooch, Border, Gavaskar and Vengsarkar all scored their fair share of runs against the Windies, but no one took their runs more aggressively and more confrontationally than Lamby. In fact, of the players who played most of their Caribbean cricket against teams captained by Clive Lloyd and Viv Richards, only Gavaskar with 13, scored more hundreds against them than Lamby, and that is a big rap for him.

It doesn't matter what sport you're playing but aggression and attitude count for a lot. From the first kick of a Lions rugby Test match to the last smash in a badminton final you have to be positive. You have to be aggressive and you have to let the opposition know that you won't be pushed over. Whoever shows weakness first will almost always be the one to lose out.

Lamby never showed weakness at the crease.

I also think that Lamby's bravery went beyond the field of play. I thought he made a brave decision coming over from

ALLAN LAMB

South Africa to qualify and represent England knowing full well how sensitive the issues surrounding cricket and South Africa were. Once he arrived, though, he made a total commitment to England that has remained to this day and that speaks volumes for his character as a player, and as a man, something I never doubted from the moment we met.

When he was first picked for England in 1982 there were some murmurings and mutterings about his background as well as question marks over whether he was good enough. Well, on both counts he showed the doubters up for the negative moaners they were.

Both of his parents were born in England anyway, which should end the matter there and then; however, having come to play for Northants and made England his home I think he made his feelings perfectly clear.

Nevertheless, on his first tour in 1982 to Australia a few of us thought we'd better make sure he knew we were on his side. Bob Willis was the captain and together with David Gower and me, took Lamby out for a lunch one afternoon early on during the tour and told him just how we felt about him. We told him that as far as we were concerned he was one of us. We were all really glad to have him in the side because we knew what he was capable of with a bat in his hand and we wanted him to show the Aussies too. From that point on we never mentioned South Africa although I know he found things quite tough having to deal with a lot of abuse from the Australian crowds. As always, though, Lamby stood up to it all and used it to his advantage to push himself to greater heights.

Right from the off though I noticed that Lamby had a very similar constitution to myself, which was a worry, and it is possibly why we ended up rooming together for quite a long time in the England team. In truth no one else wanted to room with me and no one wanted to room with him so we fell into each other's pockets and that is where we stayed for about six years.

He was always great fun to be with and I regard him as one of my best buddies. Being good mates, though, didn't stop him stitching me up on a regular basis. Whenever we left a hotel he used to say to me 'Hey Beef, when we check out let's just split the bill eh, it's too hard trying to work it all out!', and for a long time I used to go along with that because I knew I'd ordered a few drinks and bottles of nice wine on the room so I didn't mind sharing that. So we used to just hand over two credit cards, pay the bill and be on our way.

When I gave the bill a proper look I noticed the huge cost of the phone calls and Lamby used to say, 'It's always expensive ringing back to England, eh Beef!' I agreed but I thought it was faintly ridiculous that the odd call I made back to my wife Kath was so expensive. It was only when we started getting the itemised bills showing exactly who was calling where that I collared the little bugger. Next to my ten calls to Kath were about fifty of his back to South Africa to his missus Lindsay!

We have always enjoyed spending time together but I'm constantly telling him to get rid of the crocodiles he keeps in his pockets. Every time he tries to put his hands in them to get a bit of money out they try and bite them off so he can't quite get in there!

As his career took off with three memorable back-to-back hundreds against the West Indies in 1984, I became quite proud of what he was achieving; however, despite these personal milestones he wasn't exactly over the moon with things. The reason was that with each hundred he took off the Windies attack, either the rest of our batting faltered or their batting took even more runs off our bowlers and the matches usually ended in defeat. Lamby was always a real team player and would put his own personal achievements way down the list behind team success, and as we weren't beating the Windies, all those runs seemed worthless in the end. It wasn't until 1990 and his fifth hundred against them that it actually mattered when England finally beat the West Indians in Kingston 16 years and 29 matches after their last win. I wasn't playing in that match, but when I saw the result, I was beaming with pride, not only at the win but because Lamby had played such a vital role in it.

England then drew the next Test and with Goochie out with a broken hand, Lamby had to step in as captain for the first time. It was a huge honour for him and one that he thoroughly deserved. I know he was incredibly proud to do the job and he celebrated with yet another hundred for England – perfect! Only things had frustratingly reverted back to their old ways. Ton-up for Lamb, defeat for England. A final defeat in Antigua cost the lads the series and Lamby was gutted. Luckily he only had to wait a year before getting a first ever drawn series with the West Indies which was about as good as it got in those days!

Lamby's career will forever be intertwined with the Windies because it was against them that he showed what he was capable of at his very best, but he had some special moments against other sides and was a great servant to Northamptonshire cricket throughout his career too. I can remember during the 1986–87 tour to Australia, where Lamby had suffered some terrible abuse four years before, he put in some displays that showed them what a good player he really was and also what a fine one-day cricketer he was. One-day cricket has always moved with the times and Lamby was always quick to move with them too; whether it was improvised shot making or classical power hitting, he could do it. In Sydney we played Australia in a day/night match and Bruce Reid was bowling the final over when we needed about 17 to win and Lamby was at the crease.

He just stood there and hit the ball this way and that as the over went 2, 4, 6, 2, 4 with Lamby running off the hero of the hour and Australia devastated at defeat.

The next game was down at Adelaide. Lamby goes out to bat and has just taken guard as Bruce Reid is about to bowl, but before he can get to the crease Lamby spots something out of the corner of his eye in the stands and pulls away in a fit of giggles.

Bruce and the other Aussies are not happy at this and give Lamby a mouthful, asking why on earth he isn't ready to face him.

Lamby points up to the stand and tells him to have a look, whereupon he eyes the banner that reads, 'Can Bruce Reid please call Allan Lamb on 24624'. We were all doubled up with laughter, even the Aussie players too.

Lamby and I will be friends till we die; we have been through an awful lot together. I think as a result some of his bravado has rubbed off on me and some of my confidence has rubbed off on him. It is probably what drove us to pursue our case over ball tampering with Imran Khan in 1996, which ended up going against us. Hindsight is a wonderful thing, but yet again Lamby wanted to stand up for what he believed was right and so did I. Another brave decision, but perhaps a little too brave that time.

It is behind us now and instead of fighting court cases we spend more time fishing and enjoying each other's company. There isn't too much that I haven't done on a cricket field at one time or another, but Lamby always has one up on me and it is why he is a sporting hero.

ALLAN LAMB

I always wanted to be the best no matter whom I played against, but I think that the West Indians actually brought out the best in me because they were the greatest side around at that time.

I was more determined to score runs against them than I was against anyone else because they set the mark with which everyone else compared themselves. If you took the wickets of Viv Richards, Gordon Greenidge and Clive Lloyd then it meant something extra and if you could score runs against the likes of Holding, Marshall and Garner you knew you'd done so against the best in the world.

I had a few doubters around during my career who said I couldn't play and I really wanted to prove to them that I could play a little bit, and nothing said that more than runs against the Windies.

I've always been a brave cricketer and I never shirked my responsibility in the face of quick bowling or aggression on the field. I'd like to think I always stood up to be counted for my team.

If you went out to bat scared, you might as well go and play club cricket. If you had that fear factor in you then you were knackered, so there was no way I was going to let them intimidate me.

What the pace attack did was make you concentrate on what you were doing even more. I was always very positive and I worked out early on that the West Indies bowlers didn't like you rotating the strike. They just wanted to pin you down at one end and bowl full overs at you. If you could alternate the strike it really frustrated them and so I made sure we kept being positive.

Beefy has always been a very generous man, but I can assure you I paid my way with him over the years! We've had some great times together as room mates although I should point out that sharing a room with Beefy was like having a room all to myself because he was never there! He was always out doing something different, visiting this vineyard, or catching that fish or watching some other sport – he was always on the go. We're firm friends though and I'll never forget how good he was to me from the moment I joined the team, such a genuine bloke who you would go out of your way do anything for.

Throughout my career I was always labelled South African Allan Lamb, but to Beefy I was always an Englishman and that meant a lot to me.

ANDY FARRELL
SKILL

It takes a special kind of sportsman to join the best team in the land and make them better, but that is exactly what rugby league legend Andy Farrell did at the tender age of just 16.

He wasn't even a man in the eyes of the law, but from the moment he made his first-team debut for Wigan in 1991 he set new standards in the game and became a key player for both club and country – and he was a full international by the age of 18.

It is quite astonishing to think that a lad of such a tender age could be playing senior professional rugby in a sport that is as tough as it gets physically. You've got to be so strong to hold your own, but in Andy's case there was never any question of him not being able to handle it. He took it head on and flourished with cups, trophies, medals and caps to prove it.

Not much time needed to pass from the day he made his debut to the day he played for Great Britain, which goes to show just how quickly the cream rises to the top.

And it backs up a viewpoint I have held from the day I was a young cricketer myself to now. If you're good enough you're old enough and it doesn't matter what sport it is that you are playing, talent like Andy Farrell's should not be wasted waiting to see if he can get enough experience or tosh like that.

Later on in his career he switched codes to rugby union and

made a decent enough fist of it to be picked for England and become a dual-code international, but his stint in the 15-man code never quite hit the same heights so it is rugby league which is what he'll always be remembered for and it is his exploits in that code which make him stand out for me.

When you first walk into a senior dressing room it can be daunting. If you are moving from the junior side to the reserve side you feel it. If you're moving from the reserve side to the first team you feel it, and if you're stepping into an international dressing-room for the first time it can send shivers down your spine.

How do you cope? Do you look your heroes and your idols in the eye as an equal or do you shy away from the situation and hope they don't notice you? If you're good enough and you're confident enough you do the former and you back it up with your performance. You train hard, you play hard and you perform – and if you do that every single dressing-room will accept you. In Andy Farrell's case he did just that. He was only a teenager sharing changing space with serial winner and intense competitor Shaun Edwards, he was lining up alongside legends such as Ellery Hanley and Denis Betts, so he had to have something about him to stay there and he made sure they saw it. He has said of his early time there: 'When I was growing up you trained with your own team and had to earn your right to make it into the top dressing room. There was so much hunger to prove yourself against someone like Shaun Edwards. He was very dominant at Wigan. Shaun was the ultimate winner.'

A big bonus for him was that he had size on his side; he was big for his age and therefore he wasn't easily intimidated, and with that size he had strength, stamina and enough pace to be a handful. Where he stood out in my book was his level of skill. It is one thing for a loose forward to make his tackles and put the legs on a run, but to have the skill and vision to pass the way he did and to kick the way he did was remarkable. Here was a six foot plus, sixteen stone beast of a rugby player who was stepping up to slot in penalties and conversions with ease. I know John Eales did pretty well for Australia, but Andy was in the Jonny Wilkinson class of kicking and it was great to see.

He just belonged on a rugby league pitch because he could do everything. He was the complete player, a guy that the Australians would have been proud to have in their rugby league side, that is how good he was. To my mind I'd put him in the top five English rugby league players we've ever seen and some would go further and say he was the best.

He achieved so much at such a young age it could have been easy for him to let his standards slip as he got older. He won three Challenge Cups in a row as the legendary Wigan team of the late 1980s and 1990s rumbled on with him and he also contributed hugely to their repeated success in the Championship.

By 1995 he had won almost everything in the game, but international success on the biggest scale had eluded him and his countrymen. He had just been a part of the Wigan team that had gone to Brisbane and won the World Club Challenge on Australian soil for the first time, but with the Rugby League World Cup at home in 1995 that was the ultimate prize in his sights. Playing for England rather than Great Britain in the tournament, he led from the front under captain Denis Betts, and with him in the side and playing with such gusto at the time I thought they just might have a chance of upsetting the record books. It was in the opening match of the tournament against Australia that he impressed me most on the pitch with a try-scoring display full of vim and vigour that shook the World Cup holders and let them know we meant business. Every tackle he put in and every pass he made seemed to be perfectly timed and so when England won 20–16 I was absolutely delighted.

England's march to the final was almost a procession, beating Wales and my old mate Jonathan Davies in the semi-finals, and inevitably Australia were again the opponents. England didn't get things their own way and in that rather annoying style of theirs Australia raised their game to become World Champions again.

Without international success Andy turned back to his home-town club for solace, and in 1998 they won the first ever Super League grand final as the game took on a new structure and competition. By now, though, their halcyon days were over with the departures and the retirements of some great players. Gone were Martin Offiah, Shaun Edwards, Denis Betts and Henry

Paul, but Farrell remained. As the captain and leader of men, he continued to put in one towering performance after another despite the club's success drying up. The most glamorous and successful club the game had ever seen was struggling, but Andy refused to be dimmed by it. He continued to skipper Great Britain and he continued to perform head and shoulders above the rest, and for four long years the club won nothing. His perseverance paid off in 2002 when the Challenge Cup was theirs again. It was the last trophy Andy was to win with the team, yet such was his character and his determination he picked up the 'Man of Steel' title for the second time in 2004. It goes to the best player in the league and fully 13 years after his professional debut he was still at the top of his game and that told me everything I needed to know about Andy Farrell.

It is why in 2005 I was so excited by his decision to switch to rugby union and just like the people who orchestrated it I thought he would be a roaring success. The fact that he has been beset by injuries since his move and hasn't quite had the impact that was envisaged is a crying shame.

When he left Wigan I remember his coach at the time saying he would need three players to replace just one Andy Farrell because that is how talented and all-round a player he was.

Like all great sportsmen he wanted the challenge of testing himself in a new environment. It is a bigger arena in the UK with more attention and more coverage than league and perhaps he felt he had done all he could in league and wanted a taste of something bigger. After watching the England rugby union team beating Australia in a World Cup final in 2003 maybe he wanted a taste of that.

Whatever his ultimate reasons for the switch he did so knowing that the chances of success could well be slim.

The players that are most successful are those who go from union to league rather than the other way round and only Jason Robinson of the rugby league converts has really made as big a success of his union career as he did of his league career. Guys like Iestyn Harris and Henry Paul only had moderate success in union before him, yet he still wanted to come across and try it for himself.

MY SPORTING HEROES

Spending 18 months on the sidelines due to injury certainly didn't help him. Everything that could go wrong did go wrong and perhaps a little bit like Wilkinson his body was telling him to stop after so many years at the coal face. Once he did start playing and he got his position sorted as an inside centre he showed flashes of his old brilliance. He made it into the England side and let's not forget that he played a part in them getting to the final of the World Cup in 2007, which is no mean feat.

I also admire him for the way he rose above the ridiculous claims that he didn't belong in union or in the England side. He was a world-class player with unbelievable skill and sometimes you have to take a gamble on people like that. I know that I would rather put my faith in a player like Andy Farrell on a rugby union pitch than just another 'solid' performer.

I don't really know him; I've met him once or twice at sporting functions, but I've never really spent any time with him socially, so my admiration for him as a sportsman stems from watching him play and reading about him and his achievements.

From what I hear he is a dedicated family man as much as anything else having had children pretty early during his career. He has clearly done a good job along the way, with his son Owen determined to follow in his father's footsteps having become the youngest Premiership player in history when he turned out for Saracens against Llanelli in 2008. He didn't get the chance to play with his dad though since another injury had kept him out. At least he'll be keeping an eye on him as a skills coach at the club.

He has now retired from the game and it will be poorer for it; however, it is good to hear that he is staying involved as a coach, because he will have so much to pass on. If there is one thing Andy and the rest of that Wigan side knows about it is being successful. It is interesting though how rugby union is benefiting from all that success. Andy Farrell, Shaun Edwards, Denis Betts and Jason Robinson are all coaches at Premiership rugby clubs. It wouldn't surprise me to see Andy take his knowledge back to Wigan one day and bring back their glory years.

ANDY MURRAY
COMPOSURE

Everyone in this book has achieved some amazing things in their sports. They've won world titles, Grand Slams, Majors, World Cups and gold medals. They've almost all achieved something that very few people ever get to do and in most cases they've achieved it more than once too. I say almost all, because Andy Murray represents one of the very few guys that I watch at the moment in the total belief that there is so much more to come. His potential is quite extraordinary and I am convinced that he will go on to achieve some very special things in tennis by the time he is done. He has already made an impressive mark in the game and after moving to number two in the World rankings last year he did something no British tennis player had ever done before. He has won big tournaments, beaten the very best in the game and taken home a stack of prize money. Yet the biggest prize – a Grand Slam tournament – is yet to be added to his list of honours. So why does he make my list ahead of so many other sportsmen and women who have captured the ultimate glory in their sport?

It is the way that he has developed from a gangly awkward youngster with talent into a mature, fit and focused man in such a short space of time that has really knocked me sideways. I can't quite believe I'm watching the same player now as the one who sed to cramp up and fall short any time the game went into a fourth set just a few years ago.

He clearly had a lot of ability, but he just seemed to be wrestling with himself and his fitness. He didn't seem to fully embrace the idea of being the very best tennis player from these shores, but the speed with which he has matured in the last 24 months is just phenomenal. The guy is fitter and stronger than ever before; most importantly he is fitter and stronger than most of the other players on the circuit and he is taking them apart on the court to prove it.

At 23 he is still relatively young in most people's eyes, but in tennis terms he has entered his peak years and it wasn't that long ago that I thought he might well waste the golden opportunity he has to do something no British male tennis player has done since Fred Perry in 1936 and win a Grand Slam.

What he has shown me is that he is prepared to fight for what he wants and he will go to the ends of the earth to get it.

There was a glimpse of his desire even as a really young lad when he upped sticks from his native Scotland to go and further his tennis education in Barcelona. He went to the Schiller International School at 15 because the level of competition for him in the UK was no longer pushing him as hard as he needed. That was a good sign from him that he understood what it might take to be the very best, and unlike a lot of junior tennis stars he wasn't happy to remain in his comfort zone.

A series of junior successes showed that he could mix it with the best of his age group, especially when he won the junior US Open title in 2004, but once he turned professional the following year the hard work was about to begin.

His performance at the 2005 Wimbledon Championships also announced him properly to the wider British public. By beating 14th seed Radek Stepanek to get to the third round all eyes were on him. With Tim Henman and Greg Rusedski both going out in the second round he was the only Brit left and considering his age, he was now the great tennis hope for the entire nation. That is quite a lot for an 18 year old to have to deal with and I'm not sure he really knew how to cope. I suppose he would have known from watching Tim carry the burden on his shoulders for a

ANDY MURRAY

decade that it was bound to happen to him sooner or later because he knew he was the best British tennis player of his generation. However, there is still nothing that can properly prepare you for the attention, the expectation and the intrusion that comes with being such a high-profile sportsman. Of course some love it and relish it, but for others it takes a bit of time to grow into that skin and I think Andy is a case in point.

Once he'd burst into the consciousness of everyone, every success or failure would be magnified and when you've got someone like John McEnroe saying in that same year that 'the sky's the limit' for Andy then the goldfish bowl becomes even smaller.

I think 2006 and 2007 were tough years for Andy, looking from the outside. It's not that he wasn't improving throughout, his steady career rankings improvements showed that much, it was that he wasn't making the strides forward that he wanted to.

His fitness was again called into question on several occasions when he cramped up during lengthy matches and I'm not sure his temperament was helping him either. It looked to me like he was fighting with himself; there were one or two verbal explosions on the court and he was starting to be cast as a surly teenager.

It didn't help that he suffered a wrist injury during 2007, which kept him out of the French Open and Wimbledon, but I think perhaps this was a low point that ignited the start of his real development as a tennis player.

Having been given Brad Gilbert as a coach by the Lawn Tennis Association, Murray was clearly being invested in heavily by the British game, but it wasn't working the way he wanted. Gilbert had taken Andre Agassi and Andy Roddick to the top of the world rankings as a coach and it was thought he might be able to do the same with Murray, but it wasn't to be. I'm sure Murray learnt a few important things from him, but their split at the end of 2007 signalled a new start for Murray and for things to be done the way he wanted them. I wasn't sure whether Andy had the wherewithal to keep pushing himself the way he did as a 15 year old, or whether he had the stomach to put himself through the mill of public expectation, but the work he put in during the close season of 2007 tells the complete story.

MY SPORTING HEROES

He got himself fit, not just tennis fit, but super fit to the point where he could play a five-set match and be ready to go again the next day. He surrounded himself with a team of people that could get the best out of him in every department. He'd earned enough prize money for finances not to be an issue and he took full control of his tennis future. The really interesting decision that impressed me was his withdrawal from the GB Davis Cup side for a tie so that he could focus and play in another individual event. There were some people who were disgruntled with that decision, and I think his own brother might have taken a pop at him for it, but there are two important things to remember. Firstly the Davis Cup is not the most important tournament in tennis. Yes it means something and it is great to represent your country, but people don't remember players for winning Davis Cups; they are remembered for winning Grand Slams and so preparation and focus should go on getting one of those. Secondly it has been so long since a Brit did get one of those that if and when Andy does it, the impact on tennis in this country will be so big that his brief withdrawal will be long forgotten. And he knew it. I'm certain that Andy will be the one to ignite real interest in all the youngsters coming through at the tennis clubs around the United Kingdom. They'll all be thinking about Andy Murray and wanting to be him.

In the same way that Bjorn Borg became the icon that people like Mats Wilander and Stefan Edberg looked up to and went on to emulate, so I think Murray can do the same for British Tennis. Don't get me wrong, Tim Henman was a very good player, but we got tremendously excited if Tim got to a quarter-final. I think that is now the minimum we expect from Murray.

I think Tim was a great ambassador for the game and played above his mark, but Andy Murray has got it all.

He's got height, power, pace and the all-round skill you need to be successful. He can power hit with the best of them and he's also got the light touch you need to outwit some players. Watching him really excites me.

Even though he failed at the first hurdle of the 2008 Australian Open, he stayed firm to his belief that the hard work would pay off and so when he reached the fourth round of Wimbledon that year, I was glued to my television like everybody else. His muscle-bound show of emotion after beating Richard Gasquet was pure theatre and I loved every moment of it. I was being wrapped up in Andy's world and that is why I've got such huge respect for him.

His temperament and his mindset is another part of his make up that has come on in leaps and bounds – there appears to be plenty of emotion in his game but none of the petulance that he might have once shown.

Of course the real triumph for him and his methods came at the US Open when he made it to his first Grand Slam final, only to be beaten by Roger Federer. The fact that he beat Rafael Nadal in the semi-final was another big turning point for him because these two are the guys he will have to beat to win his first major tournament and he knows he can do that now. Until you do it for the first time there will always be that element of doubt. He won't have that any more.

He is now the guy that the rest of the tennis world doesn't want to see in their half of the draw. He is so hungry for success that he is ready to take on all comers, but I'm not sure anyone really wants to take him on at the moment because he is that good.

The finish to 2008 was as good as it gets, winning back-to-back Masters titles, but that would have counted for little if he didn't keep the improvement going and this is where we get to the crux of my admiration for Andy.

We have been so starved of success in tennis for so long that mediocrity is considered acceptable. There has been so much money pumped into so many young hopefuls and it has yielded nothing. Too many players get a taste of the good life and become lazy and stop striving. The real champions in any sport are the ones who get a taste and want more. They soon work out that success is the only thing that keeps their fire burning and that is the sort of man I believe Andy Murray to be. He enjoyed a remarkable run in 2008, including his Grand Slam final, but he is not satisfied. He will never be sated until he has the big one and that is the perfect outlook. It is why he was able to build on his success and reach a second final in the 2010 Australian Open. Again he faced the greatest of all time in the shape of Federer and again he came second. There was no disgrace in that, since Federer admitted to playing out of his skin to beat Murray. If you're pushing the greatest, then surely it is only a matter of time before the ultimate triumph is yours.

I do believe that he is now enjoying the experience of being Britain's great tennis hope. I don't think it sat too well with him a couple of years ago because it is a lot to be thrust on a young man's shoulders. I think he actually relishes it now and enjoys the pressure that comes with it.

He is beating Roger Federer more than he loses to him, he's beaten Rafael Nadal and now it is just a question of time before he beats them on the biggest stage of all at a Grand Slam final. By the time you're reading this book he may well have already done it, if not I'm convinced it won't be long before he does. I thought 2010 was going to be his year as he took a serene march towards the Wimbledon semi-finals only to be faced with a determined Nadal ready to make amends for missing the previous year's tournament through injury. Murray would have been confident of doing something special, but in the face of Nadal's genius the wait for a first Grand Slam goes on.

I think he could go on to become the best British player of all time. I know there are a couple of great ones out there like Fred Perry but there is something about Andy – I hope I'm right.

BARRY JOHN
INSTINCT

Dealing with expectation is one of the things that sportsmen and women learn to cope with as they get better and better at their sport. The better you are the more people expect of you and with the help of more experienced players who have been through it before you it is something most can cope with. Dealing with the fame and notoriety that comes with being the very best the game has ever seen is something altogether different and so much harder to comprehend, especially if you are the first of your kind.

In the case of legendary Welsh fly-half Barry John, it drove him to pack in the game he loved at the ridiculously young age of 27 and slip away without the career he could and should have had.

That being said, Barry John and his unbelievable talent for playing rugby was a gift the world got to see and we should be grateful for the twenty-five Welsh and five Lions caps he won in a magical era for Welsh and British rugby. His light burnt so brightly it simply couldn't be sustained for any longer, but I still feel that he finished with the game far too early.

Barry, though, was and is governed by his instincts, both on the pitch and off it. He always did what he felt was right at a given time and even though he now regrets some of the decisions he made, he made them in the same way that he glided by defenders on the pitch because he felt that was the way to go.

I was just a teenager when Barry was setting the rugby world on fire in the late '60s and early '70s and even though football was a big love of mine, he and the rest of the Welsh boys at the time got me hooked on rugby with their sheer verve and style.

They were free spirits when it came to rugby; the likes of Gareth Edwards, J.P.R. Williams, Gerald Davies and John Dawes all played the game how it was meant to be played and Barry John was their conductor.

He was such a naturally gifted rugby player who could change a game with a sudden sidestep or a turn of pace through a gap. He had wonderful hands, almost never dropping a ball that Gareth Edwards sent him. And, perhaps most crucially of all, he had a killer boot that could get his team rumbling forward or stop opposing teams in their tracks. That right boot of his was probably the difference between the sides on the 1971 Lions tour to New Zealand, but it would be so unfair to brand him a kicking machine like Neil Jenkins or Jonny Wilkinson. In fact, both of those men know how to run with a ball as well as the next, but in the 1960s and 1970s the Welsh way was all about running and passing and the fluidity of movement. Barry John made rugby look like an art form where so many struggled to stay on their feet.

He could swivel, swerve and pirouette past a would-be tackler despite there being more mud than pitch underneath and more rain clouds than sky above. I can remember watching footage of him destroying all comers in the Five Nations as Wales won title after title, and then became the first and up to now last Lions team to win in New Zealand. Barry was the heartbeat in some of the game's greatest ever teams. And then it stopped.

Having become the first real superstar of rugby, before Jonah Lomu had even been born, he realised everything that went with that lifestyle wasn't for him. Barry decided to give it all up because the price of fame became just too much for him. He was pretty cagey about why he suddenly quit the game completely and whenever I've spent time with him it is not something we've ever dwelt on. You get the impression that he'd rather talk about anything other than his career and why he stopped, so you don't ask. You don't push him on it. Since then he has offered the reason for his retirement saying that the spotlight grew too hot for him and he felt he was becoming too alienated from the Welsh people, which is something he didn't want. He thought fame was a monster that grew and grew and took him to uncharted territory as a rugby player so his only way out was to quit.

In many respects he was the George Best of rugby, and I know that the pair of them actually confided quite a bit in each other because they were the only ones who knew what the other was going through. There had been no footballer with a profile like George up to then and there had certainly not been a rugby player like Barry.

Timing has a lot to do with it. Before England's 1966 World Cup football win, there hadn't been a great deal to shout about as far as British sport was concerned, and in the 1950s and early 1960s the memory of war was still etched on many a mind. The UK was still being rebuilt, and so when the 1960s got into full swing there was a craving for success, style and extravagance. George Best and Manchester United provided it on the football field, Tony Jacklin on the golf courses, while Barry John and Wales provided it on the rugby pitch, and it was new and exciting.

By the time he went on the 1971 Lions tour Barry was already 'the king' of Welsh rugby and had forged such a devastating partnership with scrum-half Gareth Edwards. He actually nearly missed that tour after taking some heavy punishment during the Five Nations and had to be talked into going by his wife Jan. When he told legendary Lions coach Carwyn James that he'd be going he set in motion the greatest tour by any player before or since. The first Test match was won in large part because of Barry's relentless kicking to Kiwi full-back Fergie McCormick. He couldn't handle the accuracy of Barry's boot and wilted under the onslaught of Lions pressure. In the second Test the New Zealanders hit back to win 22–12, and at 1–1 with two games left to play this was the sort of crunch moment where great players either stand up to be counted or sink without a trace. I've spoken to Barry about this game many a time, and he admits the nerves and the doubts in his mind were greatest just before this crucial match. He'd been told by those who'd come out for the Test just how much interest the tour was creating back at home and that added to the pressure he was under. In many ways I guess it was just the same sort of thing that Jonny Wilkinson was going through ahead of the World Cup final in 2003 and all the expectation of a nation was on his shoulders. In Barry's case it was the hopes and dreams of four nations. He needn't have worried though – the team around him proved their worth with a sensational opening spell of rugby as good as any the game has ever seen. I read as many reports of the game as I could get my hands on and I've subsequently watched footage of it at home and it was just an exhibition of how rugby could and should be played. A 13–3 victory was more than deserved and that is when Barry moved beyond being just a rugby star to a superstar. The 14–14 draw in the final Test was enough to secure a well-earned (and still, to this day, only) series win in New Zealand and from there Barry's life was changed forever. Even my old mate the late *Daily Mirror* cricket correspondent Chris Lander, as a young hack was sent to doorstep his house to try and get an insight into this new hero. The fact that he only ever played three more international matches following that tour was so very sad.

I have my own theory as to why he stepped down when he did. I actually think that deep down he'd set such high standards that he was worried about not being able to keep up with them and maintain them. I think he had taken the game to such a level that he knew he would always be fighting with himself to try and stay there. Perhaps he lost a little bit of belief in his abilities. It happens to us all. We have those brief moments of doubt where we're not quite sure whether we can hit the same heights again, but usually it is the most fleeting of thoughts and certainly for myself I always wanted to get out there and prove to me and to others just how good I was. Being on top affects different sportsmen and women in different ways and for Barry, his personality wouldn't allow himself to enjoy the new-found fame he had earned.

When he came into rugby and started playing for Wales, I'm not sure he would have expected all the accolades that he got. He was suddenly not just Barry John from the Valleys who played a bit of rugby, he was Barry John the king of Wales. He was the man who was going to cement Welsh rugby's position in the history books.

When you see the passion in Wales for their rugby and the knowledge that they've got, it is a special atmosphere.

I used to go down to Cardiff and watch a lot of club games when my son Liam was playing there and the buzz was extraordinary. You can't go and watch a game of rugby in Wales without some kind of atmosphere. It could be the young farmers of Swansea against the plumbers of Neath and there would be a crowd there. That is the passion they have for the game and maybe, just maybe, that is what forced him out at such a young age.

The fact remains though that as fly-half Barry had no one to touch him. To stand out at any time in a team sport takes some doing, but to stand out amongst the group of players that Wales and the British Isles had at that time was incredible.

Barry wasn't just admired by the Welsh people but also by rugby fans around the world. If you go to New Zealand these days and talk about rugby or the Lions, Barry's name invariably comes up. He is held in high esteem around the world and I think everyone was shocked when he walked away.

Like a lot of players in that amateur era his career and life after rugby was hamstrung by his 'professional' activities that stopped him from being too involved in the game from a coaching or administrative point of view. He became a decent columnist for the *Daily Express* as well as a respected summariser for the BBC, but he could have taken other routes if it wasn't for his headstrong and principled attitude. After returning from the 1968 Lions tour to South Africa and before his legend was sealed he was offered a lot of money to go and play rugby league as a professional by St Helens and came within a whisker of signing the papers, but something told him he needed to think about it. Believing he still had plenty to prove in union, he rejected the overtures. The most astonishing rejection, though, came after his retirement when he was offered £120,000 to go and be a goal kicker in American football, which was a huge sum in 1973, but having given his word to the *Express* and a couple of other business ventures he decided he couldn't let them down, which I think speaks volumes for his character as a man. An honourable and decent man, who simply had a proper code of conduct and stuck to it.

To me Barry was and is a complex character, but also a man who lives by a few very simple rules. He is an ordinary bloke who was touched by greatness when it came to rugby. I don't know what he could have achieved had he stayed in the game longer than he did, but what I do know is that he was the greatest while he was there.

BARRY JOHN

Rugby shaped my life and has given me a fantastic opportunity and platform to meet people, and to a certain extent I've been spoilt to a degree. But you can only be spoilt for as long as you want to be spoilt and after a point you can let everybody else get on with the show.

I look back on my career with real fondness, but the point was that in 1971 the sports editors in Fleet Street were banging their heads because there was nothing happening in British sport. There was no Ashes or World Cup to get interested in; it was just the Open and Wimbledon. They then suddenly realised that the boys were playing rugby 12,000 miles away and weren't doing too badly and so the flights became booked as people flew in to cover it. We were commanding the back pages like never before and from there the game took off.

I'm pretty certain that chance played its part because there just wasn't much happening and we filled a spot by playing some pretty good rugby, running in some great tries and with some personality to boot.

That tour was a huge part of my life and I will never forget it, but playing for Wales was what I loved. There was nothing like running out at the Arms Park. In 1971 before the Lions we won the Grand Slam in Paris, which was the greatest game of rugby I was involved in. Both sides were absolutely outstanding and had won three games apiece so it was a shoot-out at the OK Corral. We won 9–5, I broke my nose, had it clicked back on the side of the pitch and then came on to score the winning try. It was an amazing game and a great night. We were applauded into the dinner that night by the French and to be a part of something like that was just incredible.

I love cricket and I can remember going to a sporting dinner with Alec Bedser there and being asked who my sporting hero was. They all expected me to say Cliff Morgan or Carwyn James, but instead I said Garry Sobers! I saw him play at Swansea for the West Indies and I read the line in the paper that said, 'I would pay the entrance money just to see Garry Sobers swagger to the wicket', and I couldn't agree more!

I used to play for Cowbridge down in the Vale of Glamorgan, a beautiful club that I was able to play for in 1970 in between tours, but certainly didn't get to do in 1971 when I went to New Zealand with the Lions and I missed it.

What a great player Beefy was, though. I wish I could have done what he did on the cricket pitch, but there could only be one! He was a fantastic cricketer and is a lovely man. He knows all about being in the spotlight and having his life shaped by the game and he earned that by being so bloody good!

BARRY McGUIGAN
PASSION

I firmly believe that our differences as people should be celebrated and the same goes for sportsmen and women, so whenever I find someone who dares to play their sport in their own way and is a clear individual I like that. If they can be their own person and still be successful I like it even more. There is no question that Barry McGuigan is a one of a kind and I admire him for the way he did things his own way, – has his own forthright views on things and is completely his own man – and whatever he gets himself into he does it wholeheartedly and with such passion that it puts the rest of us to shame.

His standing in boxing and sport is guaranteed by virtue of his featherweight world title success against Eusebio Pedroza in 1985, but he is also a national icon and treasure in Northern Ireland thanks to his success coming at a time when the troubles in that part of the world were at a frenzy.

He became a symbol for cross-party and cross-religious success. Everyone supported Barry and it is why he is still such a much loved son of Northern Ireland today. I'm not sure how many people could have been such a binding force as he was and that is a credit to him.

Barry McGuigan is one of those people in sport who makes you tired just by watching him. He is such a bundle of energy and has such huge enthusiasm for everything that he does, you have to sit down every now and then just trying to keep up with him.

He has a lust for life that makes him a man after my own heart and after reaching the top in the ring as a boxer he has continued to take life on with such gusto he makes the Duracell bunny look lethargic.

Barry's career beyond his last fight has also been impressive with a stellar media career dovetailing with a role as the head of the Professional Boxers Association which campaigns tirelessly for the good of fighters to help them make the most of their lives once their careers are over.

The massed ranks of professional boxers could not wish to have a better man in their corner fighting on their behalf outside of the ring while they get on with the business of knocking each other out inside it.

It is as a boxer though that Barry impressed me, and one of my big regrets is that I never got to see him fight in person.

It is a real disappointment for me that I never managed to see any of his fights live because I just didn't have the time to get along to watch him while I was still playing cricket, but I followed his career like everyone else on television and in the newspapers and was in awe of some of his classic dust-ups.

What impressed me most about the fights I saw on television was his agility, speed and intelligence. As a featherweight boxer he had such quick feet and hands. He could move around the ring with such ease, but whenever he landed a punch there was a whole lot of power behind it.

He was a clever boxer who I think was a little bit ahead of his time in terms of his tactics. He wasn't a wild workhorse throwing more punches than he needed to. He seemed to be a smart boxer who would at times knock someone out rather than play around and drag out a contest longer than necessary.

He had control over his emotions. In a sport that has the fighters right on the edge of human endeavour and baring their souls for all to see, he was able to keep it all in check.

Like most decent fighters he learnt his trade in the amateur ranks, honing his skills and his mental toughness at the big events like the Commonwealth Games, where he won gold, and the Olympics, but in 1981 he turned professional and that is where the real work started. And it wasn't straightforward.

I think it takes a certain amount of ability and talent to make it to the top, but getting there after a setback takes some doing and after losing an early fight to Peter Eubanks, Barry had his work cut out.

Things got even worse for Barry when he beat a Nigerian fighter called Young Ali in 1982. After losing to Barry he slipped into a coma following the fight and sadly died six months later, and that rocked Barry to the core, to the point where he nearly gave up boxing altogether.

The fact that he didn't meant he could get his career moving in a constant upward trajectory during the early 1980s, winning nearly all his fights by knockout, building up to his shot at World Champion glory. Pedroza stood in his way for that world title and so when it was announced that the fight would take place at Loftus Road in June 1985 the buzz around the place was astonishing.

All of Ireland were rooting for him, as was the rest of the UK, and for the duration of the week surrounding that fight, west London became a little piece of Northern Irish territory and he delivered in the most special way.

I can remember gearing up for an Ashes battle that summer of 1985 and when Barry's fight came along I was down in Bath playing for Somerset against Gloucestershire in a West Country clash that was usually a little spicy, but at the end of the first day everyone just wanted to do one thing and that was to watch Barry. Pedroza the Panamanian had branded Barry 'scared' during the pre-fight press conference, yet he was anything but, and by the time his dad Pat had finished singing 'Danny Boy' on his way into the ring he was absolutely chomping at the bit.

Along with 19 million others we watched him give absolutely everything to secure the belt. He was patient in his assault on Pedroza, using his tactical nous to outbox his opponent, but when he knocked him down in the seventh we thought it would be all over by another knockout. Champions don't go down that easily however, and Barry had to keep working hard to earn his win by unanimous points decision. It was a fantastic fight and I know I sank a Guinness or two that night in his honour! He had scaled the highest heights by doing things his own way. He had married his childhood sweetheart despite her being a Protestant to his Catholic and he fought under a flag of peace while violence often flared up back in his homeland. It is hard to imagine just what kind of pressure he would have been under inside and outside the ring, but his focus, his determination and his undoubted skill made sure he got to the very top. I was in awe of his achievements. He turned White City into a suburb of Ireland for the night and it was just one of the most memorable and astonishing pieces of British sporting theatre we have ever had.

He was rightly named the BBC Sports Personality of the Year because he had a sense of style to go with the raw nature of boxing, but it wasn't in your face. I always felt that Barry was an unassuming world champion and was happy in the knowledge that he was better than his opponent. He didn't have to ram that fact down your throat and I must admit it was a pleasure for me to come second to him when he won that award in 1985.

He was never one to go looking for the money, the lights and the fame of boxing. He always seemed to be a bit purer than that. To him it was about the contest. Putting your body on the line, man against man to see who had the better skills and who was tougher. It wasn't about the pre-fight hype and the pay-per-view event, it was about what you did in the ring.

I laugh at some of the antics that go on these days with so much trash talk before and after fights. Boxers who are happier talking a good fight rather than delivering one – that wasn't the way for Barry.

In his slipstream you had the likes of Chris Eubank, Nigel Benn and Naseem Hamed who were all decent fighters, but who all loved the trappings that came with boxing perhaps a little too much.

I first met Barry on *A Question of Sport* and he really knew his stuff to the extent I thought he was a bit geeky about boxing, but that was just his passion for it coming out.

I love listening to him talk about boxing, because he gets so excited by it; it is a real passion for him and that comes across in what he says. He gets emotionally involved in what is going on with boxing even now so many years after he's retired. The same enthusiasm he had as a prize fighter remains to this day and it captures the imagination when you hear him talk.

But he never talks about himself. He never talks about how good he was and about how tough his fights were, it is always about the sport in general and about other boxers, largely because he doesn't have to. He's always been comfortable with himself and what he's achieved so he doesn't need to bang a drum to remind people about his place in boxing history. It had already been secured.

In fact I had to really push him to talk about his own fights and whenever I did that he was always very generous to his opponents. He would always say that each fighter was 'very tough' or a 'very hard puncher' and I would sit there thinking, 'Yeah, but you won.'

Barry is just a very unassuming guy who didn't want it all to be about him. If you want him to tell you about his career you've got to ask him a specific question. Otherwise he'll start talking to you about cricket or rugby or football.

Barry and I have a few things in common; unfortunately one of them is getting embroiled in libel cases and I know it was quite a sad and tough time for him when he fell out with his promoter Barney Eastwood. Yet it is how you come back from the tough times that mark you out and there can be no tougher time for someone than when they find out one of their children is seriously ill.

For Barry and his wife Sandra to be told that their daughter Danika had leukaemia at age 11 was as big a blow as anyone can take. Barry is such a doting dad that I know it hit him harder than any of his fights and he knew this was a battle he couldn't win, he just had to help his daughter get through it, which she did with his support.

He has always supported me on my charity walks in aid of Leukaemia Research, but now he has a heartfelt connection with what we do and I can tell you he is the first person to call me up asking about my walks and the itineraries. He wants to know when they might be swinging past Belfast or in Ireland and he promises he'll be there. He's still a fit little so and so keeping pace right at the front even though he has to do two paces to my one because he's not the biggest.

We are actually colleagues these days too on the *Daily Mirror*. I think he is one of the best columnists around, not just offering some real insight into the fight game, but making people aware of the issues surrounding boxing that need to be looked at. He is a fighter in more than one sense, he is one of the most passionate men I know and he will continue to work tirelessly for his family and for other boxers to make sure that his sport and the people in it are treated properly. That in itself is quite heroic, and he wasn't a bad boxer either.

BARRY McGUIGAN

There are a few things that go into a successful sportsman, like determination and a desire to push yourself to the limit, but I would also suggest that having such a supportive family around me was crucial. My dad was a rock and my mum was so supportive too. My wife was brilliant, washing my kit morning, noon and night because I would train two or three times a day and everything would be drenched in sweat.

I had great people around me and in fairness to my ex-manager, even though we fell out acrimoniously at the end of my career, he did a fantastic job in getting me the right sparring partners and the right fights while I was boxing.

I had enjoyed a decent amateur career, but I had the ideal style for the pro game. I was lucky to have a longer reach than normal, a big engine with pace, and I punched hard for my size. They were the qualities that allowed me to get to the top, but it wasn't easy getting there. The honest truth is that I trained exceptionally hard, and when I was with the Irish team the others thought I was barmy. I'd run an extra mile, I'd push myself harder and longer in the gym and the others would scratch their heads and wonder why I was doing that. I did it because I could and because I felt I had to.

My manager would source Central and South American boxers who were the most dominant in the world at my weight and we'd bring them over to Ireland, making my gym work phenomenally hard but necessary.

As a coach now I can tell you I want a kid with a bit of ability, but most importantly I want a kid with the right attitude. Give me a boxer with bundles of talent but who doesn't work hard, I will take a lesser natural fighter who has the right drive and we'll overtake the guy with the talent any day of the week. You've got to have the desire to be successful. The Pedroza fight was the best night I had in the game and because it was the first live outside broadcast that the BBC had ever done so many people watched it. The whole atmosphere of the night was incredible. Coming up against the established champion, being a Catholic married to a Protestant, wearing the colours of peace on my shorts, having the slogan 'leave the fighting to McGuigan' in the middle of the troubles all added up to a magical night.

It was why I managed to sneak in ahead of Beefy for the Sports Personality of the Year award – sorry Beefy! What a phenomenal guy he is though. He was a great cricketer, of course, but could have been a great sportsman at anything, and I think he could have been a fantastic fighter because he has a great attitude.

I walked with him in 1986 in Ireland and he is just a salt of the earth bloke. There's no faffing about with him, he just gets up and gets on with whatever it is he has to do. He's made a real difference to people's lives and it doesn't matter how painful it is, he'll get up the next day and start walking all over again and raising more money. I walked with him before my daughter had even been born and so when she had leukaemia it really brought it all home to me. It makes it all the more special to walk with him and I'm proud to know him.

BARRY SHEENE
BRAVERY

It takes a special kind of sportsman or woman to knowingly put their lives in danger for the sport they love. And by danger I don't mean the possibility of being hit by a Malcolm Marshall bouncer – I mean mortal danger. There aren't that many sports where you literally take your life in your hands every time you take part. Of course you could get seriously injured playing football or rugby, but the kind of people who take part in boxing or any kind of motor sport know that they are taking a huge risk to become the best at what they do. For Barry Sheene it was a risk he was more than willing to take on a motorcycle and in doing so he not only became the very best on two wheels, but he did it in such style that you almost forgot that there was anything dangerous about what he was doing – until of course he crashed!

Barry Sheene was the first pin-up boy for motorcycle racing in the British Isles. We had had world champions before like John Surtees, Mike Hailwood and Phil Read, but they were for the petrol heads. They didn't cross over to mass appeal like Barry did and I have no qualms in revealing that until Barry came along I had never even glanced at the results of a motorcycling race, let alone watched one. That all changed with Barry, and the only reason I've got any idea who the likes of Michael Doohan or Valentino Rossi are is because of him.

MY SPORTING HEROES

He was everything a biker should be. Brave, good looking, quick witted, and oozing confidence out of every pore. He put his body on the line more often than anybody has a reasonable right to, yet he managed to come through with an incredible racing career that gripped the public not only thanks to his style and swagger, but because he was one of the very best the sport had ever seen.

In the 1970s Barry was the sportsman every man wanted to be and every woman wanted to be with. Just like the club singers up and down the country wanted to be Mick Jagger, anyone who had ridden a pedal cycle wanted to be Barry Sheene, but there could be only one.

His racing life was about being on the edge and pushing the limits of his bikes and his body, and how he consistently shrugged off fall after fall with the aplomb of a true champion is beyond me. He was a complete individual doing things his own way and that is something I love in a sportsman. It didn't matter how many bones he broke, and there were a few of those, nor did it matter how fast the other riders were going, Barry forged a remarkable career by doing it his way.

Considering his high-octane career and lifestyle, it was incredible how his body managed to survive such a battering, and I know he laid a lot of thanks at the feet of the surgeons who consistently put him back together again.

So when he was tragically taken away from his family and the racing community in 2003 at the age of just 52 thanks to stomach cancer, it was a sad day not just for motor sport, but for British sport in general, and beyond because he transcended the track. His feats in winning two 500 cc world titles are only part of the story and part of the legend that is Barry Sheene.

I actually got to meet him a few times out in Australia where he had settled with his wife Stephanie and their two kids following his racing career. I met him during the odd charity and sporting functions during Ashes tours, usually organised by the television companies out there where he'd become the voice of motorcycling. I always found him to be great fun, chatty and full of life, just like the character he seemed to me from afar while he was winning on two wheels.

BARRY SHEENE

Like most people I first became aware of Barry and his racing exploits in 1975 following a near death crash at Daytona. He lost control of his 750 cc bike and was thrown about 300 yards onto the tarmac, tumbling and sliding along the ground until he came to a complete stop.

If anything highlighted just how dangerous motor sport and motorcycling in particular was then this was it. Thanks to a documentary being filmed of Barry we got to see that crash in such graphic detail that you couldn't have anything but wholehearted admiration for the guy, not only for being brave enough to put himself in that position in the first place, but to then recover from the crash to continue with his career.

I've only ever been to the odd motor sport event and it certainly took me by surprise just how quickly these souped up vehicles and bikes can go. I like a bit of speed in my own motors, but these are something else.

When Barry had that crash in 1975 I can remember watching it and thinking just how terrifying it must have been. I used to travel in a car to cricket matches with Brian Close, who drove his car like a racing driver, except with one hand holding a coffee, and that scared the life out of me, so I can't imagine what it must have been like on a bike.

It is fascinating to think what makes a national hero. In so many cases it isn't the success of an individual that takes them into our hearts but their failures. I'm not sure whether people knew too much about Barry and how good he was as a rider, but having seen him take such a fall in which he broke a leg, an arm, several vertebrae, two ribs and peeled off most of the skin from his back, he was our gallant but accident-prone hero.

Having gone through such a devastating accident he would have been forgiven if he'd retired there and then, just happy to be alive. At least he could have taken the rest of the season off to recover fully – not Barry. The man was as fearless as they come and he loved what he did too much to spend more time convalescing than he needed to. Within seven weeks he was back on his bike racing in an event at Cadwell Park. Seven weeks!!!!

It was a national event, since in those days there was a World Championship to contest as well as home races which brought in a lot of extra money for Barry thanks to his popularity.

Thanks to his unbelievable thirst for action he became one of the most recognisable sportsmen in the land and his swift return to the track made sure the public's fascination with him grew and grew.

The summer of 1976 was all about motor sport with Barry firmly established as one half of a golden speed-loving pair. He took the 500 cc world by storm with his successes on his Suzuki bike while James Hunt was making all the waves in Formula One. While the West Indies were busy giving our cricketers what for with the bat and ball, by the end of the year England would have two racing champions on both four and two wheels.

It looked like a life of sex, drugs and rock 'n' roll, plus plenty of successful racing thrown in. With a chirpy cockney accent that made it clear he was a 'man of the people', this heady mixture had the British public eating out of his hand. He had worked hard to get where he was and he deserved the good things that were coming his way. He became the epitome of British cool just like George Best was in the 1960s; Barry was the marketing man's dream and who can forget those Brut aftershave adverts he used to do with boxing legend Henry Cooper.

I've always said that winning at the very top just once is hard enough but to do it twice or more takes something special. It is why serial winners like Sir Alex Ferguson and Sir Nick Faldo deserve their own categories in sporting folklore, so having won the 1976 world title, Barry's task became that much harder. There are plenty of special sportsmen who don't get to climb their Everest a second time and it is no disgrace to be in that group. So when Barry retained his World Champion title in 1977 he secured his superstar status forever.

I remember him struggling a little bit after that as the American Kenny Roberts became the number one racer, but they then began a duel that was as captivating as any great clash. It was a McEnroe versus Borg on wheels, a rubberised Coe versus Ovett if you will.

Ultimately Barry couldn't get past his rival no matter how hard he strived, yet he never seemed to show how much it was hurting. The pair actually ended up cancelling each other out so that neither won the title after 1981 and that was a shame.

BARRY SHEENE

Barry came across as this 'cheeky chappie' who looked like he just strolled in off the street smoking a Gitane before hopping on a bike and leaving everyone in his wake. But there was more to Barry than that. His numerous accidents actually had a profound impact on the sport and on him. The safety record in motorcycling wasn't that great when Barry first started, with life-threatening accidents a real concern at every race; however, thanks to him and a real crusade for safety at tracks the number of serious incidents was gradually reduced. In fact he was a bit of a stickler for safety to the point where he used to make sure he had the best and most protective leathers money could buy and he also wore the first back protector, which he invented and made himself. It is now a regular part of a rider's kit, but in Barry's day he was well ahead of his time, and boy did he need it.

He used to joke openly about the problems he had getting through airport security with the metal detectors; well you can imagine what he would have to go through these days if he was still with us. He'd have to give himself five or six hours just to get to the departure lounge!

Barry was also a pretty smart character. Not necessarily measured in degrees and certificates, but in a good old-fashioned street sense and even though he lived a fast and at times loose life, he made sure he got what he deserved from his sport.

He was always the main attraction at racing meets and an appearance by Barry would swell the gate and therefore the receipts beyond belief. So it was only fair that he got his share of the cake even if it came in a brown envelope. Up until Barry came along promoters were milking the racing drivers for all they were worth without paying them a decent fee for putting their lives on the line. Barry changed all that and even though he took home more than most, his efforts still saw every other racer far better off than they had been. It was a testament to him that I've seen and heard plenty of other former racers declare how much of a team man Barry was despite being such an obvious individual. Too many sportsmen have been paid far too little for far too long and it takes someone like Barry to knock the administrators into line when it comes to how they treat their major assets, namely the competitors. I'm all for a bit of player power when it comes to things like that.

Following another serious crash at Silverstone in 1982 Barry eventually retired in 1984 and moved to the Gold Coast in Australia. The warmer climate would certainly have helped those aching bones of his.

His quick wit and gift of the gab would have been a major reason why he became the voice of motor sport commentary in Australia, but he also knew his stuff better than most. To get to the top of any sport you have to have a deep understanding of what it is all about and Barry knew bikes forwards, backwards and inside out as he had to.

With a wife and two kids it seemed that he was living out the perfect end to a remarkable life, and then it was all taken away. I was truly shocked when I heard that cancer had got him. I know it is indiscriminate and I know Barry also smoked an awful lot so perhaps it shouldn't have been that big a surprise, but this was Barry Sheene we were talking about. The guy was indestructible – wasn't he?

In the end he was human like the rest of us, but I will always remember him as the motorcyclist I wanted to be.

BILL BEAUMONT
COMPOSURE

When it comes to the perfect ambassador for his sport the same name always pops into my head. That of William Beaumont, the inspirational captain of England and then the Lions who took his side to a Grand Slam in 1980 before becoming one of the most respected and admired men in rugby administration.

Bill has always had a calm air about him and for a big man, rarely if ever showed his temper, even when tumbling backside over chest down a nursery ski slope!

Bill and I will forever be intertwined thanks to our stint as opposing captains on *A Question of Sport* but our friendship goes back far further than that and it was one of our first meetings that actually revealed to me his character and his composure as a man.

It was the evening of that Grand Slam-winning match up in Edinburgh, and after a hard-fought game in which England unexpectedly won their first Grand Slam for 23 years.

I had been up there watching it with my father-in-law Gerry who I used to go to a lot of rugby with, and the England centre Tony Bond, who had broken his leg earlier in the season and was still on crutches. Having spotted the three of us in the hotel bar afterwards, Bill invited us to come and join the party and celebrate with the team. Obviously we were delighted at this generous offer to enjoy a glass at a reception hosted by the home side. Now I don't know whether or not we had actually done anything wrong other than be English, but apparently our mere presence at the party was taken as some kind of affront by the Scottish Rugby Union as one of their minions came over and demanded that we leave.

He told us that we weren't wanted because it was the SRU who were paying for the function and they decided who did and didn't get an invite to it, not the England team.

Well, I've never been one to back down from rudeness or downright jobsworths so I told him, 'If it is your party and you paid for everything, then you better have this gin and tonic back hadn't you,' as I proceeded to tip the drink over his head.

With that we were frogmarched out of the reception and on to the streets. Bill was absolutely incensed that guests of his were being treated in this way and he stormed out with us along with most of the England team.

He didn't have to do that but it just shows the mark of the man that he was prepared to deal with confrontation in his own way and it is why the Grand Slam-winning England captain spent most of that evening on the steps of a Scottish hotel as players took it in turns to pop inside and ferry drinks out to us on trays!

As a player Bill was a competitive second-rower who loved the game and loved getting his hands dirty, but, is a softly spoken gentle giant off the pitch. I used to ask him why he ended up at the bottom of so many rucks and he just smiled and said, 'It is where the real work gets done.' And he's right. Back in the 1970s and 1980s rugby wasn't anywhere near the glamour game it has become today. It was an amateur sport that you played for nothing else but a love of the game. There certainly wasn't any real financial rewards for what you did and in Bill's case he certainly didn't go down the brown paper bag route of being employed for his rugby, nor playing for a club that lined his pockets. His association with Fylde rugby club was as pure as it comes.

What impresses me most with Bill is his ability to take things in his stride and not let sudden changes either good or bad affect the sort of person he is or the sort of performance he delivers, whether that has been on a rugby pitch, on a quiz show or in a board room. He is consistent in everything he does and it is always to a high standard. He was a tough man on the field too, and I remember that like so many other powerful England second rows he never went looking for trouble, but if it came his way he was able to handle himself.

He was the obvious choice to lead the Lions to South Africa in 1980 at a politically very sensitive time but he did it with the good calm authority that the tour needed and I think the way in which a lot of new things were thrown at him as a rugby player stood him in good stead for the job.

When he made his debut for England it came as a bit of a surprise because Roger Uttley was supposed to play, but having injured his back eating apple pie the road was clear for Bill and he coped admirably. Again two years after that in 1977 he thought he had missed out on selection for the Lions, but then Nigel Horton broke his thumb and Bill was called up to the squad in New Zealand and ended up in the Test side. In each case he didn't lose sight of what he was about and when the opportunities presented themselves he grabbed them with both hands.

If we're honest English rugby was in the doldrums throughout the 1970s as the great Welsh wizards of the time weaved their magic, but in 1980 under Bill, the England team enjoyed their golden moment. They had a bit of consistency and stability with their selection, and with Bill having a couple of years', experience as captain under his belt he was another steadying influence on things. He told me that it was actually the first time they had named him as captain for the whole year rather than on an ad hoc basis and he said that made a big difference to him; it gave him the confidence boost he needed to be able to really shape the team how he wanted.

There were a few other senior players at their peak together in that team too, such as Steve Smith, Roger Uttley and Dusty Hare, and Bill got the very best out of them. It was a case of getting the right blend together at the right time, but having Bill in charge meant the opportunity wasn't wasted.

The game in which Bill sealed his position as a rugby legend and a British hero in my eyes was the battle in Cardiff where tempers ran high, players were sent off, but somewhere through the red mist Bill kept his cool and guided his side to glory. It could have all ended in tears though after Steve Smith's late clearance kick was charged down, leading to a try by Elgan Rees. Showing the true skill of a composed captain, Bill reassured his scrum half that there was still time left to snatch a win and in the closing moments Dusty Hare knocked over the winning penalty. With just Scotland to come, and with three wins out of three, everyone knew a Grand Slam could be England's and that is when I knew I had to get to the game myself.

Perhaps it would be a bit fanciful to suggest that Bill's early retirement from the game in 1982 at the age of just 29 cast a dark shadow over the national side, but it certainly can't have helped things as England went on to struggle until the Will Carling years.

The thing that I found quite sad though and showed how rugby needed to change into the professional game we have now, is how Bill was exiled from the game at all levels following his retirement in 1982 all because of a book. Having been banged on the head one too many times at the bottom of those rucks, Bill had given up the game early and so decided to write his autobiography. Yet even though it was an account of his life as well as his rugby career, the Rugby Football Union told him he had to either hand over the cheque to them or give it to charity. It was a ridiculous stance and one that has thankfully long gone, but that is what it was like in the amateur days. Bill was exiled from the game he loved and it meant he wasn't allowed to take part in any coaching or anything like that at his club and certainly not with England, even though he would have been useful. At least his easygoing nature, which came across so readily on *A Question of Sport*, was also being used in the commentary box for the BBC, and it kept him in contact with the game until eventually in 1989 he was welcomed back into the fold.

I can remember how happy he was that he could officially play a part in rugby again, but I also remember how upset he was that he wasn't allowed to get involved in coaching, which is something he wanted to do. To be cast as an outsider for six years was tough to take, but ever the gentleman he didn't let the stuffiness of the game get in the way of his love for it. I've certainly had my run-ins with cricketing authorities over the years and have given the traditionalists plenty of headaches, but no matter how many times you clash, nothing can take away the pure love you have for your sport that is sewn into you as a child, and Bill was the same with rugby.

What was good to see was his elevation to the RFU council when in 1995 the game went professional. It was a fitting position for Bill knowing how volatile the situation in the game was about to get. He was exactly the right sort of calm influence that the game needed as battle lines were drawn between the RFU, the clubs, the players and the rest of the international game. It is a row that has gone on since that day, yet despite being in the thick of it as a rugby administrator you never have and never will hear a bad word spoken about Bill because of the way he handles people. He has worked tirelessly behind the scenes for the good of English rugby for nearly 15 years now and his motivation has only ever been a good one, to see our country's rugby side do as well as they can. It was the same motivation he had when he took over the Lions manager role for the ill-fated 2005 tour to New Zealand. Bill was again working alongside Clive Woodward, who had made his debut under Bill in 1980 for England. But this time the roles were slightly reversed with Clive having the major responsibility on the tour and Bill being the respected face of the tour party. It is a funny role, but one that takes a certain type of person. It has to be someone who can go into the committee rooms and bars of rugby clubs around the world and be welcomed with open arms win, lose or draw and that is Bill. You won't find him finger-jabbing at the opposition in the same way that Clive and Alastair Campbell were over Brian O'Driscoll's unfortunate tackle. You won't find him snubbing receptions and dinners because it takes too much effort. With Bill you get complete dedication, professionalism and good humour from start to finish and it is why he is so highly regarded in the game. He is now involved with the International Rugby Board at the highest levels rather than with the domestic unions, but his love and loyalty to the game will never change.

He was a fine rugby player, of that there is no doubt, but you'll be hard pressed to find a better bloke full stop and that is impressive to me.

MY SPORTING HEROES

BILL BEAUMONT

I always felt I was an honest player and an honest captain. I made sure that I did my fair share of the work for the team and made sure that I carried my weight. I couldn't ask someone to do something if I wasn't prepared to do it myself so I liked to get my hands dirty. I worked hard for my teams as a player and was passionate about what I was doing on the field; rugby really was my life, and so to be told at 29 that you can't play any more really was a kick in the teeth.

It is why I'm so glad of what we managed to achieve despite the Welsh dominance of the time. A stable environment goes a long way in top-level sport and for the first time in a long time we had that in 1980.

The more you do anything the better you get at it and you learn from your experience. You also get more confidence with that experience too, because you are able to trust those around you more and you can delegate a lot better. I've always found in rugby that players perform to their best when they buy into the environment around them and there is no better way to do that than to give them some responsibility for it.

We slipped away again after that 1980 Grand Slam because it is hard to repeat success, although not impossible. The team sort of disintegrated after that season with a lot of players getting injured and then retiring. It is why I have so much admiration and respect for someone like Sir Alex Ferguson who does it year in year out over an incredibly long period of time.

My period as a 'professional' after retiring from the game allowed me to pursue other careers. I didn't know at the time that it would come full circle but I'm glad it did. Nothing will ever replace playing, but because I was out of the game for so long I wasn't really allowed to get involved in coaching and I missed out on that. I would really have liked to have got involved in coaching more.

Circumstances haven't allowed that and so I've just got on with it and have done my bit as an administrator, but I never really set out with an ambition to do what I've done – I've always thought if it happens, it happens.

BILL BEAUMONT

Beefy and I have known each other for 30 years and we've always got on well. He was a great cricketer in his time, but as a bloke he is one of the best I know. Our paths had crossed a few times before becoming opposing captains on *A Question of Sport*, but that is where we got to know each other really well and even though the programme was competitive it was great fun. Although I only caught him trying to cheat once – because so was I!

BOB WILLIS
DETERMINATION

It might sound strange to say this about a sporting hero of mine, but how on earth Bob Willis took 325 Test wickets I will never know! How he took more than 50 still baffles me, but the fact that he did puts him in a very special bracket as a sportsman who battled against the odds to achieve something great.

Bob Willis was always going to be good enough to take those wickets and have the impact on cricket that he had; it's just that his body looked like giving up on him at any stage. There was not a day in Bob's sporting life when he didn't wake up without some kind of pain or discomfort. His knees were completely shot to pieces and after major surgery on both of them it was incredible that he managed to come back and perform the way he did over the next decade.

Bob was my opening bowling buddy for several years and I've not seen a finer example of an English fast bowler in my lifetime and this is despite his injury woes. He nearly died on the operating table after suffering a thrombosis on one occasion and his knees looked like spaghetti junction from the amount of times they were sliced and diced. There wasn't such a thing as micro surgery when they went into his knees, it was the big knife and he got cut to ribbons. That is why his determination to return to the game at the highest level and then deliver his best performances for years to come rates as something special as far as I'm concerned.

His talent was rarely in doubt. Even though it was hardly an orthodox approach to bowling Bob, or rather Goose as we called him thanks to his arms and legs flailing all over the shop as he bowled, was the best fast bowler England had produced in a long time and I don't think we've seen another to beat him yet.

Guys like Angus Fraser, Darren Gough, Matthew Hoggard and Steve Harmison have all had their moments and have all done great things for England over the years, but in terms of consistency, durability and sheer hostility none of them can claim to be in the same league as Bob. They've all experienced the pain and hard work involved in injuries and getting back out on the park, but these players have been lucky in how medical procedures have improved since Bob's time. 'Goughie' in particular will know what dodgy knees are all about, but the techniques used by Dr Richard Steadman on him were a million miles away from what Bob had to go through, although he came out on the other side alright.

After having that surgery early in 1975 Bob returned to the England team during the latter part of summer 1976 and he struck right away with eight wickets in the match against the West Indies at Headingley. That was a great effort by him because it proved to everyone that he could do the job that he feared might be over for him.

By the time I joined the England side in 1977 Bob was a well-established senior member of the side and I looked up to him in more ways than one. Standing at six feet six most people had to do that to him, but to me he was the fearsome England fast bowler that struck fear into the hearts of the opposition. So imagine my surprise when I first walked into the England dressing-room and found this ferocious fast bowler to be one of the funniest and most generous men I'd ever met. Bob was so very good to me when I joined the side and his dry laconic sense of humour had us all in stitches most of the time.

His current role as Sky Sports' curmudgeon in the studio is one that he plays ever so well, but I can assure you he is anything but sour in person. He is a genuinely funny bloke who is great company to have around.

MY SPORTING HEROES

His kindness to me meant we struck it off pretty well from the beginning. There was a bit of a bowler's union with Bob, JK Lever, Mike Hendrick and myself, and as the junior member they made me feel at home.

We had quite a lot of the same interests. He used to drag me to Bob Dylan concerts all around the world and although I liked a few songs it was nothing compared to his obsession. Someone who changes their name by deed poll to Dylan after their hero shows a certain amount of devotion. You knew which room belonged to Goose on tour because he would have Dylan's songs blaring from under the door at all hours. It would be at strange times too because he never slept. A good night's kip for Bob is about three hours; he just cannot sleep. As a result he had to be in a single room on his own rather than share with other players and keep them up all night.

Our other great common interest was and is wine, so we soon slipped into a very easy relationship as far as that went and it provided us with some great memories, one of which has actually resulted in a little business venture.

It was on the 1978–79 tour to Australia that we met a man who was to play a big part in both our lives, but before we got to that part of the trip, I remember the only game in which I witnessed Bob wilt under the strain his body was handling, and I must admit I thought that was it for him. Bizarrely for a cricketer Bob doesn't really like the sun much and during the fourth Test at Sydney we found ourselves playing in 42 degree heat with the sun beating down. We bowled 158 at the Aussies during that match but Bob bowled just 11 of them. You knew if Bob left the field something was seriously wrong and on this occasion he thought 'Oh this is a bit hot' so he trotted off the field and sat on a metal chair underneath the shower for about three hours! He said he just needed to 'cool the engine down'; meanwhile his buddy at the other end whom he shared the new ball with was busy running in for his 28th over! Luckily for us he'd cooled down enough by the time we got to Adelaide for the next Test and it was in a bar there one evening that we met wine maker extraordinaire Geoff Merrill for the very first time.

We were just having a drink and Bob said, 'Geez, I just can't drink any more of this weasel beer,' or something even less complimentary than that; overhearing this an enormous bloke sat just next to us with a giant moustache turned round and Bob thought he was going to thump him for being rude about Aussie beer. But instead he just said, 'Oh well, don't worry about that, you should come and try our wines!' and it turned out to be Geoff. So we took him up on his offer and he took us to see his vineyard and let us taste some very good wines and a close friendship was started which has continued to this day. A few years after that we had the idea that we'd quite like to do our own wine and Geoff was the ideal man to go to. It was all a bit of a pipe dream really but seventeen years after the first discussion we produced our first bottle of 'Botham, Merrill and Willis' wine which is going strong with about seven vintages to date. The wine has done pretty well, but for us it is not about making money, it is just a passion of ours.

Two mates who shared the new ball for England are now sharing a wine label, but we had a couple of obstacles to get over along the way. The wine got nicknamed BMW for obvious reasons and one afternoon I got a strange call from a German who said, 'I am the lawyer from the BMW car company and we understand you are using our name for the wine.' I said, 'No it has nothing to do with you, it is called Botham, Merrill, Willis and some people in the media have decided to abbreviate it.'

'This is not good enough.' he said in a bit of a flap. 'Well listen mate, I'll tell you what, I promise I won't make any cars if you promise not to make any wine,' and with that I put the phone down. Bob got very twitchy about it all, but as yet we've been OK.

Bob's finest hour as an England bowler will be forever entwined with me at the Headingley Test of 1981 and I've said it before and I'll keep on saying it, there should have been two man-of-the-match awards there. I got the runs and took a few wickets but his 8–43 to wrap the game up was just a phenomenal piece of bowling and put him into exalted company. For those who don't remember Australia needed just 130 to win and were cruising at 56–1 when Bob changed the course of history. Having been told to run up the hill to bowl because I was being given my head following my 149, Bob went up to Mike Brearley the captain and said, 'Look, at my age I'm too old to be running up the hill, give me a blast down it and I'll see what I can do.'

It didn't take long for Bob to show Mike and the world what he could do as he found edge after edge, had short-leg pouncing on the fended ball and then in rampant style knocked back Ray Bright's stumps to bring about the most remarkable England win.

It was a completely mesmerising spell of fast, hostile and brutally accurate fast bowling that made the hours of toil on dodgy knees worthwhile.

The thing about Bob was that every time we went out to play I just expected to see him fall in a heap at any stage, but he just kept on going, he was a seriously tough competitor. And perhaps with that unique style of his with arms and legs all over the place, I don't think people actually realise just how good he was. He might not have had the grooved action of a Dennis Lillee or the rhythmic grace of a Michael Holding, but with his Buckingham Palace guard hairstyle flapping in the wind he was so effective.

If you want to talk to someone about Bob Dylan he's your man and if you're looking for someone who knows about real mental toughness then Bob's your man on that too because I don't know if he ever got out of bed feeling 100 per cent. His body just wasn't designed for the pummelling he gave it, but he did it anyway.

He rarely complained, he just got on with terrorising opposition batsmen and some found it particularly painful, like Aussie opener Rick McCosker who had to bat with a head full of bandages in 1977 after Bob had broken his jaw with a bouncer. Rick Darling also had a near-death experience against Bob after being struck on the chest by a bouncer which caused him to swallow his chewing gum, but it got stuck in his throat and he couldn't breathe properly. He had a real aggression that all fast bowlers need, but off the field he just had this laid back demeanour where very little would get him upset. Of course if you watch him on television now you'd think that having his tea too hot would send him into a lengthy rage against the tea growers of China!

BOB WILLIS

There was a distinct dividing line in my career. I started playing for England in 1971 but I couldn't string many games together at all until 1976.

After the Centenary Test in Melbourne in 1977 I was spending a few days' holiday in Sydney and Tony Greig our captain, who I found particularly inspirational, basically told me I'd let him down in that Test after he'd looked after me in the run up to the match by not making me play and bowl too much.

At that time I met a chap at a barbecue called Arthur Jackson who was a hypnotherapist and he put me onto a new mental and physical training regime, which transformed my career as my long-term fitness dramatically improved.

Although I had a constant battle with fitness, thanks to my bowling action which didn't really lend itself to treating my knees very well, I got a lot more determined and mentally much tougher following that Centenary Test. And you need to be to play top-level sport, so in many ways I got better physically and mentally the longer I played.

I got into a regime of slow long-distance running which did an awful lot for my stamina and transformed my career in every possible way.

Once I broke into first-class cricket and then got an early opportunity with England I felt I could succeed at that level. I had raw pace and it was a weapon that was and is very hard to find. For a long time I only had to turn up fit to get picked because I was an out-and-out fast bowler. I was fortunate that they generally wanted me to play, which is a real advantage for a player, and the fact I was taking wickets for England as well obviously helped.

As I got fitter the England team was joined by a certain 'Beefy' Botham at that time and we steamrollered the Aussies in 1977 before forging probably the most devastating opening partnership England had enjoyed for decades.

It was terrific to bowl with Beefy because the pressure was taken off me. Beefy would bowl into the wind all day long and have to get the ball ripped out of his hands, while I could be used in short sharp bursts down the hill. Beefy was just so strong and hungry for work it made the perfect combination.

Headingley in 1981 was just about the best I ever bowled. It was the last chance saloon and thanks to Beefy's knock it gave us something to bowl at. His performance was incredible that summer and he will admit his knock in Leeds didn't really start out as much other than a slog. His innings at Old Trafford – where he again scored a century – was a far more stylish innings, but together with his bowling they were 'Beefy's Ashes' no question.

I've had some great times with Beefy on and off the field and in our day the tours provided much more spare time for us so we could get out and about and enjoy ourselves. We spent far more time with the opposition than they do now and we used to go out to wineries and things like that during our rest day in the middle of a Test!

It was during those times that long-term friendships were made and Beefy slots right into the middle of that group.

SIR BOBBY CHARLTON
PASSION

At times life can be so complicated that it can drive you crazy and you long for the simplest of days when you had no worries and no pressures. Of course you think back to your childhood and to days either playing in the park or at the beach and just being able to run around carefree throughout. Whenever I do that my mind takes me back to the '60s and a time when I still dreamt of playing for England – football that is and being the next Bobby Charlton.

He was one of my big schoolboy heroes. I used to have pictures of him on my wall and I can remember trying to recreate those booming shots of his in the playground – to less success of course.

He was everything I wanted to be as a sportsman. He was fierce, competitive and bloody good at what he did, but he also seemed to have a gentle manner about him. A proper Englishman with decency and class, winning with humility and losing (rarely) with good grace.

Whether it was for Manchester United or England he delivered the goods so many times there is no point really keeping score, and as a result he became the most successful English footballer in history. He won 106 caps, scored a still record 49 goals and of course helped England win their one and so far only World Cup success. Apart from the pinnacle of international achievement he also helped turn Manchester United from being one of the bigger clubs in England to being the biggest club in the world, winning domestic titles and cups as well as the coveted European Cup for the first time by an English club. His anointment in becoming Sir Bobby Charlton was entirely justified as a footballer, but his subsequent dedication to good causes and charities makes him all the more deserving.

I have since got to know him as a person and he has completely lived up to the image I had of him and has continued to be a real hero of mine in the way that he goes about his business to this day. However, I must stress that it was Bobby the footballer that won a place in my heart when I was just a little boy.

His story is a heart-warming one based on the awful tragedy he lived through. It is hard to think of Bobby without recalling the terrible Munich air disaster in 1958 where 23 people died on a flight returning from a European tie in Belgrade that crashed on take-off in Germany. It not only robbed Manchester United of a team of talented players, but it also shaped the way that he has lived the rest of his life.

I know that being on the plane and coming through the other side when so many of his friends and team-mates didn't had a deep effect on him as it would anyone, and he can be an emotional guy. One of the things he has talked about and I know he still asks himself is the question 'why me?' when it comes to the Munich air disaster. 'Why was I spared?'

It is a question that he will continue to ask until the end, but with plenty of time still left on the clock he has made and is making the most of the chance he was given. He knows he was given a second chance when a lot of his mates like Duncan Edwards were not. So to come through the horror and confusion of an incident like that and to have the career he then did reveals an inner strength that I don't think many of us can comprehend. They do say that survivors of horrific accidents like that often struggle to come to terms with why they've survived and others haven't, but he has coped with it as well as I think anyone could have.

Getting picked for England soon after the event must have been quite a bittersweet moment for him especially as he scored against

SIR BOBBY CHARLTON

Scotland on his debut too. I think from then on every glorious moment he enjoyed as a footballer must have been tinged with a little sadness for his departed colleagues, but it did not deter him from making the most of the chances he was given and in many ways it drove him on.

I've known a lot of people who have come back from adversity in sport to enjoy fantastic careers and I've got a lot of respect for that, but in truth once you decide to get back out there and show what you can do then there is a burning desire not to let anybody down and to give your all – sportsmen and women know no other way and Bobby Charlton was the epitome of this.

With Manchester United decimated by the disaster Sir Matt Busby rightly turned to Bobby to be his rock around which the team would be rebuilt. Throughout the '60s Bobby cemented himself as the footballer to be compared to. He was strong in the tackle, clever with the pass, fit as a butcher's dog and could run all day long, and when it came to shooting . . . I don't think I'm doing anyone a disservice when I say no one has ever kicked a ball as well as Bobby. I know some of the current players like Cristiano Ronaldo can do some special things with a ball, and who can forget Roberto Carlos' banana kick against England in 1998. However, for me the truest striker of a ball was Bobby and by all accounts he actually still is!

Not too long ago he was involved in a funny drinks advert with a number of great England players from the past like Chris Waddle, Peter Reid and Peter Beardsley. Of course Bobby banged one in to remind us all of what he could do even into his late 60s, but it was in between the match filming that he really turned it on. They needed to get some shots of Peter Shilton making some great saves for the camera so asked if someone would shoot at him, and in a flash Bobby was there taking aim. He let them fly this way and that, to the point where both Waddle and Beardsley had to step up and shoot too so as not to be outdone by a pensioner!

I saw him do something similar close up a few years back through our work with the Laureus Sport for Good Foundation. We were two of the original forty founders of the organisation and I've been glad to get to know him properly as a result.

Bobby has been very conscientious when it comes to getting

involved and on one occasion we were both involved in a project in Northern Ireland, which was about bringing Protestants and Catholics together in Derry. It is a difficult situation, but differences can often be put to one side through sport. He was revered by all who met him whether they were adults or kids and I just marvelled at the way he went about the day. He just had this infectious enthusiasm for what was happening and was a real livewire with the kids. He went and had a kickabout with them and for a guy who is not young he could still hold his own. He just loves playing football, whatever the circumstances. And you can imagine the thrill they all had at sharing a football pitch with a World Cup winner.

The thing that comes across most with Bobby is his passion, and if he gets involved with something it gets his full commitment. He will stay the course all the way with whatever he is doing. His love of Manchester United and of English football courses through his veins and his involvement throughout his life has shaped him into the wonderful man he is. He is a bit like a stick of Blackpool rock with Manchester United and England written all the way through the core of it.

Bobby's ability as a footballer was never in doubt and when he played his goal-scoring part in England winning the World Cup and then Manchester United winning the European Cup in 1968 he got all the plaudits he deserved. However, even in those great moments his thoughts were never too far away from Munich and rather than celebrate wildly after a side that included George Best had won Europe's premier trophy he had a quiet night of reflection on what had happened ten years before. It was fitting though that he managed to be a part of the successful era that picked the club off its knees and took them forward with such purpose and it is why his subsequent role as a director, and ambassador and figurehead for the club is such a perfect one for him.

In one man Manchester United have someone that embodies the history and traditions of their club, yet looks forward to bigger and better things and embraces the new stars of the game.

The fame and the money sloshing about in football isn't a problem for Bobby; he doesn't resent what the players get these days and he accepts that he had a great career and a great time, but everything moves on with time and there is no point looking back wishing you were still playing.

I know that he likes Wayne Rooney because he plays with passion and gusto. The game has changed a touch since he played but I think he likes the way Rooney goes about his game and sees a little bit of himself in him.

I was only a young lad of ten when England won the World Cup and I can remember being over the moon at our team being champions of the world. Four years later I was heartbroken as we failed to retain the trophy that should have been ours and should have been a fitting send-off for Bobby. There have been endless debates about it since, but I still can't believe that Bobby was taken off against West Germany in the quarter-finals. I'm not saying that England would have won with him there because with Gordon Banks in goal we were already in trouble, but for Bobby to be taken off when the game was still very much alive at 2–1 was a shocker. I always find it amazing when teams 'rest' their big players for tougher challenges to come in a tournament because as we all know those challenges disappear if you don't deal with what's in front of you, and in 1970 Sir Alf Ramsey got it wrong.

It should have been a huge night of celebration for Bobby having overtaken Billy Wright as England's most capped player that day, but instead of looking forward to a semi-final he was left to ponder the end of his international career and he deserved a better send-off than that.

Whenever I think of Bobby Charlton three things pop into my head: world champion footballer, world champion bloke and that hammer of a right boot! He is everything we could possibly want in a sporting hero and more – I'm just proud to have got to know him.

BOBBY MOORE
LEADERSHIP

Bobby Moore is one of the few people to have made my list despite my having never met them. His life was cruelly cut short by cancer in 1993; however, his deeds as an England football player and captain remain an inspiration to me and to millions of people who regard him as a truly special man.

Your opinion of people can change quite dramatically when you get to meet them in person, either for better or worse, but it is always a joy when people simply confirm what you thought about them in the first place, and I've got no doubt that Bobby Moore would have fitted into that category had I had the chance to share some time with him.

His achievements as a footballer are there in black and white and are as important to our sporting heritage today as they were back in 1966. I got to play in two World Cup finals, but never ended up on the winning side, so I can only imagine what Bobby must have felt to be the first and only Englishman to get his hands on the Jules Rimet trophy.

That image of him holding the World Cup aloft while his team-mates carried him on their shoulders is an iconic one for anybody with even a passing interest in sport and for me it was the last thing I saw of that day before being yanked off on holiday to Devon.

BOBBY MOORE

We used to go on a caravan holiday down to the south-west every summer for a couple of weeks and being just ten at the time I was crazy about England making the World Cup final at Wembley. So the whole family were getting ready to go except for my dad and I who had to watch the final. So as my mum and my sisters got the car packed, the men watched one of the greatest games the world has ever seen. As the game headed towards the end of the 90 minutes all the women were now in the car waiting to go, but unfortunately for them there was a long way to go yet. Every ten minutes one of my sisters or my mum would stomp into the living room and try to nudge us into the car so we could start our holiday, but I just refused to move and anyone who knows me can understand how stubborn I'd have been even then! But it was all worth it to watch England win the trophy in the end and even though I can't remember exactly what happened on that holiday, I always think of it as one of the best simply because of how it started.

Bobby Moore was a hero to me as a young lad and as I grew up to play a bit of football he was the person I idolised and most wanted to be like. Being a centre-half myself for Scunthorpe United, I'd like to think I modelled my game on him! Maybe I didn't quite have the assuredness on the ball that Bobby had, or the ability to read the game quicker than anyone else, but I'm pretty sure there are a few former centre-forwards who felt the full force of our crunching tackles, even though I'm sure Bobby actually came away with the ball rather than bruised ankles.

It is important to remember that with or without that World Cup win in 1966 Bobby Moore was a great footballer full stop. Of course sport is about winning things and Bobby did just that with both England and West Ham, but even if he hadn't, his ability on a football pitch was second to none and his peers knew it.

In 1964 he captained West Ham to an FA Cup win that then paved the way for a European Cup Winners' Cup triumph a year later. I remember hearing a lot about West Ham in those days and Bobby Moore was the kingpin as far as I was concerned. He was the captain of England and the player that most embodied what football in England was about.

You had to be tough, strong and athletic, but in Bobby there was this classic gentlemanly nature about him. He was gracious in defeat and magnanimous in victory and that is why he made such a good leader.

In many respects it is difficult to prove yourself to be an outstanding leader in football because of the nature of the game. You don't have to make too many game-altering decisions on the pitch and there isn't the chance to say too much to the rest of your players because they are scattered across the pitch and the noise from the crowd is deafening. So unlike a cricket captain whose job can be quite cerebral and measured, a football captain has to inspire by deeds much more than words. He is the man who should set the tone for the rest of the players to follow and I think that is what Bobby Moore did so well. He led by doing and that is something no one can argue with.

It meant that his position in the game was a hugely respected one and he proved to be the perfect ambassador for our country.

That photo of Bobby and Pele together at the 1970 World Cup reflects what his contemporaries thought of him. He was and is held in the highest regard by those he played against and in some ways was probably appreciated more in his heyday by those he competed with than by the great British public. Pele called him 'my friend as well as the greatest defender I ever played against,' and having spoken to the likes of Sir Bobby Charlton about him, I am in no doubt about his calibre as a player and as a man.

After winning the World Cup he received all the accolades he deserved such as the BBC Sports Personality of the Year as well as an OBE, but as with most of the World Cup winning squad I don't think his achievements were fully appreciated until much later.

When England won the World Cup there was no doubt that we thought the trophy would find its way back to our shores on a regular basis, so while it was a special occasion it certainly wasn't treated with the reverence a win now would be. Could you imagine the fuss that would be made over the players now if they were to win the trophy?

Bobby Moore played in an era of understatement and when British reserve was still a huge part of our lives as a nation. I know things were beginning to change with the swinging '60s and with the likes of George Best becoming a huge celebrity as well as a footballer, but these were new themes and ideas; they weren't as ingrained as they are now.

For someone like Bobby Moore it would not have been what he was used to. He always struck me as being a straightforwardly decent man and not someone who needed others to tell him how good he was, he knew.

And it is that easy manner and belief in his own abilities that made him an ideal captain and the perfect man for team-mates to follow. He set the example and everybody else tried to get up to his standards because they admired him, respected him and wanted to do well for him.

It is curious therefore that when he retired and clearly had his eyes on moving into management things didn't work out so well. In fact he was virtually ignored by the football establishment and just couldn't get the sort of job that the likes of Alan Shearer, Tony Adams, Paul Ince and Bryan Robson have been able to enjoy following their successful careers.

He thought he had got a look-in at Watford before Graham Taylor came along, but no. Instead he had to have a go with a club called Herning in the Danish third division!! Can you believe that?

We've got the former World Cup-winning rugby captain in charge of the national side just three years after his retirement and yet our football version couldn't even get a gig in English league football. It was nothing short of an insult.

Perhaps there was too much jealousy flying around the FA and the clubs in those days, and seeing as Bobby was his own man he clearly didn't fit into the mould those in power were looking for.

As it turned out his attempt at management didn't work out at all, although he can at least rest happy in the knowledge that his brief tenure at non-league Oxford City gave his assistant Harry Redknapp a first step on the ladder to where he is now as a successful Premiership manager.

Even though he led from the front as a player for both West Ham and England he just couldn't do the same off the field as he then moved to a club in Hong Kong. I still can't quite believe how the game collectively turned its back on him in England.

MY SPORTING HEROES

In the end he moved into the media where his insight as a summariser on the radio showed just how well he knew the game and what clubs had missed out on. He read the game so well as a player that he was always going to see something that ordinary people wouldn't.

His achievement though at leading England to our one and only World Cup is something that just brings back great memories and never fails to bring a smile to my face, and I will always associate it with him as captain more than with anyone else, hat-trick or not!

BRIAN CLOSE
BRAVERY

I would say that apart from my parents, Brian Close had the biggest influence on my career and in a cricketing sense it was he and Tom Cartwright who had the major say in my early development.

Brian led from the front and the thing with 'Closey' that you admired from a player's point of view was that if he gave you a bollocking you probably deserved it, but at the end of play he'd be the first person to buy you a beer in the bar afterwards. That was it, the telling off was done and it was all a part of your learning curve. You might have thought at the time that it was a bit harsh, but he had his reasons and they were always good ones.

During my early days at Somerset under him along with a certain I.V.A. Richards, Closey guided us at just the right time. When you're a kid in your late teens, it is easy to go off the rails but that was never going to happen with him around. He was as tough as old boots on and off the field and there would be no messing around on Closey's watch, but boy was he supportive. You wanted to do well for him and you wanted to prove your worth, and if he rated you he let you know it, which was the ideal confidence boost for Viv and I. We were told early on that we'd make a success of ourselves at international level and that spurred us on to prove him right.

MY SPORTING HEROES

In the early days for my sins I used to have to travel with him and his driving didn't exactly make for the most calming of journeys. Let's just say that it is an experience that you'd never forget – somewhere between scared out of your wits and the white-knuckle territory for me. He would drive as quickly as the banger he had at the time would take him and he would always be up to something else, whether it was eating a sandwich, drinking some coffee or checking out the form guides for the races. I would always offer to drive for him, hoping and praying he'd say yes, but he'd just look at me and say, 'You're alright lad, it helps me relax.' Well I'm glad someone felt relaxed!

My wife Kath grew up with Closey as Uncle Brian, as he was her godfather and very close to her family. One day he'd had a prang in his car which was nothing unusual in itself – he had more prangs than hot dinners.

He'd had one of these little accidents and asked Gerry, my father-in-law, whether he could drive him down to the garage so that he could pick his car up.

Gerry said, 'Of course I will, let's go and get it now.' So they drove off to the garage and when they got there the car was just being given a last polish and the mechanic was rubbing the bonnet as Closey got out of the car.

'Here you go, Mr Closey. The car is all ready for you.'

'Thanks lad,' said Closey, because to him everyone was called lad. He got in the car, drove it out of the garage up to the roundabout at the top of the road, went straight into the back of another car, drove round the roundabout and straight back down into the garage. All this before Gerry had even moved off himself, so he just climbed out of the car, gave the mechanic the keys and said, 'Gerry, can I get a lift home, the car's not quite ready yet!'

I have such a soft spot for Closey, but that is not why he makes my list. He makes it in his own right as an outstanding sportsman that I looked up to as much for his ability as anything else.

He makes it for his all-round excellence, his leadership, his durability, his skill as a cricketer, but more than anything in my mind he makes it as the bravest man I ever played with.

He was a remarkable player right up until his mid-40s and a fine all-round sportsman who could play golf right-handed and left-handed off single figures.

He played football for Arsenal and Bradford city and still holds the record for being the youngest person ever to play a Test match for England at just 18 years and 149 days old.

But with Closey we're talking about one of the bravest players the game has ever seen. The vision of him standing firm and taking the blows on the body is an image attached to him for good reason, because he took an awful lot and not once complained or shied away from them.

Colin Cowdrey rightly got a lot of accolades for going out and playing with a broken arm against the West Indies in 1963, but it shouldn't be forgotten that it was Closey who battled and top scored in that innings with 70 after taking blow after blow from a ferocious pace attack.

It wasn't the last time he would stand firm in the face of a West Indian barrage either. At Old Trafford in 1976 he and John Edrich got called back into the side on that uneven, quick wicket and took the body blows yet again. After that match he came back to the county on Tuesday night and we were playing in a one-day game on the Wednesday and he was black and blue. He was incredibly proud of his bruises and actually got someone to take a photograph of his 'medals'.

The next day though facing Steve Rouse, who was no more than a little medium-pace seamer, one of his deliveries just kicked up a little bit and hit Closey on the side of his ribs and he buckled. He almost went down in absolute agony, which was unlike him, and we knew something was up. Despite his protestations we made him go to the hospital and get the bruises checked out for internal bleeding, but he wouldn't go until the day's play was over. Nowadays a player only needs the toilet to rush off the field, but Closey refused to leave the ground until the end and then he got it all checked out.

When we asked him about the blows and the bruises he didn't really talk about it at all, he just shrugged it off as part and parcel of being a cricketer. To him it wasn't even a case of being brave, it was just what you did and there was no point in complaining about it. If you didn't like it then you could go and find something else to do, it was as simple as that.

He was a great character, a teak-tough sportsman who would field anywhere around the bat without fear of getting hit. There used to be an award for the player who took the most first class catches in the season and he and Phil Sharp were neck and neck one year. 'Sharpie' was always at slip when the spinners were on and Closey fielded at short-leg, and in one of the last matches a batsman swept the ball fairly hard and it struck Closey right between the eyes. He rocked back holding his head while the ball looped up straight to Sharpie at slip, but no sooner had the umpire raised his finger than Closey tried to claim the catch. 'It's my head, it's my catch!' he kept saying. 'That's my catch! That's my catch!' until Sharpie just relented and gave it to him, even though the book says differently.

He never ever asked you to do something he couldn't do or hadn't done himself and that is why he had so much respect from his teams and those in the game. He was as solid a man as you will ever find and he is a bloke I looked up to from the moment I got to know him and will do so until the day I die; he was and is a hero to me.

He commanded total respect in the Somerset dressing-room, and it didn't matter how young or old you were, Closey was the man we all looked to.

We held him in such high esteem, and even though he could be strict and stern with you at times it was for your own good. He was there to teach us and to pass on his wealth of knowledge and experience. He did that and more for us.

It is easy to forget how fantastic a player he was as well. Bravery is one thing, but bravery without ability is little more than stupidity. He was brave because he also had the talent and the skill to back it up. He could go to the coal face and stand up to whatever was being thrown at him because he was actually good enough to deal with it and dish it out with the bat as well. Closey was a superb cricketer who would score runs for fun.

When I first joined Somerset I remember him scoring runs willy-nilly and he was our best batsman at the time. Viv learnt under his wing and blossomed into the great player he became as Closey wound down his career.

There was a reason he got called back into the England side at 45 and don't think he didn't have the ability to be there. He had bags of it. He was a special player.

BRIAN CLOSE

His bravery didn't just extend to the physical; he was also mentally and tactically brave too. The faith he used to show in the likes of Viv and myself as young players coming through was a joy for us. He trusted us and gave us responsibility when the easy thing would have been to look to older, more experienced players. He was brave enough to trust his instincts and what he knew about us as players to give us our head and that takes some doing.

On those car journeys he and I would talk a lot about cricket. We would spend hours sharing ideas and talking cricket and just because I was a youngster he didn't dismiss me which would have been easy for him to do. Instead I fed off him and learnt more and more about the game, which turned me into a better player as I got older.

I like to think I took a bit of his bravery with me when I made it into the England side. I used to relish the combative nature of international cricket and I used to love going toe-to-toe with opponents. At those times you've got to be brave and you've got to stand firm; no one taught me that more than Brian Close.

BRYAN ROBSON
BRAVERY

Sport is constantly changing from one era to the next and it annoys me when people try to compare one generation to another. Of course you can suggest that someone would have been successful if they had been born at another time because of their ability, but I think it is unfair to say that W.G. Grace was a better player than Donald Bradman or that Bjorn Borg is a better player than Roger Federer because it is not an equal comparison. How do you know how good Federer would have been with a wooden racquet? You don't. You play the sport in front of you and you don't worry about what it used to be like or what might happen in the future. You live in the here and now and you should get judged on that alone, so as far as I'm concerned the finest midfield footballer in the game during the 1980s was Bryan Robson and he was perfect for his time. When 'Robbo' was in a football side it was always better for it full stop.

In many respects he changed the nature of what being a midfielder meant and I'm convinced the term box-to-box was born as a result of Robbo. What an engine! The guy could run and run all game and when other players got tired he was able to take advantage, even though he had been purring around the field just as long as they had.

He really was the complete midfield dynamo who could run

like the wind, tackle like a JCB digger and pass like a precision laser; he was the whole package. And to top it all he did it while enjoying himself off the pitch too.

I've known Robbo a long time and I know he won't mind me saying that in our era of sport you could give it everything on the field and enjoy yourself off it. I'm not saying you were reckless, but it was all part and parcel of sport where the social side mixed with the physical side and you got on with it. You'd earned the right to sink a couple of drinks if you won, but you knew that come the next game or the next training session you had to be able to perform. You couldn't let that get in the way of your sport because you'd be found out and Robbo knew that better than anyone. He was always one of the first to training and always one of the last to leave and he never offered any excuses for his football – not that he needed to. He would always be able to turn it on when it mattered and that is what it was about, and what I mean about being right for your own time. He wouldn't get away with it now because the game has become far quicker and more scientific as far as diets and nutrition goes, but I'm absolutely convinced that Robbo was such a committed footballer that he would have been a triumph in the game whenever he grew up in it.

The thing that I admired most about Robbo was that you knew what you were getting with him – total commitment. There are no airs or graces, just complete dedication to producing the goods on the football field.

Having started off at West Bromwich Albion, his career really took off and came to my attention when he moved to Manchester United to follow his manager Ron Atkinson. It was a big move for him and I remember there being a big price tag with it, £1.5 million, which was such a big amount in 1981. But if anyone could live up to it Robbo could.

He quickly established himself not only as Manchester United's midfield maestro, but also as their captain because he was a terrific leader of men, the sort of bloke that others would follow.

Because he was fit, strong, fast and athletic it wasn't difficult for him to set an example. He wouldn't ask players to do anything he couldn't do and with every aspect of his game in working order he could do everything. I like that about sportsmen. The more you can do as a player to help your team win, the better and in Robbo, Manchester United got an all-action hero who defended as if his life depended on it yet could sweep forward in attack and score some devastating goals both from long range or with a precise header.

It was inevitable that he would suffer injury problems as a player because of his incredible high-octane style, but when you're fit and firing you don't think about things like that.

At times when I was struggling with injuries I used to wonder whether it was my own fault for doing as much as I did batting and bowling, but in truth I wouldn't have had it any other way. Top-flight sport is not for the faint-hearted and actually the more you can do to help your team win the better. And that was what Robbo was about too. Getting out there, getting stuck in and giving it everything – the injuries can take care of themselves another time. By 1984 he was the club's captain and managed to lift his first trophy in the famous number 7 shirt – the FA Cup.

The legend of the number 7 shirt at Manchester United has much to do with another man featured in this book – George Best. Yet even though Robbo didn't quite have the sexy swerve of the hips that 'Besty' enjoyed, his efforts in that shirt added to the legend and in many ways secured it before Eric Cantona, David Beckham and Cristiano Ronaldo took it on.

For England too he was a giant among men, probing and cajoling his team onwards in what was a difficult time for the national side, who really should have won something with the players they had at their disposal. Clearly the 1986 World Cup will forever be remembered for the quarter-final defeat thanks to Diego Maradona's handballed goal, but the absence of Robbo from the side following the second game made a huge difference. A persistent shoulder injury reared its ugly head and cut short his World Cup and when I think how good a player he was then, along with Gary Lineker, Terry Butcher and Peter Beardsley, that should have been England and Robson's World Cup. Would Maradona have cut England in half the way he did if Robbo had been there? I'd like to think not, but that is what injury can do to a player and a team and unfortunately it cost him.

The way he tackled and put his body on the line was a lesson to footballers everywhere and told them just what he was capable of at the highest level. The only unfortunate thing for him was the toll his style of football took on his body and at one stage his shoulder used to pop out for fun at times.

He was still a magnificent player for England though and his nickname 'Captain Marvel' was absolutely spot on in my book. He was driving both England and Manchester United forward and when Sir Alex Ferguson took over at the club he could spot that as easily as anyone.

Towards the late 1980s things were starting to change in football with hooliganism rife and the Hillsborough disaster round the corner. The game was ready to be shaken up on and off the field and that is exactly what Fergie was doing at United. He was ready to have a revolution at the club and get rid of the drinking culture which was going on at a lot of clubs up and down the country. Players like Paul McGrath were eased out of action, but not Robbo. He was always able to focus on what mattered most which was the football, and I think that is why Sir Alex Ferguson rates him as one of the finest players to have been at the club during his managerial career. Robbo really laid the foundations for what has become English football's greatest dynasty.

He would have been the player that Fergie put up in front of the rest of the squad and said, 'That is what I want from the rest of you guys.' He is the guy that played the game hard, trained hard and then celebrated hard. There was little in between.

When the game was said and done he'd let his hair down, but he'd be the first on the training ground the next morning without fail.

I really got to know Robbo at length on *A Question of Sport*, when I started on the programme, and he was an absolute blast. A really good guy to be around and what I would call a salt of the earth sportsman. He was a great player on the pitch and remains a great bloke off it and he knows what the game is all about.

I remember going to the BBC Sports Personality of the Year awards and seeing Robbo and before I'd even shaken his hand he was leading me over to the Manchester United team to introduce me to someone. He was so excited about this new player they'd got. He said he had never been surer of a player in his life and he insisted I meet someone who was going to be the future of the club and would be a household name. 'Come and say hello to Ryan Giggs.'

Robbo is also a very generous soul who really helped out when we had a couple of charity games at Scunthorpe against Manchester United and thanks to him they would send over their best team, full of their stars of the time which helped us raise a lot of money. And while Robbo would patrol and control the pitch, I would hang around the centre circle and watch in wonderment at this fast, strong and skilful footballer who just dominated the game around him. He was awesome.

He lifted two more FA Cups for Manchester United as well as the Cup Winners' Cup, which was a taste of the European success Fergie was to have at the club, but the real prize was to come in the twilight of his career.

Normally I'm not too bothered who wins the league championship – unless of course it is the mighty Scunny! – but in 1993, I actually took great delight in seeing Robbo win the title with Manchester United. He hardly played for them as injuries took their toll, but it was such a deserved reward for all his years of hard work as a professional footballer. He behaved the way sportsmen of that time were supposed to behave. He was hard-working, he was committed, he was dedicated to football and to life and I loved that about him. And when the club ended their drought to lift the first ever Premier League, I thought his work had been worth it and he could finish his career a satisfied footballer. Of course he wasn't to know at the time just what kind of a dynasty he would help start, but every time I see Rio Ferdinand or Gary Neville lift another trophy at Old Trafford I do have a little chuckle and think it is what Robbo started.

Of course he is back at the club now as an ambassador which is a dream role for him. He will undoubtedly take over from Bobby Charlton as the club's figurehead in due course. It is his career as a footballer that I really admire him for, and although I don't think he did an awful lot wrong as a manager, it didn't come as naturally to him as running around on the park.

I used to see a bit of him when he managed Middlesbrough,

which is not too far away from me, and so I'd give him a buzz to go and watch the odd game. It struck me that he was doing all he could to get the team playing the way he wanted but you can only work with the tools at your disposal and I think he was always going to find it tough at the clubs he was at.

He had some good seasons with Middlesbrough and the way he helped West Brom stay up in 2005 was something to be really proud of, but I think the role he has taken on with Manchester United now is perfect for him.

His full-throttle style of football caught up with him as a player with a succession of injuries that diminished his later years, but the real price might have been much more severe. Having suffered with serious back pain for a while, Robbo underwent some major surgery to correct a problem with a fused vertebra – if things hadn't worked out for him he could have been paralysed from the neck down. It wasn't a likely outcome, but when you know that is a risk of the surgery it makes you think twice. Thankfully he came through it and can still play in his legends games and get around the golf course, even if he takes in more of the course than some! He was a teak-tough competitor who summed up what top-level football could be about. Great fun, hard work and immense satisfaction over a pint.

COLIN MONTGOMERIE
PASSION

Colin Montgomerie has puzzled me for years. He is one of the finest golfers Scotland has ever produced and has enjoyed some of the greatest successes any professional sportsman could want, yet he still appears to be restless and unfulfilled. Even though he has won the European tour Order of Merit eight times, including a record seven in a row, plus enjoyed five Ryder Cup wins he still seems agitated by the game. Not even the ultimate honour of captaining the Ryder Cup side in 2010 at Celtic Manor appears to have relaxed him, and I put it all down to one thing . . . no not missing out on a major, but passion.

'Monty' has a passion for golf that is hard to believe. His love for golf goes beyond any real sensible explanation, it is a ferocious consuming passion and I think it is what makes him the player he is, for good and bad.

I would class Monty as a dogged and determined competitor, but I would also call him moody because he is moody and that side of him has an incredible effect on how he plays his golf.

If it is a good day then he can play some exquisite golf that will take your breath away. He strikes such a sweet ball and has lovely control around the greens. You will see that great big grin of his as he walks with that little bit of a spring in his step; however, on a bad day it is probably best just to leave him be and get out of his way.

Luckily for Monty his bad days haven't been too plentiful over a magnificent career that might be missing a major, but more than makes up for it thanks to his other tournament wins and his Ryder Cup exploits. His achievements in the game stand up against anyone who has played and I include major winners in that bracket.

Of course his biggest bugbear is that he hasn't won a major even though he has come close on a few occasions. I know that is the thing he covets more than any other and I still think he could do it.

I think of someone like Goran Ivanisevic who came so close to winning Wimbledon so many times until eventually, when all hope seemed lost, he triumphed and I could see the same thing happening for Monty.

It would be the crowning moment of his career and I would love to see him do it. And if it could be the British Open up in Scotland it would make the perfect fairytale for his career.

I really do believe that his record is amazing, he has bestridden European and world golf for years and I've constantly been impressed with what he has achieved. His doubters and his critics will constantly chuck the major-less record back in his face, but so many times when he has come close, he really has done enough to win the thing, but has been beaten at the post by some extraordinary golf from someone else. Five times he has come second, five times!! At that level it is still a remarkable record.

Nowadays young British golfers going to America to play in their college system are two a penny, but Monty was one of the first to go out there and try something different when he went to Houston Baptist University in a bid to set himself the highest possible standards he could.

As one of the pioneers of that trend it again shows his passion for the game to do whatever he could to be the best. And if I remember rightly there were a lot of eyebrows raised at the time as to why a player with obvious potential would choose to finish their sporting education abroad rather than at home, but it paid off for him.

MY SPORTING HEROES

To me that is part and parcel of reaching your goals. Going wherever you have to in order to become the best you can be. It is not to say that facilities, coaches or teams in the UK are poor, they're not, but sometimes sportsmen and women need to go outside the bubble and outside their comfort zone to find out what top-level and world-class competition is all about.

Look at Martin Johnson who went to New Zealand, Andy Murray who went to Spain and Alec Stewart who went to Australia. They all went and got something they couldn't get in the UK and when they came back, it was our sporting heritage that became enriched by it and that is what Monty did. It is hard to argue against it.

For me Monty's passion for the sport shone through most of all after his seven years of dominance on the European tour. Having achieved what he did, he endured a bit of a rough time professionally and personally, ending up with him slipping not only out of the top ten in the world but down as far as number eighty-two, which is mind-boggling to think of.

From there he could have never come back. He could have finished with the game at the highest level safe in the knowledge that his record of seven straight Order of Merits was as good as anything anyone has done in the game.

Yet he couldn't and didn't let go because he loved the game so much. Sometimes you come across these sportsmen and women who are good at their chosen sport and they like playing it, but it becomes a bit of a chore and they lose the love they started out with. Not Monty, the fire keeps on burning inside him and to see him climb back up the rankings and win his eighth Order of Merit in 2005 was something special.

His individual career record is something to be proud of, but what really sets him apart for me is what he's done and hopefully is going to do in the Ryder Cup. There is an old saying that cricket is a team game for individuals, but there can be no greater example of that than in the Ryder Cup and it is where Monty comes alive. It is where his passion shines brighter than ever and it is where he has found the true appreciation of his talents.

Having been invited to both the 2002 and 2006 Ryder Cups by the respective captains Sam Torrance and Ian Woosnam, I've seen Monty operate up close in that environment and he is an absolute inspiration. At times he can be aloof and almost over-focused when he is at a tournament on his own, but at a Ryder Cup he gives it absolutely everything he's got for the team cause. He is helping out the rookies, he is signing autographs for fans, he is giving the captains the odd bit of advice here and there, plus he is bringing home the points that the team needs to win. In 2002 he was a revelation for Sam Torrance, picking points out of the American pockets as if they were little pieces of Scottish shortbread for tea. I was so impressed by him during that tournament that he instilled confidence in me that we'd win. In 2004 his legend grew even more, and again in 2006 under 'Woosie' at The K Club in Dublin he was so impressive. Just like Sam Torrance had wanted in 2002, Woosie repeated the tactic and sent him out first in 2006 to strike fear into the Americans and get some blue colour up on the scoreboard as early as possible, and once again it worked. For Monty to have played in eight Ryder Cups and never lost a singles match is a mind-blowing statistic and one that Sir Nick Faldo might wish he'd relied on in 2008 when the Americans finally triumphed after nine losing years. To be fair to Nick, his wildcard picks of Ian Poulter and Paul Casey didn't let him down, but how I bet he would have loved to have had Monty there too.

He is the European linchpin whenever he plays and he is the player that the rest of the team rally around. He was the player no American golfer wanted to draw in a Ryder Cup match and he was the player that the American public loved to hate.

They tried to get under his skin with name calling and poor etiquette to try and knock him off his game, and there is only one reason you do that – if you're scared. They tried to disrupt him and make him fail, but their taunts so often fell on deaf ears and that is all credit to him, especially when you concede he has the ability to lose it at times. From his position as European talisman when he played, he must now translate that team ethos and ability he has into something altogether trickier as the non-playing captain at Celtic Manor.

I know the captaincy means the world to him and I know that he will do whatever it takes to bring the trophy back to Europe.

MY SPORTING HEROES

My guess is that he will have learnt a lot from the likes of Sam, Ian and Seve Ballesteros who fostered a great atmosphere amongst the team. The European players always seemed to be enjoying themselves at the Ryder Cup and Monty will go far if he can make sure they have plenty of fun in 2010.

To spend time with him is to understand his passion for golf, but he is also very warm and friendly. There is another side to Monty that isn't often seen. People always assume he is a miserable old so and so, but he's not. He's thoroughly entertaining and decent company. I feel that he is a much maligned personality and wrongly so. Whenever I've spent time with him he has been great company all around the world.

I can remember going to a tapas bar with him, Woosie and Peter Baker one year in Madrid. It was during the Spanish Open and we all decided to go out for a nice meal. It just so happened that there was some bullfighting going on at the same time and there were a few locals gathered at the bar watching it on TV.

As the food came over Monty started tucking in and then noticed what was on the telly and, being a sensitive soul, he said, 'Oh no, that bullfighting is terrible, we must get them to turn it off!'

As he motioned to the waiter to come over, Woosie quickly pointed out that he was in the middle of Madrid, there were rather a few gruff looking locals watching the fight intently and he was also busy chomping down on some rather rare beef. 'It might not be such a good idea for you to get upset about the bullfighting mate, I reckon a change of channel might just make you the matador to these local bulls,' said Woosie.

When the waiter got to the table to ask what Monty wanted, he simply said, 'I really like the bullfighting on the TV, do you know whether we might be able to go and watch it live?' We were all in stitches, but from that moment on the waiter became our best friend and anything Monty wanted was done within seconds.

DALEY THOMPSON
DEDICATION

I think it is sometimes difficult to compare different Olympic champions. They say a gold medal is a gold medal regardless of how you got it, but I beg to differ. For example, how can you compare the chances of a swimmer like Michael Phelps, who gets to compete in eight or nine events with a medal on offer for each, with those of a cyclist like Victoria Pendleton, who gets one shot at one medal and that's her lot. Or how do you go about comparing the athlete who picks up five gold medals at five different games like Sir Steve Redgrave with the gymnast who peaks just in time for one Olympic Games, picks up five and then disappears without a trace. In my book winning a gold medal is special, but retaining it is where the real glory lies. And that is why the likes of Redgrave, Sir Matthew Pinsent and Seb Coe are my kind of heroes. To that list you can add the greatest all-round athlete England have ever produced – double Olympic decathlon champion Daley Thompson.

At the 1980 and 1984 Olympic Games he proved beyond doubt just how good an athlete he was, setting world records and claiming gold medals for fun. In fact at one point in 1983 he had every major decathlon gold medal hanging at his home because he was simply the best.

Some sportsmen and women set new benchmarks in their sport which puts them out on their own, but they are not particularly original in what they are doing or how they are doing it. Too often in sport one decent competitor is replaced by another and while their success is well earned and means an awful lot to them there is something missing.

Nothing was missing where Daley Thompson was concerned and he is simply one of a kind. I don't think I know anyone that is more of an individual than him and that is a good thing. He is a once in a lifetime sportsman who accepted nothing but the very best of himself and did whatever he could to achieve it. But where Daley was and is different is that he does it all in his own way; he doesn't care what people think of him, he doesn't care if he looks silly, if it helps him become a winner then he'll do it. If it helps him push someone else into second place and makes them feel bad about themselves he'll do it. It is a no-compromise attitude to sport and life and that is why I love Daley Thompson.

Daley is the most complete athlete England has ever produced by the very nature of his competition. If all-rounders are the multi-skilled stars of cricket and running, kicking and tackling fly-halves are the kings of rugby then the decathletes are the heroes of athletics. Daley was an absolute master, able to run, jump and throw in one event after another better than anyone else in the world had done before him and he proved just how good he was time and again.

Daley has become a very good friend of mine since we first met during an appearance on *Superstars*. There was myself, Jonny Francome the jockey, Brian Jacks the judo champion – who set all the records in the gym test – Danny Nightingale, who was the modern pentathlon champion of England, and Daley Thompson the then current Olympic decathlon champion.

Jonny and I worked out pretty early on that we weren't going to figure too well in *Superstars*. In those days most of the competitions all revolved around athletics and endurance rather than much else so the two of us thought we might as well enjoy the trip because we knew we weren't going to win.

That became even more clear after the decision on which sports to drop. Everyone had to drop one event which was as close to their own sport as possible and in our competition there was both pistol shooting and fencing, so even though they were both included in the modern pentathlon Danny Nightingale only had to drop one of them because he was slightly better at one than the other, so he completely destroyed the rest of us. Jonny and I were determined to enjoy ourselves and so we came back to the hotel one night after going to a very nice bistro with some mates for a long one.

We had to go down to the Thames to do some canoeing the following morning, but as we arrived back, the other three were all outside jogging, stretching and getting themselves ready so we tried to sneak into the hotel without anyone seeing us and luckily we managed it. About two hours and one ropey snooze later I have to get into my canoe and the starter gun goes and everyone goes powering off. The next thing I know is that I've got these frogmen pulling me out of the water – much to Daley's amusement. 'That's what you get for hitting the clubs till all hours!' he shouts at me in between guffaws and he has never let me forget it.

During his pomp in the late 1970s and 1980s he was virtually unstoppable, but for one man – the German Jürgen Hingsen. Like all great individual athletes who produce their best when another rival pushes them, Daley was no different. In Hingsen he had a man who he could use as a focus to spur himself to greater heights. Just as Bjorn Borg and John McEnroe did and Roger Federer and Rafael Nadal are doing now in tennis, Daley had Hingsen to keep pushing him. Three times in the early 1980s Hingsen broke the decathlon world record and four times Daley broke it back, but the most brutal demolitions of Hingsen during two decathlon competitions came at the 1984 Olympics and the 1986 European Championships. This was where Daley secured his legend.

Having been unbeaten for six years Daley was under real pressure from Hingsen who had just broken his world record again. As a powerful sprinter and jumper the decathlon has always been set up to favour those type of athletes with the 100 metres and the long jump coming first and second so it enabled Daley to get himself in a strong position from the start. Hingsen responded and on the second day a big discus throw made sure there were only thirty-two points between them with three events to go. The pole vault was something to behold and as Daley put in an incredible five metre leap followed by his memorable celebratory somersault, poor old Hingsen was feeling the heat in more ways than one and was throwing up in the stadium tunnel. Not only had he taken Hingsen apart mentally and physically, he then caused a huge furore by wearing a T-shirt with the slogan 'Is the world's second best athlete gay?', which everyone took as a swipe at Carl Lewis. I thought that was hilarious and showed Daley at his most individualistic and antagonistic, and with a gold medal dangling around his neck he had every right to be. He was doing what he wanted to do and he had the talent to back it up.

From there he and Hingsen continued their duel and in a fantastic climax they met on the German's home turf in Stuttgart in 1986, and in another fantastic show of his ability and strength of character Daley put Hingsen and his countryman 'Siggy' Wentz to the sword over two days. The home crowd absolutely hated it. Here was this English athlete daring to embarrass their own and they let him know about it with booing and catcalls throughout. Hingsen even went so far as to apologise for his home fans. Daley didn't care though. The louder they booed the better he got and when he had clinched the gold out came another T-shirt saying 'Bernhard, Boris and Daley, Germany's favourite sons', suggesting he was on a par with Bernhard Langer and Boris Becker!

It was another example of Daley's unbelievable faith in his own ability and he had every reason to hold that self-belief. The Great Britain head coach of the time, Frank Dick, summed Daley up so perfectly when he said, 'Daley was far and away the best I ever came across for making the most, competitively, of what he had physically, intellectually and emotionally. He linked those strengths and built on them, compensating for areas that were not so strong, rather than focusing on them. He had great character, charisma and self belief.'

There was one element of the decathlon though that he really struggled with and actually hated. The 1,500 metres that closes the event is the thing that Daley would wilfully have got rid of, he hated it. His aim was to build up enough of a lead so that he could just jog round without pushing too hard. He always made sure he knew exactly what time he had to run to win and he would make sure he was never more than a second inside it, no more. He really didn't like it, pumping those little legs round the track. I used to crack up watching him do it, because I knew he hated it so much. It is much the same response when I get him to come and help me with my charity walks.

I get to see Daley fairly regularly these days because we both have a place out in Spain on the same golf course and he runs his fitness camps from there – he's always trying to get me involved but he hasn't managed that yet.

The other thing we do together is the Laureus Sport for Good charity work and so we meet up at the odd function and in my book he is the best person to have dinner with. He never touches a drop of alcohol so as the waiter comes round with the wine he has his lemonade and he leans over to me and says, 'What do you reckon Beefy, white or red?' I'll tell him, 'Just a drop more white please,' and when the waiter gets to him that's exactly what he asks for.

He loves his cricket and he is quite protective of me at times. We go to the odd sporting dinner where there are a few American sportsmen who aren't really cricket buffs and if they haven't seen me for a while they sometimes forget who I am and they'll be standing there stuttering, 'Oh hi, er, er, it's er, er,' and in a flash Daley jumps in and with a finger jab and a cheeky smile, he says, 'It's Ian Botham, cricketer, England's greatest all-rounder, that's Sir Ian Botham, the best!'

And I have to say, 'Thank you Daley, you're most kind, now stop it!' as we giggle about it. He never wears a jacket and tie though. Even if it is the blackest of black tie events he will turn up in a tracksuit or a set of Adidas shorts and a T-shirt.

Seb Coe is one of Daley's best mates and even at his wedding, Daley turned up in a tracksuit, although to be fair to Seb he did come in a new tracksuit. At my 'Knight of Knights' dinner in London to celebrate a knighthood with the cream of English sportsmen, businessmen and politicians, what was Daley wearing? You need not ask.

I don't actually think he owns any shirts or trousers because I have never seen him wearing them. I've known Daley for 30 years and the only suit I've ever seen him in is his birthday suit. He's just a good buddy, a generous man who gives up a lot of his time for charity and is a bit of an unsung hero.

MY SPORTING HEROES

He has never courted the limelight, but I still cannot fathom why he has not been given a major role in the running of British athletics. I know he is doing a few bits and pieces for the London Games, but he should be front and centre alongside his great mate Seb Coe. He should have had a high-profile role within British sport years ago, but for some reason he didn't quite fit in. That is such a narrow-minded attitude from those in power. Just because Daley is a bit different and a bit of an individual doesn't mean he hasn't got plenty to offer. He knows what it takes to reach the top and he knows what it takes to be a winner. If he had been involved over the last ten years would we be scraping the barrel for athletics heroes now? The jealousy that runs through British sport has suffocated too many great sportsmen and women and it has been to our cost. Daley is a true hero and should be treated as such.

DALEY THOMPSON

I enjoyed my career as an athlete, but I don't talk about myself now that is over; I think that is for others to do and I'm sure my old mate Beefy will put it in his own words just fine. What a character Beefy is though. I can remember when I first met him on *Superstars* and I had got up to go for my early-morning jog, and as I set off from the hotel along the river I spotted him coming in from the nightclubs. We had a good laugh that week, but most importantly, I beat him! He and John Francombe became known as the nightclub boys and apart from when we competed we only saw them at breakfast staggering home.

His effervescence and lust for life is what impressed me about him and to me he has always been one of these larger than life characters. He works hard, he plays hard and what you see is what you get.

We got on well and we stayed in touch because he used to invite me along to some cricket games which was kind of him and was great fun. I got to know his family and we became close friends.

In later years we've both become involved in the Laureus Sport for Good charity which allows us to spend a bit more time with each other and I must say the more I see of him the more I like him. He's got a good heart and he is a real giver. I'd like to be more like him. Although he does get his benefits out of me like extra wine at dinner, and I'm still waiting for him to pay me back for all those glasses he's had over the years; it must be quite a vineyard by now.

I consider him to be a friend and if he is prepared to get off his backside and get out there walking for twenty or thirty days at a time to raise money for charity, the least I can do is turn up for two or three of them. Although for some reason he always gives me all the really hilly legs to do because he knows I'm going to hate it, so why not make it worse!

He is not one of those guys who has just taken from his position in the public affection; he has given plenty back and I think you can hold him up as a proper role model. He is someone that I've always looked up to, but what I will say is as far as my career goes, he is lucky I never decided to take up cricket!

As for my issue with clothing, I think at my age it is better for me to be comfortable wherever I go so I think it is better that I'm there rather than be uncomfortable. I always give people a choice, if they want me there I've got to be able to wear what I like, if not no big deal. I will say now though that I am prepared to wear a suit for the first time just for Beefy – at his funeral.

When Ian was at his best in the 1980s he really was rock 'n' roll and he took cricket to another level, not just because of his performances but because of his personality, and kids wanted to be him. It was a great time for sports people in the 1980s and Ian was right at the forefront of that, he is yet to be surpassed, and so are his dodgy clothes and haircuts!

DAVID BECKHAM
COMPOSURE

There is a well-used sporting truism that says it isn't the success of an individual that tells you about their character, but the defeats and the tough times that tell you who they are. It is how they come back from those tough times that reveal just what sort of a champion or not they are. I've heard it from the likes of Martin Johnson and Sir Alex Ferguson and it is something I believe in too. It is all well and good when things are going well, life is easy when you're in form or your team are winning and the whole world loves you.

Your real ability as a sportsman and as a person shines through when life gets hard and you're out of nick, the team are faltering and the public are no longer on your side. It is those situations for which David Beckham was born. If ever there was a sporting hero who could write the book about coming back from a disappointment it would be him. His incredible career has been filled with so much success, yet it has been slapped about with huge collective and personal failure too. On the surface I think it would be easy to say that he has led a charmed life and things have fallen into his lap; the real truth from where I'm standing is that David Beckham's career in football is a story of always coming back for more, and equally one of redemption too.

It all started off so well for him from his very young days as a winner of a soccer skills camp to being picked up by Manchester United as a 14 year old. His first little setback came when he didn't break straight into the United first team after playing in a dominant academy side and was sent out on loan to Preston North End; it didn't do him any harm though as he played his way back into United colours. It was the first example of him proving a point to those who doubted him and to me it seems like this has been a feature of his career. In the 1995–96 season he came alive along with the other young Manchester United starlets of the time like Gary and Phil Neville, Nicky Butt and Ryan Giggs. Together they swept to the title despite Alan Hansen's famous phrase on *Match of the Day* that 'you'll never win anything with kids!' How wrong he was proved and again David found himself completely vindicated and justified in the eyes of doubters.

I suppose the day I really sat up and took notice of David was following his goal against Wimbledon, where he slotted an inch-perfect shot over the bemused keeper – from the halfway line! It was almost a seminal moment in English football let alone in his life and it announced him to the world. That strike pretty much summed up David's ability as a footballer for me. He was never blessed with great pace or great dribbling skill, but boy can he strike a football. Next to Sir Bobby Charlton he is probably the best pure kicker of a football I have ever seen. Those adverts he did with Jonny Wilkinson told a story about how to strike a ball and Jonny told me just how impressed he was with David's timing. That, together with a set of lungs that just allows him to run and run, is what made him into such a great footballer.

With the skill that he had, he turned himself into an invaluable source of goals for both Manchester United and then England either from crosses or free kicks. His vision is another asset that set him apart, yet you can have all the vision in the world, but if you can't produce the right pass to make the most of it then what good is it to you?

With everything going so well for him, winning trophies with United and making his England debut in 1996, it was hard to see where it would go wrong. The real blow came in 1998 when he was handled pretty poorly by Glenn Hoddle, the then England manager, and left out of the side at the World Cup finals despite playing a huge part in getting them there.

In the end he had to play and I remember another of his trademark free-kicks helped England beat Colombia. Then came the nightmare as his petulant kick out at Diego Simeone got him sent off as England crashed out of the tournament. It is hard to remember just how bad he was made to feel for that mistake, but he became the most hated man in Britain. Probably a little harsh considering we're talking about a football match here, but that is how close to the bone the England football team can get. He was a walking target for every English football fan in the country, but this is where he earned my total respect. He faced up to his tormentors and began playing football again for United, letting his performances do the talking. He didn't hide or cower in the face of adversity, he stuck his chest out and made a conscious decision to prove people wrong. Of course he felt bad about what had happened; he is clearly a proud Englishman like the rest of us, he just made a mistake. Thankfully the English public are a forgiving bunch, and after a while his displays for United and then for England started turning the tide, and a first European Cup for an English team in 1999 certainly helped.

By the time he was made England captain in 2000 he had shown enough remorse and subsequent talent to be accepted as the nation's new footballing leader, but it wasn't until after a couple of extraordinary performances that his rehabilitation from pantomime villain to national hero was complete. The first was something that couldn't fail to get everyone on your side; a 5–1 thumping of the Germans is just a footballing dreamland, and even though Michael Owen scored the hat-trick, David's contribution was telling.

The second and most important was his last-minute free-kick against Greece in 2001 that booked England's place at the 2002 World Cup finals. When I watched that game and that final goal the way he celebrated with his arms outstretched and in utter delight I thought I could visibly see the demons from three years previously leave his body. Thanks to his composure and steady improvement as a player and as a man it was the most complete personal turnaround in sport and you have to give him all the credit in the world for that.

A huge part of his comeback was down to Fergie and I think he acknowledges that. Whenever I've heard him talk about Sir Alex it has always been in a respectful way. I know that their relationship took a turn for the worse towards the end of his time at Manchester United. The boot to the eye was probably the low point, but subsequently I know that they both still hold a lot of respect for each other.

I saw Sir Alex quoted as saying at a Q&A evening in 2007, 'He was never a problem until he got married. He used to go into work with the academy coaches in the evenings, he was a fantastic young lad. Getting married into that entertainment scene was a difficult thing.'

Of course he was referring to his marriage to the former Spice Girl Victoria Adams and in a way you can see how David's life has changed completely from being just a well-known footballer to becoming one of the world's most valuable and marketable brands. I guess that cut across the relationship with Fergie and so he was allowed to leave for Real Madrid. I could understand Fergie's mantra that no player is bigger than the team.

I do think that his move from footballer to global superstar has added huge pressure to him and to his family, but the way he has appeared to cope with it is nothing short of remarkable. His agents and the team behind him have done a fantastic job as far as that goes, and no matter what anyone says, if he didn't want to be a part of it all he wouldn't do it. He has signed up for a life in the spotlight and he has handled it all with real class.

I think he realises though that without his football he wouldn't have got his opportunities off the field. He needs football and he has used it to take himself to another level. It is true for all sportsmen who find themselves in the public eye and who appeal to sponsors etc; without our sport as a vehicle we would be far less marketable.

At Real Madrid the pressure was still on him to live up to his status as a 'Galactico' next to Zinedine Zidane and Ronaldo, and he started off pretty well, scoring for fun to begin with. However, after three years at the club he had failed to win the all-important league title. Having won six titles, two FA Cups and a European Cup with Manchester United, to get nothing in

Spain would have been a failure. By the end of his final season he wasn't even being picked for the side by Fabio Capello. He could have sulked at yet another knock, but he kept on working hard, waiting for his chance to impress and even though he was off to Los Angeles at the end of the season he forced his way back into the side and played a huge role in a late-season charge to the title. It was yet another impressive comeback for David.

I've never met him. I've been in the same room as him in Lisbon at a Laureus sports awards dinner, but I didn't speak to him. I read somewhere that he was quoted as saying that I was one of his sporting heroes, so I would love to spend some time with him and work out what makes him tick. All the boys I know who have played with him and know him well say he is a good lad in the dressing-room and he is a fine player.

The only regret I think he could have is that he went to America too soon. I think he should have stayed at a top European club whether it was Real Madrid or a move back to England. In the end he had to fight to get himself to AC Milan and then stay there so he could keep impressing the England manager.

It is funny how things work out sometimes. After giving up the England captaincy in 2006 his international career looked like being over when Capello took charge of the England side. Here was the guy who wouldn't even pick him for his club, so why would he pick him for England? Yet he has gone on to pass Bobby Moore's caps record, which is a testament to him.

It takes some guts and determination to come back and make another fist of his international career, and it is almost a fatherly role he's got now, closing out games and adding an air of calm to the dressing-room. His aim of course was to play in one last World Cup in South Africa, and that is what he would have done had injury not robbed him of the chance. I felt for him when he ruptured his Achilles tendon playing for Milan, because we all knew that was the end of his dream. He could have been forgiven for turning his back on the tournament and moping about not being there, but that is not in his nature. His desire to do whatever he could to help his country continued to burn and although he wasn't playing he was supporting, cajoling

DAVID BECKHAM

and encouraging from the sidelines in a desperate attempt to add something to England's cause. We all know it didn't work out, but what you cannot argue with is David's commitment to England and to their success. It wouldn't surprise me to see him continue his involvement with the game long after he has retired, because he is that passionate. I think, though, if you sat him down and talked to him honestly about his career he would see the move to LA Galaxy as the one hiccup that could have been avoided. I mean, here is a world-class international footballer playing the sort of football I think I played in and he is better than that. I think he got that wrong, but since then he has shown his determination to put things right.

David Beckham has never excited me in the way that George Best or Paul Gascoigne did on a football field, but when I look at what he has achieved and what he has come through to do so I feel quite proud of him. I think he has taken some difficult roads in his life and has managed to get through them with a strong character that puts our country in the best of lights.

DAVID GOWER
SKILL

I played nearly all my cricketing life with David Gower and he was without doubt the most elegant and skilful batsman I ever played with. He is a man I admire for so many reasons both on and off the field of play, but his batting ability left me breathless and in awe every time he walked to the crease.

And despite my preference to watch anything but cricket while I was waiting to go in to bat, David was the exception that proved the rule – I would happily watch him bat anywhere and at any time.

David, or 'Lubo' as he's known, after an Adelaide steak house that he fell in love with, was an enormous talent and just so relaxed with it. In fact if he was any more laid-back he'd be horizontal. I can't think of anyone who has played the game who has been more laid-back about things. Chris Gayle springs to mind with his laconic West Indian swagger, but I don't think anyone else comes close to David when it comes to being languid on the cricket field.

Very little ever seemed to fluster him or get him upset; however, he did have a blue touch paper as well and I've seen him go off on a few occasions – such as when I got out against the Australians in 1989 with an impetuous hoick and my apology went down like a fart in a lift. Lubo tore a strip off me then and even though his spark of aggression didn't come out that often, when it did you knew about it.

Despite his cool and relaxed exterior I can assure you there was and is a rod of steel running through David Gower, and make no mistake that in the big games when it really mattered under huge pressure he was as switched on as anybody. You can't do what he did without having that tough inner core which made him a bloody tough competitor. He played 117 Test matches, scoring 8,231 runs at an average of 44.25 with 18 hundreds. His record speaks for itself and of all the players I've played with and against he would most definitely be in my team.

The reason I wanted to watch him from the team balcony though was because of the almost heavenly way in which he batted. He took the skill of batting to new levels and made a notoriously difficult game appear ridiculously easy. It is a gift that he was blessed with, but when he got out it seemed like a curse because it always looked worse than it was. He has played some of the best innings I have ever seen live and I consider myself lucky to have been in the same dressing-room when he played them.

I can remember a knock he played against New Zealand in the Benson and Hedges World Series Cup in 1983 and he seemed to score a ridiculous number of runs. I had never seen a better exhibition of one-day batting at the time; he just stood there and delivered, smashing the ball this way and that. He took 158 off the Kiwi bowlers from just 118 balls, which was unheard of at the time. I just watched with incredulity as he took them apart with such ease. When it came for my turn to bat I thought it would be a breeze; after all Lubo had made it look like one, and anything he could do . . . well not quite. I lasted for 13 balls and scored precisely no runs! If ever there was a lesson as to how skilful a batsman David Gower was, that was it.

In his pomp, before his shoulder fell apart, he was also one of the best fielders around. He was one of the very best in the Derek Randall 'cat-like' mould.

As a player I couldn't fault him and as a captain I loved him to bits because he invented the phrase 'optional nets' which I thought was just magnificent and that would do for me. I was never one for endless hours of practice. I didn't want to waste my best balls or my best shots in the nets, I wanted to produce them out in the middle and David saw that the same way.

As a captain I thought Lubo had the right theories and the right principles, but unfortunately for him he got blown away by a pretty impressive side called the West Indies. For me though he encouraged the individual within the team environment and I think that is the right way to do it. Some things are not for everyone and if you make players do things they don't want to they will resent it and turn away from you. David encouraged freedom and I applaud that approach – one that Andrew Strauss is trying to instil within the England side at present, personal responsibility.

David's lust for the good things in life and for life in general always went down well with me and we've had some great times together, although not everyone has had a happy ending. I can remember touring the West Indies with him in 1986 and we knew that we would be playing in all the internationals on that trip so when we got to St Vincent for a practice match that we weren't playing in I persuaded him to get in touch with a mate of his that had a yacht in the harbour.

The suggestion was that we'd take the yacht out for an afternoon's sail and do a bit of fishing just to get away from the cricket for a bit, nothing wrong with that. But when we got back we found out that England had been bowled out for next to nothing and suddenly the story wasn't about the cricket, it was how Gower and Botham were seen on a yacht as England collapsed. It was sod's law as far as we were concerned and David got lambasted for it which I thought was a bit unfair.

Cricket meant a lot to him, but he also values living one's life and so getting out and about to see things and do things was just as important to him as anything else, and I like that in him. I was so glad that the West Indies incident didn't put him off though as he continued to enjoy life as much as cricket with little jaunts, as the well-told 'Tiger Moth' adventure in Australia during the 1990–91 tour proved.

The one time I wasn't with him when I wish I had been was when he drove a hire car onto the ice in St Moritz, which is normal, except it is done when the ice is thicker than one of the modern-day bats and can carry the weight, not as they're heading into spring and the ice is rapidly melting. He told me he only just managed to get out of the car in time before it sank to the bottom of the lake, which didn't go down too well with the hire company Hertz. As a result I still don't think he is allowed to hire a car from them even today! I wish I'd seen him scrambling over the ice on that day – I'm sure he would have lost his laid-back demeanour during that little episode.

Something else I've always loved about David is his passion for wines which is something we both share. We're very lucky in that we have both done an enormous amount of travelling around the world to all parts and have come across some of the finest wines known to man.

We both enjoy that part of life and David never stops trying to sell me the merits of French wine, which I poo-poo, and I try to open him up to Australian and New Zealand wines that usually stomp all over his Châteaux 'La la la'.

His bottle of choice is obviously Bollinger RD and he generally aims for the fine wines with the fine price tags on them too, while I try to convince him that there are plenty more like that at half the price if only he'd look outside the traditional order of things. He is a throw-back to the Empire days and a Francophile to boot, who just needs a beret and some garlic round his neck to finish the look! I think years of discussions have finally got him coming round to some of the New World wines, but I know I'll have to keep on at him until the end.

When he was captain we were staying at Mottram Hall for the Old Trafford Test one year and we all gathered one evening around dinner for our big team meeting. Peter May was the chairman of selectors and Mickey Stewart was the manager and they had arranged everything including the wine. Midway through the meal the house wine we had been drinking ran out and so Mickey asked David as captain to choose some new wine for the table.

Being a bit of a connoisseur David surveyed the list and picked out a lovely drop called Cheval Blanc which went down a treat. As the evening drew to a close the management signed off on the whole thing and I remember Mickey seeing the price and saying,

'Oh that is very reasonable indeed. All the wine for tonight has come to just £145, marvellous news!'

When it then came to checking out and paying the final bill at the hotel, there was a bit of a disagreement between Mickey and the hotel staff over the total. Mickey was adamant that they'd made a mistake, 'How can it be this much when the total price for the extra wine was only £145?' To which the lady at the desk replied, 'No, Mr Manager, that is the price per bottle.'

After much coughing and spluttering Mickey was ready to throttle David for spending nearly the summer budget on one night of wine, but he stopped himself only to ask Lubo for a whipround. Well, David's response was typical of him, and completely right. With a sarcastic glance he took £20 out of his pocket and offered it to Mickey saying, 'That should about cover it.'

The England management learnt a few valuable lessons that night; firstly make sure that there is more than enough wine for your guests when you host a dinner, secondly if you run out, don't give the wine list to a Mr D. Gower, and should you fail to do both of them, just suck it up and put it down to experience.

On the field though is where I truly admired him. His batting was exceptional. All the very best players, in whichever sport it is, always seem to have that split second longer than everyone else to do what they want and David had more than a split second.

He was so smooth in the way that he played, he just caressed the ball to this boundary and that, just full of wonderful timing, which is a skill you simply cannot teach. He had that gift and put it to fantastic use for England over so many years – although we should have seen him use it for longer than we did. His clash of styles with Graham Gooch probably cost him at least another ten Test matches and another couple of centuries, but even though he had grounds to vent some frustration over it, he never did. He simply got on with the rest of his life and has made the most of that too, from his cricket media work to the successful stint he had on the hit BBC quiz show *They Think It's All Over*.

We have been good friends for years and years and our lives are still connected in much the same way. We used to tour together as players and now we do it as commentators for Sky Sports. We go back forever and if I am honest I would find it strange if I wasn't to work with him. We have been a part of each other's lives for that long I'm not sure how we'd cope if we were to be cut off.

Our relationship is built on solid foundations and we know each other so well, but at the same time David does keep a lot of things to himself and he is a very private person in that sense, but he's always been a good mate to me and I'm sure that will stay the same for ever and ever which is great.

He's now got an interest in shooting so I've told him I will take him out and see if he's any good with the pheasants, but I would imagine with his natural skill and superb hand–eye coordination he should be quite good at it.

DAVID GOWER

Whenever I batted anywhere near my best, it was because I allowed my natural instincts to take over; allied to that I needed the determination to battle through against a West Indies attack or whichever attack it might be. As long as I let my natural game take over and didn't try to hit the ball too hard then invariably it would go where I wanted it to.

The crucial time of my career was when I was trying to go from being a talented amateur to being a talented professional. I had a way to go and it didn't just click into place without trying. I had things to learn about the quality of the oppositions and the mental demands of making things work. You can't just wander into a professional sport and think you can do it all there and then. I had to learn about making hundreds, then making bigger hundreds, then making them more often and then making them on the international stage – there is always another step to take.

My natural ability obviously helped but it's not the only thing you need. I can look back on days when my talent would still be there, but the rest of the stuff you need to make it work like desire on the day, a clear mind and focus were not. It was difficult to sustain the highest levels of application day in day out and there were bad days when I would sometimes let it go and have to work hard to get it back. On the good days when everything was working, the drive was there, the application, the determination were all in place, I could let my natural skill take over and my batting worked very, very well and I managed to put in performances to be proud of – the hard part was doing it again the next day.

I always admired Ian for having the most unshakeable self-belief in the world. If there was even the slightest doubt in his mind he got rid of it incredibly quickly. He has been ready to play on and off the field ever since we first met back in 1978 and whenever we've played, his complete self-confidence has rubbed off on everybody around him. At times I wished I had the same level of confidence in my own game, but it was something unique to Ian. I relied on my ability to play the game a certain way and that worked well for me; I tried not to make things too complicated and let my natural skill together with the work I'd put in speak for me on the pitch.

As a captain I firmly believed in allowing players room to breathe and think for themselves; that is what I did with Beefy and it is what should be done with Kevin Pietersen in this generation. They are special people and as such the normal rules don't apply; you have to account for their personality and their talent. If you risk upsetting one or two as a result, well I think that is worth it.

Being friends with Beefy is a lot of fun and our exchanges over wines are even more interesting today than they've ever been since we no longer have to take on the world's quickest bowlers. Following a trip to see some tigers in India I've managed to turn him on to wildlife and safaris in a big way and that same wide-eyed enthusiasm that he had for cricket is there in hobbies like that. What he will get me into next is anyone's guess.

DEREK UNDERWOOD
SKILL

One of the beauties of sport is that it sparks such fierce debate over the merits of one team or another, one player or another and one generation over another. But sometimes it is hard to argue with the statistics and with 297 Test wickets to his name, I would say that Derek Underwood is the best post-war spinner we've ever produced.

There you go, I've shown my hand and am waiting to see if anyone has got something else to trump it. However, I feel that I could be waiting for a very long time because unless an English clone of Shane Warne is ready to pop out and surprise us all I think Derek's record will stand the test of time for quite a while yet.

There could be an argument for some of the old spinners of yesteryear such as off-spinner Jim Laker, who has always been a favourite of mine for his 19-wicket demolition of Australia; however, I still put 'Deadly' Derek Underwood at the top of the pile. And can there have ever been a more perfect nickname for a player than 'Deadly'? That is exactly what he was when he had the ball in his hands and too many batsmen to mention simply had no answer to him.

The thing that struck me about Deadly's left arm-orthodox spin bowling was just how much control and accuracy he possessed. He knew exactly where he wanted to pitch the ball, exactly how much he wanted it to spin and exactly how much pace he wanted to put on it. And in each case he got it exactly right. Not before, or since, have I ever seen an English slow bowler with more control than he had. It was a marvel to watch, and I was glad that he was always on my team until his final Test in 1982.

He was a genuine world-class spinner who had a remarkable cricket brain to go with his ability. He could out-think batsmen in such a wonderful way that it almost seemed as if he was toying with them, much like Shane Warne did in his pomp. The thing that slightly annoys me where Derek is concerned is that people often suggested that he was only a real danger or threat when the conditions suited him. Utter tosh. Deadly was a magnificent bowler in all conditions and his record supports that.

The conditions people referred to were pitches that were wet or damp, because in those days we used to play on uncovered pitches. So whenever a touch of rain had got onto the surface it would produce what we called a 'sticky dog' and on that kind of pitch Deadly was virtually unplayable; however, what that doesn't mean is that on dry pitches he was no good.

Arguably his greatest performance for England came quite early on in his career, and I can remember watching it as a 12 year old, as he secured a famous series draw against the Australians in 1968 at the Oval. Needing just five more wickets to win the game on the fifth day, Australia looked like being saved by the rain as a thunderstorm broke out over London, but late in the afternoon the sun was back, and by the time the ground staff and a few of the crowd had got the place mopped up play could resume with just an hour and fifteen minutes left to play. They held out for a time, but with 35 minutes left on the clock Basil D'Oliveira made the breakthrough and Deadly was on. Half an hour was all it took as he claimed the last four wickets in thrilling style to secure the win. It was a remarkable piece of pressure bowling and it helped secure his place in the England line-up for the next 14 years, and I'm glad it gave me the chance to play with him before he retired.

I took plenty of slip catches during my career, but early on I used to field at short cover to Deadly's bowling and from there I had a ringside view to his art. He would tangle his opponents up in knots and I used to love watching the batsman tempted forward before the ball turned and spat to give me a catch. It was mesmerising even for his team-mates.

Whatever happened though, at the end of play he would sit in the dressing-room and he would always look like he'd been sat in an oven. It didn't matter if we were playing in Leeds in April or Delhi in October, he would still look like he'd been squeezed into an oven on full blast by which time he felt he'd earned his half of beer and a fag. He never changed.

I must say he was always a happy man in the dressing-room and around the team. I can hardly remember him ever losing his temper, he just enjoyed what he was doing and almost always had a smile on his face. I think he seemed contented to be playing cricket for England, trying his hardest and doing his best. Knowing he always did just that I think he could always be satisfied that whether he took a hatful of wickets or not he'd given his all and that was something to be cheerful about.

His bowling was his best asset, but he could also hold a bat, as I found out to my cost during an Ashes Test in 1980. I always remember how in Sydney he went in as the night watchman in a low-scoring game and I said to him, 'Deadly, if you bat until lunch today I will buy you a case of beer.' The cheeky so and so only went and did it. He batted through to lunch and got what we thought was a really valuable 43. David Gower batted beautifully on a pitch that had been tricky to score runs on, but was getting easier. In the end the target of 216 was easily overhauled by the Aussies.

The one and only time we roomed together was for the Jubilee Test match in India on the way home from that tour of Australia. Deadly asked me, 'What shall we get from duty free?', to which I replied, 'I don't mind, as long as there's plenty of it.'

So he went round and filled up the bag with gin, and maybe a drop of medicinal whisky, and walked through Indian customs clunking his bag as he walked. As we strolled through he got stopped and asked if he had anything to declare.

'No,' he said.

'Are you sure?', at which point he was about to say what we'd bought, and so I just ushered him through saying, 'No no no, nothing to declare here!' and they let us pass through.

MY SPORTING HEROES

We got to our room and settled in, but by day five I hadn't seen him at all and wondered where he had got to. He was found sleeping on a complete stranger's floor, just to hide from me! It was a chap he'd only met that evening in the bar and he said to him, 'Look, I need your help, I've got to sleep on your floor and get a decent night's kip.' The bloke wasn't sure why England's best spinner wanted to bed down in his room, but poor old Deadly had already had his fill of late nights with me and just needed a rest.

Maybe subconsciously it was my way of getting him back for his massive error on the first night. I had a lovely pair of blue crocodile-skin shoes that I'd got in Australia. I was so proud of them, they were really snazzy and cost an arm and a leg, so they were my pride and joy at the time. Deadly said to me, if you want them looking tip top, in India you just leave your shoes outside the room, they'll come and pick them up, clean them and then have them back outside the room in the morning. I was on my first ever trip to India so knowing no better I took the word of the senior pro and left them outside the room. Those lovely soft shoes were never seen again! There is probably some bloke still walking around Mumbai with a slightly faded pair of blue crocodile-skin shoes on now!

Deadly was a good man to have in the dressing-room, because he could always be relied upon to do his bit. He was an absolute master of his trade, and I wonder whether some of the spinners today have truly learnt their art in the same way that Deadly did, bowling over after over and progressively learning as he went. He managed to figure out what worked well for him and what didn't. He knew when to flight the ball and when to bowl it flatter and with a bit more pace. He was a multi-dimensional bowler who used every tool that he had plus the conditions at his disposal to make the most of a situation.

There aren't too many spin bowlers who think about the game enough to make sure they do the same. Perhaps the closest to him at the moment is the New Zealand captain Daniel Vettori, who varies his pace, his angles and his flight beautifully to make the most out of what he's got, but he is not as big a spinner of the ball as Deadly was and struggles to take big wicket hauls.

DEREK UNDERWOOD

For England 'Monty' Panesar got his career off to an absolute flyer and I thought he was a bowler who would go on to challenge Deadly's record, but since his electric start he hasn't kicked on in the same way. He still has time on his side and he may yet get there with the volume of cricket now being played, but it is clear that batsmen have worked him out and so he needs to think a bit more about how he will combat them. If Monty had an 'arm-ball' half as good as Deadly's then I think we may well see a lot more from him. He would do a lot worse than to pick Deadly's brain on the art of left-arm spin bowling. He could learn so much from the best.

It was a pleasure to see Deadly be given the M.C.C. presidency following on from Mike Brearley. He is the ideal man for a position like that where you need excellent diplomatic skills as well as all-round respect from others in the game. In Deadly the M.C.C. could have picked no one more suited to that position than him.

DEREK UNDERWOOD

I think my bowling was refined by a lot of hard work through practice and practice. By bowling over after over I felt that was the best way for me to hone my skills. It gave me much more control over what I was trying to do and tied in with a fairly decent bowling action. I think I had a good recipe for becoming a good bowler.

One of the best pieces of advice I was given was that as a spinner, on each surface you play on there is an appropriate pace to bowl. There are times when you should push it through to get the most out of the pitch and there are other times when you need to flight it up and bowl more slowly. So that is what I was looking for when I first came on to bowl and in my first couple of overs I'd try to work out what that pace was. Once I'd worked that out I could then use the other things in my armoury like angles to try and get the better of the batsmen. If you don't work out what speed is right for the surface then your skills become less effective than they otherwise might be.

I was effective on wet wickets when the ball turned because I generally bowled a little quicker than most spinners, but I'd like to think that I was able to adapt on wickets in places like Australia and India in particular where I had some success on dry wickets.

I enjoyed my time as a sportsman immensely and as you get older the more philosophical you become. You learn to accept that on a given day a batsman can play really well and murder you, but on the next day it might be your turn. If you have some talent and a firm mental approach to what you're doing then you will always come back and do something better after you've had a bad day.

I also found it important to relax and unwind with your teammates after a bad day. It was worth having a few beers and talking to them at the end of a day because it often helped to get over the agony if things had gone poorly, but it was also a lot of fun when things had gone well.

I enjoyed playing in the same team as Ian and he was always a good man to have on your side. It is fair to say that he operated hours that I wasn't used to in India and our rooming experience didn't last too long together. However, I thought he might try to make me become his room mate forever after that because he managed to turn in the greatest all-round performance in the history of cricket during that match. He took 13 for 106 in the match and scored 114 when he batted as we won by 10 wickets. I would have done it too, if it had meant more performances like that. As it was it didn't really matter who he roomed with because he kept on delivering.

GARETH EDWARDS
PASSION

It is said that all men are created equal, yet when I watch some sportsmen I think distinctly otherwise. When I saw David Gower caress a ball through the covers I thought he was operating on another plane, or when I watched George Best jink his way round a defender I knew no one else could do what he had just done. Some sportsmen simply have no equals and when it came to rugby scrum-halves I can't even think of a player who you might dare to suggest comes anywhere close to Gareth Edwards. Goodness me, he was one of a kind and just thinking of some of the tries he scored or dashing breaks he made has my mind dancing in wonderment at just how good he was.

He set the standard for the position of scrum-half and from him all others follow. It is such a specialist position that you sometimes sacrifice one part of the game to get the most important parts. So you'd perhaps take someone with a quick pass but little pace over a speed demon with terrible hands. With Gareth Edwards a coach never had to make that choice because they got everything with him. Great hands, a killer pass, an eye for a gap, the pace to exploit that gap plus a ferocious ability in the tackle. He could also finish like a wing; with that low centre of gravity he was a tough man to put down despite his size and he made it count so many times, scoring 20 tries for Wales in his 53 internationals.

The fact he played all his games for Wales consecutively tells you something about him and his ability that no other player came close to edging him out of the side, even as a young 19-year-old starlet.

His feats for Wales and then the Lions played such a huge part in the development of rugby in the British Isles that I think it would be fair to say that without him and of course some of the other great Welsh players of the time then rugby union would not be viewed in anywhere near the same way it is today. Gareth and his Welsh wonders brought the game alive for so many people including me.

I must admit that even though I'm a diehard England fan in all sports and couldn't have been happier when we won the World Cup in 2003, my real love for rugby came as a result of watching the Welsh side of the 1960s and 1970s. It was the way in which they played their rugby that turned me on to it. They were stylish, full of verve and swagger and Gareth really was a huge part of that.

Together with Barry John to begin with and then Phil Bennett, Gareth provided the fulcrum of the side and really made them tick and I don't think you can underestimate the impact he had on such a team game.

While he was a Welsh international they won seven Five Nations titles, three Triple Crowns and a Grand Slam and there is no question at all that if there had been a World Cup available to win they would have claimed that too.

For Cardiff, Gareth maintained the same incredibly high standards and as a legend of the club and director, it was always great to go down to the club when my son Liam was playing there and spend a bit of time with him. Almost every person we bump into at the ground wants to tell me just how good a player he was and how proud they are that he played for them. They also reassure me that his best tries and his best games were always for Cardiff and not for Wales and the Lions!

I've known Gareth for a long time now from the moment we first got to know each other at Max Boyce's charity dinners at St Pierre in Chepstow over 30 years ago. From those early golf days to now he has been one of the most competitive men I know and tied in with that is his luck. He must be the luckiest bloke I know and I see it time and again on the golf course, but perhaps even more often when we go fishing.

We both have a real passion for fishing and every now and again we head up to the River Tweed in Scotland for a family fishing holiday, yet every single time he outdoes me on the fishing stakes. If there is one fish in the whole river system it will jump onto Gareth's line and if there are two there to be had, you can be sure he'll get the bigger of the two. I've never known anything like it.

In fact, the truth is I have two ambitions in life left. One is to catch a bigger fish than Gareth and the other is to be there when he buys a round! He won't mind me saying that because he is such a good guy and great company to be around.

Gareth was blessed with such fantastic sporting talent that he could have turned his hand to anything and been a success. He was an exceptionally gifted footballer as well as being a more than useful gymnast, and maybe that is what helped him to be such an elusive runner on the rugby pitch. What is certain is that he became one of the greatest rugby players of all time, in any era, in any side, but the fact that he stood out in a team so full of ability and talent is a testament to him. He also stood out as the very cream of the Lions too and it was his performance in the opening half of the third Test against New Zealand in 1971 that secured his legend.

With the series tied at 1–1, the Lions could easily have folded and having spoken to Gareth about it, I know he was feeling the nerves about the following game. He had already earned a reputation for being a fine scrum-half, but even he had a few doubts about whether he was as good as he could be. His performance though at the start of that match was as complete as you could want and it allowed the Lions to race to a 13–0 lead, one which they would never relinquish. It was the confirmation of his status as the world's best scrum-half as he tore the Kiwis to shreds. When you think that the Lions had never won in New Zealand before that series his performance came on the biggest stage and at the toughest time.

To me that is the definition of a great player – the man who assesses just how important a game or a contest is and delivers the biggest performance just when it is needed most. The fact that the Lions were able to draw the final match of the series and claim the only win on New Zealand soil to this date is down in large part to Gareth, and even though he is modest enough never to say it, I'm saying it for him!

I saw him play in a couple of games live, and even though it was coming towards the end of his career he was still a magical little player. There was always an element of excitement when he got the ball in open play or in broken field play because no one knew what he was going to do next and whenever I talk to players who played with him, they talk almost reverentially about him, he was that good.

Like most rugby fans I believe Gareth scored the greatest try the game has ever seen when playing for the Barbarians against the Kiwis again in 1973. It is the greatest try the game has seen for a couple of reasons. It was the most wonderfully flowing movement you could wish to see with forwards and backs getting involved throughout. It went from one end of the pitch to the other like an organically flowing piece of art and showed just how beautiful rugby can be.

Also, it capped such a wonderful generation for rugby because the game was on the up following that Lions win in 1971 and a try like this on television captured the imagination and kept the love for the game going. Of course it remains a part of British sporting folklore because it gets replayed over and over; however, having worked in television for a few years now myself, I can promise you that only great performances worth replaying ever are and the sight of Gareth diving for the corner to finish off the move is well worth it. He might not be able to sprint and dive like that any mòre, but his love for the game remains and I can think of no better person to share a drink and a story with than Gareth – an absolute hero of the game.

GARETH EDWARDS

I loved playing all sports as a young boy and I can remember having a strong desire to play rugby for my country, but I wasn't bad at football either and one day I cheekily said to my dad, 'One day I'm going to play for my country, where do you want to come and watch me, at Ninian Park or at Cardiff Arms Park?' It was a dream that I suppose every young lad has, but at the same time you think it might be beyond your reach in many ways. It was only when I saw Wales play live as a teenager that my wish to be a part of it became so strong that I felt I might be able to touch it if I wanted it enough and I certainly did.

I had to work hard for it though and just because people said you had lots of natural talent, I felt that wasn't enough on its own. I had some kind of natural skill for sport, be it rugby, gymnastics or football, but until you play something and practise it, that talent doesn't come out. I suppose it was a sacrifice not to go out with my mates every Friday night but to run up and down the slag heaps of my mining village to train, but these are the things that seemed right for me to do at the time.

In fact throughout my career I didn't realise there was anything special about what I or the teams I played for were doing. Even with the Wales and Lions teams I played for, the results told us we were doing something right and it felt good, but it is only many years down the track that I look back on it and realise that it might have been special. It is only when people come up to me and say, 'You and the Welsh team gave us so much pleasure and entertainment' that you think you might have done something great in the grand scheme of things. It is only now when you see how many Lions teams have won in New Zealand or South Africa that you realise it was very special.

One of the things I'm proud of is the way I felt able to deal with expectations. The more games we won the more the public expected and the more the fear of failure grew. We had to keep on performing to match those pressures and you had to cope with that.

For me, winning in New Zealand and South Africa with the Lions opened up the game to a much wider audience and kids wanted to play the game more than before. That was a huge achievement and I think winning a Test series against those southern hemisphere sides would possibly be the highlight for me. It is very difficult to pick something out above all others though.

MY SPORTING HEROES

It was an interesting time for rugby because we started attracting more attention than we had done in the past and things like training really improved during that time and the Welsh team became such a close family. It was a magical time for us as players, but we were all caught up in it and so it just seemed normal to us. People often ask me what was my best game, my proudest moment or my greatest try and of course they want me to say that Barbarians try against the New Zealanders in 1973, but at the time it just seemed like another try to me.

I think it is a similar sort of thing to Ian scoring that hundred at Headingley against Australia in 1981. At the time it would have been another great innings from him and he would have just enjoyed doing it as he would have enjoyed scoring lots of others, but perhaps now looking back on it he can really appreciate it and the impact of it has grown into something much bigger.

I actually played a couple of charity cricket matches with Ian when he was down at Somerset, although that is one game that I enjoy watching more than playing. He is always good fun to be around and it was great when his son Liam was playing at Cardiff because we saw a lot of him at the games. His cricket career was legendary and his charity work has made such a difference to so many; it has been a real pleasure to have such a good association with him.

GEOFFREY BOYCOTT
DETERMINATION

Geoff Boycott turned himself from a good player to a great player through his sheer force of will and determination, and whatever anybody says about him as a bloke or otherwise, nothing can cover up the fact that he made himself not just the best that he could be, but one of the best England ever had. For me 'Boycs' was never what I would call a natural player, but he was determined to be a top-class player and worked extremely hard to get there. In fact he worked harder than any person I've ever seen at his game.

I used to say to him, 'Geoffrey, you just go into those nets for hour after hour to play all your shots and get them out the way so you can go out to the middle and survive for the day!' He was so dogged when it came to batting, but his record is amazing and he did it against everybody too.

He also scored a hundred in a one-day final at Lord's, so he had the ability to score runs at a pace, he just rarely showed it. In the final of the World Cup that we played against the West Indies at Lord's in 1979 he and Mike Brearley opened the innings putting on a hundred-run partnership in 30 overs! It took him 17 overs just to reach double figures! It meant when I went into bat we needed 17.5 an over which was just a little bit out of even my reach.

MY SPORTING HEROES

Geoffrey for me was an old-style Test match cricketer who would go out there to survive and not give his wicket away for all the tea in China. He never let someone just have his wicket. If you got Geoffrey Boycott out as a bowler you knew you'd earned it because he was the most determined and cussed man at the crease.

Don't get me wrong, he could certainly play and he had one or two shots in the locker, but what I admired about him was his ability to concentrate on what he was doing and have the self-restraint to bat for such long periods of time without being frivolous with his wicket. For me it didn't look like it came that easily to him; he really had to work at being the player he was and it paid off for him.

How he would have got on with the modern game we'll never know, but I suspect that he would have worked equally hard at making himself a great player in this era too. Test matches now require batsmen to play shots almost from the first ball and for run rates to be up at 3.5 if not 4 runs per over and that is completely alien to the sort of game that Geoffrey grew up playing and became a master of. Yet such is his love for the game that I think he would still be as good a player today as he was all those years ago. Certainly if you ask him he'll tell you he could probably still do a job at his age now!

Boycs is an English cricket hero and if you see the way he is revered in India you'll understand just how good a player he was, but along with that came a character that could infuriate just as much. There is a funny but true story about Boycs, who had done something to upset his captain at Yorkshire, Brian Close. They were both sat in the old Bradford dressing room and 'Closey' had just had enough of him so he stood up over Boycs, picked him up and just hung him on the dressing-room pegs with his feet dangling down as his shirt held him up.

Boycs and I have enjoyed many ups and downs over the course of our friendship because at times he could annoy the hell out of you, but at others you could see another side to him. And I think over the past few years following his cancer scare the man I know as 'Fiery' has mellowed a little. Just a little though and I'm delighted to see him back being his old cantankerous self these days.

GEOFFREY BOYCOTT

Hearing that he had throat cancer back in 2002 came as quite a shock to him and to those of us who know him, because of all the people in the world to have a form of cancer you'd never expect it to be him because he used to look after himself so well. He looked after his diet and his fitness, and he never drank much so for him to be struck with cancer was a real surprise. But he took it on with the same burning determination that he dealt with cricket and so it came as no surprise to see him win that battle as well and get the all-clear six years after being diagnosed.

What Geoffrey had to go through with his treatments and the after-effects of it at his age was nothing short of heartbreaking, and it would have made mincemeat of a lesser man. For Boycs it was another opposition, another bowler trying to take his wicket and he wouldn't budge for anyone. He has come through that trial with flying colours and perhaps his healthy lifestyle beforehand is paying off now as he continues to travel around the world commentating and delivering those forthright views of his with the same energy as before.

Some people said that he was a selfish cricketer who only looked out for number one rather than the team, and I can see why they say that, but I don't think that was quite right, actually. I think he had a style of play and he was determined to do a job that more often than not paid off handsomely for the team. That was the job he was picked to do and he did it with astonishing regularity.

If Geoff Boycott offered more shots than a bartender for Yorkshire and then shut up shop for England then people might have a point, but he did the same things and played the same way whenever he walked to the crease and he was a valuable asset for any team to have.

He had his moments, but I generally got on well with him even though I used to fool around with him all the time. I was quite young when I got into the England side and played with him while he was coming to the end of his career, so I used to play silly jokes on him like hiding his kit and tying his shoelaces together. He'd have a bit of a sulk and a rant then he'd be back to himself again.

Perhaps the worst 'joke' I played on him was when I ran him

out in 1978 in New Zealand at the behest of Bob Willis. He was gumming up the works and something had to be done – I think my standing in the team took a bit of a step up after doing that since I was still a relative rookie in the side and so was still trying to prove myself. A lot of water has passed under the bridge since then, and I suppose I should thank him for giving me the chance to impress a few team-mates even if it was at his expense!

To my mind he was the perfect man to have at the top of the batting order. So utterly determined not to give his wicket away he really protected the rest of the batting line-up from having to deal with that new ball and the fresh and fast bowlers tearing in.

I always used to joke with Allan Lamb that if Boycs was not out overnight then you knew you could go out for a better night than normal because you knew he'd come back and bat all day the next day and you wouldn't be in for a long while.

Geoffrey remains the most determined man I have played cricket with and never was that more in evidence than in 1977. I always remember the emotional moment for him and one of the high points of his career when he got that hundredth first-class hundred against the Australians on his home ground at Headingley, and if there was any innings that you needed to put your house on it was that one. That knock was Geoff Boycott at his most determined and there wasn't a cat in hell's chance of him losing his wicket before he'd got to three figures. He'd been in good form the Test match before, scoring a hundred and an 80 so he felt confident he could put on a bit of a show. And from the moment he left the dressing-room to bat until the raise of the champagne glass on the balcony, he wasn't going to let anyone or anything stop him from reaching the goal he wanted.

It also came on the back of a self-imposed exile between 1974 and 1977 when I think he probably felt he should have been made England captain ahead of Mike Denness, but whether he'd ever completely own up to that I'm not sure. Such is his stubbornness you can see why he did it, but you can also see why he wouldn't dwell on it now.

The facts that are worth dwelling on are his incomparable statistics as an England opening batsman who scored 8,114 runs at an average of 47.72 with 22 hundreds. That to me is a career worth celebrating and admiring, especially when you know it came as the result of sheer hard work. You knew what you were getting with Geoffrey; there were no airs or graces, no hiding away from who he was, you knew what was coming and he was just a very determined man.

These guys out here work hard, but Geoffrey would play non-stop for Yorkshire, then go and play for England, come back and play a bit more for Yorkshire and then if he had a day off he'd go and play in the nets. It was a relentless pursuit to get better and make the most of what he had and his record proves how good he was at doing that.

This book is about recognising the traits that make the very best sportsmen and women just that. In Geoffrey Boycott's case determination was not just a trait, it was part of his fibre.

GEOFF BOYCOTT

A good team needs different characters who come from different points of view, but the main thing is whether you can play and that was what I made sure I could do. I wasn't going to let anybody down through a lack of preparation or discipline. The things I could take care of, I made sure I did. When you gel that together with the sort of freshness and ebullience of an Ian Botham then you've got a decent mix. In the nets when I was batting things would be done properly because I was an individual that liked things to be done a certain way, but when he went in all hell broke loose, but it was good fun.

My philosophy was that you had to work hard off the pitch in order to make sure you didn't give things away easily on it and that is why I practised the way I did and I think it paid off for me and for the teams I played for. Cricket is a serious game and I took it seriously, but whenever Ian was around you couldn't help but have a laugh and joke with him. I thoroughly enjoyed playing with him and my only regret is that we didn't get to play longer together because I was getting on a bit when he came into the side. I think we only had about four years together and I would have liked more. He did so many good things for the team and from my point of view I always liked how he would not only get batsmen out, but also tailenders. There is nothing more frustrating for an opening batsman than to have to wait to bat as some dopey tailender hangs around wafting his bat. There was none of that with Ian – they were gone.

I still see Ian as the young lad who came into the England side on my return to the team in Nottingham in 1977 and his first ball being a long hop that got rid of Greg Chappell who inside-edged it onto his stumps. That was a stroke of luck, but his talent went on to get him five wickets and a whole lot more besides. For him he had luck and talent which meant the sky was the limit and he was full of fun and life. I was the older statesman and I had to keep working at my game, while he was the young kid on the block, taking the mickey. I nicknamed him 'Guy the Gorilla' after the gorilla at London Zoo that everybody loved, and we all had great affection for Ian.

GEORGE BEST
INSTINCT

'Beefy, you won't kick me up in the air today, will you? There's a good lad.' We were in the dressing-rooms ready to come out for a Bryan Robson testimonial match and the late great George Best had just asked me not to kick him. Now this was a faintly ridiculous question to ask me for two reasons. Firstly with the game being in the early 1990s my footballing prowess at the time was seriously on the wane so inevitably I would be kicking anyone within reach of my right foot.

Secondly George Best might have only just crept into his 40s, but he still had more skill in those feet of his than any of us could ever dream of, so if he didn't want me to get near him then he had more than enough in the locker for that to be the case.

Even when he was getting on a bit and was playing in these charity games with me, he still had the touch and the skill to beat anyone. The pace had gone and the strength had gone, but the shimmy of the hips and the turn on a sixpence was still there and everyone on the pitch and in the stands could only watch on in awe. In the changing-rooms the current pros would all speak to George with a mix of respect and wonder, clearly hoping that some of his magic would rub off on them, but there was only ever going to be one George Best.

When we played in these games the teams would usually be

sorted beforehand; on the odd occasion however there would be a bit of mixing and matching, but I always made sure I was on the same team as George. I knew if I wasn't he would make me look extremely silly. Unfortunately for Bryan's game George was captaining one side and I the other so this was it, no choice for me but to face him. As we walked out through the tunnel he turned to me and said, 'Take it easy on me today mate, the legs aren't working as well as they used to.' I thought this was a wind up so I said, 'I'll promise not to kick you if you promise not to make me look stupid.'

'OK, done.'

The game started and it was cruising along at a nice easy pace – which I could handle – and I even managed to time one or two tackles in the opening exchanges. It wasn't until George came trotting towards me that our agreement blew up in my face. He twisted this way and that until I was flat on my back, and after he'd rolled the ball into the net, all I got was a cheeky smile, a shrug of the shoulders and a 'better luck next time mate!'

I couldn't be angry; after all it was George Best who to me was the most gifted footballer I have ever seen, and despite my footballing prowess with the mighty iron at Scunthorpe United it wasn't really a contest!

In the end George Best's descent into alcoholism which ended in his sad death in 2005 should serve as a lesson to us all and I only hope and pray that the other great natural footballing talent that I talk about in this book, Paul Gascoigne, doesn't end up the same way.

For George though it was all or nothing and that is perhaps part of the reason why he was such a wonderful player during his peak in the 1960s. The ability that man had with a football at his feet was frightening, and as a schoolboy, watching him play a starring role in taking Manchester United to domestic and then European glory felt like watching a fantasy footballer. It was like watching a dream where you couldn't quite be sure that what he was producing on the pitch was actually happening.

Where do you start with someone like George Best? For me he is possibly the greatest footballer that ever lived, and even when I think about the likes of Pele, Maradona or Zidane I still feel drawn more to 'Bestie' than to any of them. He was the footballer I wanted to be. He burned so brightly as a player, yet it was all over in such a short space of time because he was already on the slippery slope in his 20s.

In a way his legend and his position in the hearts of football fans who watched him around that time will be even greater because of the short time frame in which we were able to really enjoy him. And although I've talked elsewhere in the book about how some sportsmen and women have impressed me even more by some of the things they've done off the pitch as well as on it, Bestie makes an entry into this book for his golden age at Manchester United, and not for the decline in his career beyond it.

His 179 goals in 466 games is a remarkable achievement, especially when you consider that he wasn't even an out-and-out striker. He never really had the easy goals laid on for him; the tap-ins that strikers get were not for him. He usually had to beat someone to score and if he chose to he would go and beat them again just to show that he could, and then score! From the moment he truly announced himself to the world with two goals against Benfica in the 1966 European Cup quarter-final, you had to make sure you watched any game he was playing in. The skill was there of course, but it was the instinctive way he went about his football that really appealed to me. He was so unpredictable that it made for pure theatre when he got the ball. His body was light but strong and he could move with such rhythm that defenders would always get more air than Best in their challenges.

If there could be one accusation levelled against him, it was that he was perhaps too good, and therefore a little too selfish with the ball. He knew he was better than the other players on the pitch and he wanted to show it, but whereas the easier and more useful thing to do would be to pick out a pass to the likes of Denis Law, he would take someone on first before passing.

Luckily for him and for Manchester United he had such wonderful players around him that his ability wasn't wasted, and on the rare occasion that a Best twist didn't work he had the likes of Denis Law, Sir Bobby Charlton and Paddy Crerand to make up for it.

MY SPORTING HEROES

He was just a wonderful player who took life and football as he found them. He revelled in his position as the Belfast boy and epitomised the flair and flamboyance of the 1960s. He became as much a part of history by his deeds on the pitch and the superstar lifestyle off it.

I just wish there had been someone who had been stronger and taken more control of him when he became such a superstar. Someone like a Sir Alex Ferguson now would have been perfect to steer him past some of the pitfalls, but hindsight is a wonderful thing, and if we're honest, could anyone really have stopped George? In those days no one had seen anything like it and I'm sure that the Manchester United management did their best to keep him on the straight and narrow, but it was all so new to them too.

No one could understand or empathise with him because no one had been where he was going. This young lad was thrust onto a pedestal with a population of one, him. The big names before him like Stanley Matthews and Tom Finney never had to deal with what he did so they couldn't warn him about what was to come and so really he was on his own.

The 1960s enjoyed an explosion of celebrity that knocked George Best off his feet and he loved it. It might seem small fry compared to some of the attention thrust on even the 'D-listers' of today, but back then the fountains of champagne, the E-Type Jaguar, the fur coats and the women were all new territory as was the media attention which had started to boom as well.

I also don't think we truly understand just how much pressure was on the young man who had come from such a humble and down-to-earth upbringing and had to cope with being the talisman in which a club was investing their hopes and dreams following the Munich air disaster that was still so raw in everybody's minds.

I got to know George reasonably well through various charity games that we played in and of course we had a glass or two after the game and he was good company, but each time I saw him there was never an off switch or someone with him to apply the off switch. It is a free world and I'm all for people taking responsibility for themselves, but sometimes the people closest to you are the ones who can help you out of a spot of bother. For George that guidance perhaps came too little too late, and for all the help he did receive over the years, it couldn't stop the disease of alcoholism. It is an illness and one that sadly caught up with George in the end.

Maybe if he had been born 30 years later he would be today's Cristiano Ronaldo, but instead he paved the way for the Ronaldos and David Beckhams of this world to follow. For me, George Best was the first superstar of football, transcending the game to reach a level that I'm sure he didn't even realise was possible. He would have just been caught up in it and gone with the flow, having an absolute ball along the way.

He was the man who put the magic into the Manchester United number 7 shirt and for all the players that have followed him, from Bryan Robson to Eric Cantona to David Beckham, they all come second to him. Beckham's profile now is probably as close to what George had for the first time, but with all respect to him, David Beckham's got about as much footballing talent as George Best had in his big toe. Beckham's got a fair bit of ability, but in my eyes it just doesn't compare to George.

His later career was a huge disappointment and beyond football things unravelled for him beyond all measure. Embarrassing moments on television were punctuated by time spent in jail, time spent in hospital and dealing with bankruptcy. He came through all that, but the one thing he just couldn't beat was the alcoholism and despite taking every single option available to him he lost that ultimate battle.

He was a sporting genius who for a brief but glorious time actually lived up to the two most important things when it comes to top-level sport in my opinion: winning and entertainment.

If you can play sport at the highest level and win, then you've achieved all you need to. If you can play sport at the highest level and entertain the public who pay to watch you then you've achieved something everyone wants to. If you can do both, as George Best unquestionably did, then you've achieved something special and that is heroic.

GORDON BANKS
INSTINCT

There are some incidents in sport that leave you in complete disbelief. 'How did they do that?' is the question you're asking yourself and no matter how hard you root around in that brain of yours, you just can't find a reasonable explanation. Things like Shane Warne's 'Ball of the Century' against Mike Gatting in his first Ashes Test match in 1993, or Padraig Harrington's second shot at the 17th hole during the 2008 British Open are just as good as it gets. The most incredible thing I've seen lately is Usain Bolt's complete demolition of the 100-metre world record at the Beijing Olympics when he eased up before the line and still smashed it, which was something that just left me flabbergasted.

However, of all the amazing things I've seen in a lifetime of sports watching there is one example of brilliance that stands tall above all others, which is ironic since it involved him scrambling around on the floor. Gordon Banks' save from Pele in the 1970 World Cup was just about the most perfect piece of footballing artistry a goalkeeper has ever come up with. Even if Gordon had never made another save in his entire life it wouldn't have mattered; he already had the number one save to his name and to my mind it has never been bettered.

For those who didn't get to watch it first time round and who have had their heads buried in the sand and haven't seen a replay of it either, you need to log on to *YouTube* quick smart and see what I'm talking about. This was the unstoppable Brazil team of 1970 packed to the rafters with the best players on the planet. Yes, England were the defending world champions, but their crown was soon to slip. In the searing Mexican heat in Guadalajara the game was almost being played at a walking pace and I can remember mentioning to my dad that even though I preferred playing cricket in the heat rather than in the cold, I wasn't sure I wanted to pound into bowl if it was that hot. Little did I know that I'd be doing exactly that in places like Australia and India in the not too distant future!

As the game chugged along I was completely absorbed just waiting for one or other side to either break through or make a mistake and when Carlos Alberto released Jairzinho down the right I thought that was it. He got to the by-line and crossed the ball for an unmarked Pele to head it home. That is just what he did and as if to emphasise the point he shouted 'Golo!' as he did it. From nowhere Gordon dropped down to his right, and as the ball bounced off the turf and towards the net, he somehow managed to turn it over the bar. I sat there in my living room with Dad just open-mouthed and pointing at the screen in astonishment. Surely it was a trick of some sort. The replay proved my eyes hadn't deceived me and from that point on I had a new-found respect for goalkeepers. That is the kind of impact Gordon had; by virtue of that save and a pretty impressive career all round he changed people's perceptions of what a keeper can bring to a side and he forced people to look outside the strikers and the midfield players to appreciate just what a difference keepers can make.

In today's game players like Edwin van der Sar and Petr Cech get plenty of plaudits for their work, while Sir Alex Ferguson rated Peter Schmeichel as one of his most important players ever alongside Roy Keane, Bryan Robson and Eric Cantona. But when Gordon was busy diving to stop Pele's header, the lot of a goalkeeper still had some improving to do.

Of course Gordon was about more than just that one save, he was unarguably England's best keeper of a generation and I would go as far as to call him the best we've ever had. There have been keepers who have earned more caps, and who have kept more clean sheets than him, but you cannot live by statistics alone and when I think of the package that was Gordon Banks in goal I cannot believe it has been bettered.

Before we can get to that incredible save from Pele, you have to go back and look at what got him to the point where he could display such athleticism, such timing, such strength and such vision to pull off the greatest save the game has seen.

And like a lot of the people in this book his success came from a mixture of talent and hard work. In fact he was just about the hardest-working goalkeeper the game had ever seen. You have to appreciate that the game we see today with players earning megabucks and playing at clubs with dieticians, nutritionists and fitness trainers as well as more medical staff than the local hospital is a million miles away from what Gordon started out in. There weren't even goalkeeping coaches when he began so if he wanted to improve his keeping skills he had to do it off his own back. The regime for keepers in the 1960s was to do exactly what the outfield players did, which might have been useful for someone like Bruce Grobbelaar, who loved a dribble and a run, but for Gordon it didn't really help.

At Leicester City he had two willing helpers in Frank McLintock and Davie Gibson to help turn himself into the best goalkeeper he could be and for ninety minutes on each Sunday after a match the three of them would work at the ground trying to improve.

Gordon puts these sessions at the heart of his improvement as a keeper and I admire his dedication to the cause. In five seasons at Leicester between 1958 and 1963 they conceded fewer and fewer goals each time and that had plenty to do with Gordon Banks. He was so hell bent on improving his keeping skills, such as reading the game, positional sense and straightforward shot-stopping, that he paid the apprentices a few cheeky shillings to stay behind and help him work out too. He really was a student of keeping and no doubt he would have got a few questionable glances as he went about his business because he was doing something different. Somewhere else in this book Graham Gooch talks eloquently about how he stayed one step ahead of the game by not being scared to change and improve. That is exactly what Gordon was about too. He calls it a voyage of self discovery, I call it bloody hard work, but it was paying off both for him and for his country when in 1963 he was called up by England.

It was the first of a long and fruitful association with Sir Alf Ramsay, who was busy starting to mastermind England's assault on the 1966 World Cup, and it was that attention to detail from Ramsay that Gordon loved so much. England weren't actually given that much of a chance of winning the 1966 World Cup, but I was just a young lad enjoying my summer holidays when it happened so my thoughts were only of being able to watch the thing and of course assuming England were going to win. As it turned out I was right! My attention though was on the likes of Sir Bobby Charlton and Martin Peters rather than Gordon Banks, and it was a testament to him and his defenders that he wasn't really needed until the later stages of the tournament. It took a penalty from the great Eusebio to actually beat him for the first time in the tournament; he had just been unflappable in between the sticks. The World Cup final itself wasn't Gordon's finest moment as West Germany scored two of their softer goals to take the game into extra time where Geoff Hurst created history.

The thing about Gordon Banks in my memory as a child was that I didn't really notice him. I think that is a huge compliment for a goalkeeper because you only really notice keepers when they make mistakes. The fact I never really noticed him until he made that extraordinary save in 1970 is a huge testament to him. I think of goalkeepers in much the same way as wicketkeepers in that they're all slightly further down the scale of madness than the rest of us, but also in that they can either complete a team or be a complete nightmare for a team. I think of Gordon Banks in much the same way as I think of Bob Taylor and Alan Knott – reassuringly good at what they did from day to day, making sure they didn't cost the team anything, and then every now and again coming up with something remarkable to take your breath away.

By 1970 Gordon was untouchable as a keeper and his value to the England team was almost summed up in that save against Brazil in the early rounds of the World Cup. I think his real value to the team was actually summed up by what happened when he wasn't there in the quarter-final with West Germany. His stomach upset that ruled him out effectively cost England their chance of retaining the World Cup. It is not because Peter Bonetti was a bad keeper – he wasn't. It was the sheer awful timing of the news, just before the game. Peter had no time to get himself properly prepared and was thrown in at the deep end. Their 3–2 defeat after leading 2–0 was a sad day for absolutely everyone, except for West Germany, of course.

Gordon's career was as stellar as it got for a goalkeeper in those days, and as a player with Leicester City and Stoke he set the standard which Peter Shilton then followed, but not even he could get his hands on the sort of medal that the 1966 vintage did.

Football is big business these days and there is no question that the team of 1966 were given a raw deal when it came to money, but that is the way things were and it takes time to change the status quo. Even in cricket the sort of money being earned in the Indian Premier League is enough to make your eyes water, but I don't begrudge them any of it. Players deserve what people are willing to pay them and probably a little bit more besides. Gordon certainly didn't win a World Cup for England for the money, and on the few occasions that I've met him, he always strikes me as an incredibly humble and personable man.

When he made the decision to sell some football memorabilia, including his World Cup winner's medal in 2001, they made a huge sum of money that he and the rest of the team deserved, but I thought it was a shame that he decided to sell them. I know he said that it would save his children from the agony of deciding what to do with the medal when he was gone, but still, there aren't many Englishmen with one of those!

A lot of the people in this book have shown tremendous character throughout their careers and I've long said it is how you deal with disappointment that marks you out as a champion. In 1972 Gordon suffered a terrible car accident that cost him his sight in his right eye. For a goalkeeper that should signal the end of that because your perspective is completely altered with just one eye. But such was his love for the game and his ability that he still managed to play on, albeit away from English football, over in America. I thought that really showed what sort of player he was.

GORDON BANKS

Of course he wouldn't get the chance to make another save like he did in 1970 on the world stage, but as I said it didn't matter to me because Gordon Banks had shown me what was possible and I still can't believe what I saw.

GRAHAM GOOCH
DURABILITY

I literally thought Graham Gooch was going to play cricket for England forever. When I started my career he was playing cricket for England, when I finished my career he was playing cricket for England and each time I pick up a microphone to commentate these days I half expect to see Andrew Strauss walking out to bat with 'Goochie' and not his Essex protégé Alastair Cook. I reckon Alastair has to beat Goochie off with his bat just to stop him from getting out there before him!

No other England cricketer pushed himself harder, further or longer in the pursuit of excellence than Graham Gooch. His dedication to batting, to fitness and to England put him at the top of a very impressive pile and that is where he remains to this day as the scorer of more Test runs than any Englishman before or after him.

That is an unarguable fact and it is why Goochie makes it as one of my sporting heroes. His non-stop commitment to the game and to what he could produce seemed to go on for a lifetime and when he actually retired from international cricket 20 years after making his debut I couldn't quite believe what I heard.

When I came to deciding on who would make this list of 50 there were some names that I really struggled with, constantly questioning whether or not they'd quite impressed me enough

Master of his domain. Sir Alex holds yet another top-flight trophy, this one being for the Champions League, which United won in thrilling fashion against Bayern Munich in 1999.
(© PA Photos)

Allan Lamb takes the fight to the fearsome West Indies pace attack in 1984. He would go on to score three top-class centuries against them that summer.
(© PA Photos)

The 'Lion Rampant'. Andy Murray has broken into the world top three and it must only be a matter of time before he wins that coveted Grand Slam title. (© PA Photos)

The sheer willpower and courage of Barry McGuigan was too much for the legendary champion Eusebio Pedroza, who was overwhelmed in their world-title fight in June 1984. (© PA Photos)

Bill Beaumont leads out England at Twickenham during their Grand Slam year of 1981. (© PA Photos)

Arguably one of the greatest players to come out of the British Isles, and a gentleman too. Sir Bobby Charlton lifts the European Cup for his beloved Manchester United in 1968. (© PA Photos)

The backbone of many Ryder Cup teams over the past 18 years, Colin Montgomerie tees off against the USA at the K Club in 2006. (© PA Photos)

What can you say about Daley Thompson other than 'superhero in a tracksuit'. The man will not wear a suit! (© PA Photos)

One of the best things about my work with Sky Sports is that I still get to sit alongside my old buddy David Gower. Here we are interviewing the England players at the Recreation Ground in the West Indies, winter 2008. (© PA Photos)

The maestro in action. Gareth Edwards was the fulcrum of the legendary Grand Slam-winning Wales teams of the 1970s, as well as serving the British and Irish Lions with great distinction.
(© PA Photos)

One of the greatest strikers of a golf ball I have seen, and also not too bad at taking on Olympians in a standing jump! 'Woosie' led a superb Ryder Cup campaign that inflicted one of the heaviest defeats on the USA.
(© PA Photos)

Arguably the best British boxer since the war. Joe Calzaghe was class – inside and outside the ring. (© PA Photos)

An iconic captain and an inspirational leader – whether for his country, his club or for the British and Irish Lions in South Africa in 1997. Martin Johnson deserves every success as the coach of the national side. (© PA Photos)

Padraig Harrington is well on the way to becoming the main contender to beat Tiger Woods in any major. (© PA Photos)

One of the funniest guys to share 18 holes with, Sam is a great man, professional player, winning Ryder Cup captain and, of course, a friend. Here we see him with his victorious team in 2002. (© PA Photos)

Determined, focused and a proven winner. Dame Tanni Grey-Thompson is an athlete this country should be very proud of.
(© PA Photos)

'Leader of the Pride.' Willie John McBride is rightly held up to be all that is good and honest in terms of what the concept of the British and Irish Lions is about. What a man!
(© PA Photos)

to be ranked above a whole host of others, but there was simply no doubt that Goochie belonged here. His record speaks for itself but I want to bring it to your attention a little more closely because it is by looking at Goochie's record that it is possible to understand why he should inspire such admiration for a career that lasted a lifetime.

As the scorer of 8,900 Test runs he is England's most prolific batsman and he has sat atop the pile for nearly 15 years. That is more than the Huttons, the Hammonds and Hobbs of the game, or the Gowers, Boycotts and Athertons too. And of the current crop of England players no one is even close just yet. I know that a lot of people have tipped Kevin Pietersen to go on and break his record – and he may well do – but no one can see into the future and while those runs are yet to be scored they remain no more than a pipe dream. Let's not forget either that Graham's record came largely as an opening batsman, up against the new ball and possibly the greatest generation of fast-bowling talent the world has ever seen, from the Lillees, Thompsons, Holdings and Roberts. At the beginning of his Test career he was up against Dennis Lillee, Jeff Thompson, Michael Holding, Andy Roberts and Richard Hadlee. Then came the latter half, he was battling the likes of Wasim Akram, Courtney Walsh, Curtly Ambrose, Waqar Yunis and Allan Donald – that deserves a round of applause!

You would have thought that after taking on the full might of the '70s and '80s pace attacks you might just want to ease into retirement before someone really does knock your block off – not Goochie. He carried on batting, and batting exceptionally well against all comers into his 40s almost to prove just how long he could keep going.

Goochie has been there and done it with that relentless attitude that made him the prize wicket for every team he played against. Yet unlike most sportsmen whose light begins to dim over the second half of their career when they have hit a peak and are on the way down, his career simply got better and better the longer he played, although by starting off with a pair against Australia you could argue he had nowhere else to go but upwards!

It took him twenty-two matches to score his first hundred for

England and by the time he had won seventy-eight caps he had only scored nine Test tons – a modest record for his talent, I think he would agree.

But in the summer of 1990, fully 15 years after his debut, Goochie made the sort of breakthrough he had threatened to make years before. He went on a run-scoring rampage starting with his 333 and 123 against India at Lord's in the same match, before reeling off another 11 centuries in his next 30 Tests – a 'Bradmanesque' rate of scoring if there ever was one, totally justifying his years of toil and hard work. Within that period he also scored a hundred and to this day I cannot remember seeing a better one of its kind.

His 154 not out against the West Indies in 1991, when they still had a fast-bowling quartet that was the envy of the world, was sensational. Up against the late, great Malcolm Marshall, as well as Patrick Patterson, Courtney Walsh and Curtly Ambrose, Goochie single-handedly won that match for England – allowing us to avoid a series defeat for the first time in nearly two decades. I might only have played in the final Test of that series at the Oval (when I didn't quite get my leg over the stumps!) and was out hit-wicket, but thanks to Goochie's knock at Headingley that was the only time in my career that I didn't get beaten in a series by the Windies and that meant something to me, and to the rest of the side.

That was one of the high points of our relationship as team-mates, but I have to make it clear that even though I respected Goochie as a batsman and as a cricketer, we didn't always see eye to eye on everything. We got on well enough, but the truth is we moved in different social circles and we had a completely different outlook on life.

Goochie's dedication to pre- and post-match fitness and my dedication to saving my effort for the match itself was probably the biggest difference between us. He was not a naturally fit man; he had to work so hard at it to maintain the levels he believed he needed. As a result he would go running almost every day whether there was a game on or not. At times he would get up at 6 a.m. to go for a run before a day's play and then go out to the middle and bat all day. It meant come dinner time Goochie was so knackered his head would be in the soup by 7 p.m.! And don't think I'm joking here, Goochie would fall asleep at the dinner table so often that the rest of us opened a book on it and in the absence of regular horse racing, would gamble on what time he would conk out. It would take a brave man to suggest any later than 8 p.m.

It got so ridiculous that on the 1980 tour to the Caribbean as captain I had to ban him from jogging. The last thing I wanted was for my best opening batsman to be nodding off as the most terrifying set of fast bowlers ran in to knock his head off and then his wicket over. The thing with Graham was that unlike bowlers who get fit and keep fit by bowling, he had to make sure he got his running in regardless, just in case he didn't spend too long at the crease; he had the ultimate sparrow's legs. It just baffled me that when he did spend an age batting, as he often did, he still felt he needed to do more. I didn't agree and we fell out about it later on when he became England captain and I was one of his players.

He was the man in charge during the 1992 World Cup, and I still believe we had the best team of the lot and that trophy should have been ours. But by the time we got to the final against Pakistan we were out on our feet thanks to the fitness regime of Goochie and coach Mickey Stewart. Some of us were carrying little niggles that just needed to be rested, but instead we were made to keep a relentless fitness routine, as much to please the watching media as anything, and I felt it cost us.

It is a subject Goochie and I have talked about and a lot of water has passed under the bridge since then; we just have to chalk it up to experience in the same way that David Gower has over his omission from the England side under Gooch in 1993 that caused an outcry. We just came from different places on the spectrum, where you had Goochie and John Emburey together at one end and David and I at the other – it is as simple as that.

What I would say though is no matter where we were coming from we all had one aim and that was to do whatever we could for an England win, and in that respect Goochie and I were like two peas in a pod – we are both fiercely patriotic. I'll never forget how, on the eve of that World Cup final in 1992 in Australia, our shared disgust at a far from funny comic in drag making rude and offensive jokes about the Queen motivated the pair of us to walk out.

MY SPORTING HEROES

There are those who will criticise him for leading a rebel tour to South Africa which ended up with his exile from international cricket for three years, but it wasn't a decision he reached lightly. The financial stability a tour like that would give to players and their families made it such a tough choice. But once it happened he didn't sink into the background never to be heard of again; it seemed to drive him to greater heights, as if to prove that his loyalty to England and the cricketing cause was never lost. The whole episode added up to make him the player he then went on to be for England. He just kept going like one of his interminable jogs!

That is where Goochie really impresses me. He had the ability, the technique and the mental strength to be a fine England cricketer, but he did not stop until he became the best. He did not quit until he had squeezed every last drop out of himself and given it to the cause of England and indeed Essex cricket. That motivation, that drive and that durability set him apart from the rest of the chasing pack and it is why I respect him more than he realises.

Since our days as team-mates Goochie has continued to live and breathe cricket, first as Essex head coach, and now as their batting coach, ambassador and part-time media pundit. I don't know what he would do if cricket didn't continue to be a major part of his life, but I think he has also mellowed a little bit in his retirement from the game. He would always celebrate a win in good style when he played, but he seems more relaxed to me these days and perhaps he is just a little less strict on himself than he used to be. He is also not afraid to make fun of himself these days either, as a piece to camera wearing a red hard-hat during the World Twenty20 in South Africa in 2007 displayed.

Goochie might not be playing much proper cricket any more but that hasn't dimmed his competitive instincts. During the 2006–07 Ashes tour, he was asked to captain an 'old' England side in a beach cricket event against the Aussies and the West Indies. They played these round robin tournaments wherever the Ashes matches were taking place and with a side that included the likes of Darren Gough, Graeme Hick and Robin Smith England didn't do as well as they hoped. The following year they went back to play the Aussies and the New Zealanders and this time Goochie was ready for it. He got his team as well drilled as possible despite the best efforts of the sponsors Castlemaine XXXX who provided plenty of their product for the teams to sample. Using taped-up tennis balls that would swing outrageously, Goochie made sure all his bowlers hid the ball to bamboozle the batsmen and it worked. England not only won everything up for grabs, but on the final day of the tournament when they could have lost their penultimate match to ensure that Australia had a game to play in front of their fans, he was ruthless in making sure they could only watch from the sidelines. Some old habits die hard, but I did have a chuckle about that!

GRAHAM GOOCH

I think a big factor in me having the career that I did was the ability to adapt my game and make changes to it right up to the very end that I felt would improve my play.

I changed things like the way I picked the bat up and I think any sportsman can't be scared of change. You have to always be looking for things that can improve you and take you to a different level. Players generally like to stick to what they know and what has been successful in the past, but you mustn't be frightened of a bit of a gamble that can take you forward.

When I started out in 1973 I could never have imagined how long I was going to play, I just wanted to survive as a county player and be a first-class cricketer. Doing that and then playing for England was always the dream and even though it didn't start that well for me with a pair on debut, I took it on the chin and tried to improve myself. I instituted a fitness regime for myself and when people ask me about it, I tell them that all the work I did in those middle years enabled me to play on longer than most people.

I was left out of the side after first making my debut in 1975, and when I got back into the England side as an opener in 1978 I realised that I needed to be fitter, stronger and more alert. I thought it was going to assist my cricket and I didn't think I could go on being a reasonably talented batsman but with no structure or method. How I prepared myself was crucial to me and it paid off, especially against the West Indies who seemed to bring out the best in me.

The success I enjoyed in the latter part of my career was also down to the hard work I'd done because it meant that I could stay at my peak beyond the age of 35, but I would say that having the captaincy also made me a stronger player. It made me more responsible and lead from the front in terms of performance and also in terms of what I demanded from my players.

Admittedly that caused me to have one or two run-ins with players who I didn't think were doing things the right way and the way I wanted them to be done. As captain you get to have the side play cricket in your style, you get to dictate the tone and the style of play. A captain is there to set the example and he is the person the team should look up to. That was a really positive thing for me to have and it meant my play went to a different level as captain. My only regret as a cricketer was that I played in all of England's World Cup finals and didn't win one of them.

I enjoyed some great times with Ian as a cricketer and I think we were lucky to come through as players together at the same time. We had the likes of 'Beefy', myself, David Gower, Mike Gatting and John Emburey all around at the same age. There is no doubt that Ian was the most influential cricketer I ever played with and his belief in his own ability was just astonishing. It was based on some solid ground too because if he ever failed with one aspect of the game he'd invariably do something special with another. I sometimes didn't see eye to eye with him towards the end when he wasn't quite the cricketer he was at his peak, but I continued to have and still have the utmost respect for him. He was the ultimate match-winner pure and simple.

We have a laugh about a few things that we didn't agree on in the past and I can confirm that it is true he did once ban me from early-morning runs in the Caribbean. Under Ian's captaincy, falling asleep at the bar was not part of his game plan!

IAN WOOSNAM

HUMOUR

Little squat powerful Welshmen are supposed to be good for one thing in sport and that is being a tough tackling scrum-half; at least that is what I thought until I met Ian Woosnam. Since then I now believe they are good for two things, golf and standing jumps.

The first is obvious after 'Woosie' claimed a Masters famous green jacket in 1991 which took some doing; the second was something that I had to see to believe, and not only did I see it with my own eyes but I made a bit of money out of it too – happy days!

Back in the 1970s and 1980s I used to go to various sporting dinners and occasions and one of my favourites was a Welsh rugby dinner hosted by Max Boyce down at the St Pierre club in Chepstow. It was there that I first met Woosie properly and over a few drinks we realised we had a pretty similar philosophy on life and we became firm friends.

One evening we were sat in the bar having a few drinks with a group of different Welsh sporting stars, mostly from the rugby side of that era, but also with Lynn 'The Leap' Davies, who had won an Olympic gold medal in the long jump back in 1964. Now there is always a bit of bravado when Woosie and I are around because we both have a huge amount of belief in ourselves and after he'd had a few drinks he reckoned that he could outjump an Olympic gold medallist from a standing start.

Of course no one believed him so he challenged Lynn and at first he refused. Woosie just wouldn't let it lie and as he kept on taunting Lynn I decided to open a book on it until the challenge was accepted. We cleared a space in the bar and everyone backed Lynn, bar me of course. Short little Woosie crouched down as low as he could and with the spring of a grasshopper jumped way out across the bar! It was impressive stuff, but we all expected Lynn to just sail past it. He crouched, swung his arms and leapt . . . nowhere near Woosie's distance. The bar erupted and Woosie and I enjoyed the spoils of victory.

Lynn wouldn't let it go though and challenged Ian to a rematch. He was only too happy to accept and I opened up the betting again. This time everyone was convinced that Lynn would put things right so even more money went on him and there was just myself backing Woosie. This time Lynn went first and put in a solid jump that would have beaten Woosie's first winning attempt. Everyone thought it was game up, but Ian crouched and jumped right past Lynn's effort to win again, 2–0!

About half an hour later all the lights went off in the bar apart from one flickering flame that was coming round the corner. Lynn had gone and got changed into full training kit, found a lighter and used it as his Olympic flame to challenge Woosie to a final round. The atmosphere was electric and there was no way Lynn was going to fail in an Olympic challenge, that was until Woosie put in the biggest jump of the night to crush a gold medallist at his own sport despite being three sheets to the wind! He had me in stitches, which is pretty much what time with Woosie is like – full of fun and laughter.

It is nights like that with Ian which hold him very dear to my heart and I consider him to be a very personal friend of mine after all these years. As a result I followed his career very closely and having played many a round of golf with him I know just how special a golfer he was and still is.

For him to be a major winner at Augusta National Park – arguably the most beautiful golf course in the world – is one thing, but he also then went on to be a record-equalling Ryder

IAN WOOSNAM

Cup captain too which is another huge feather in his cap. It is for those two reasons that I admire him so much, but it is important to remember his career was filled with success. Woosie's career is the sort that people dream about when they take up golf, and with a couple of senior tour victories in his back pocket he is now nearing 50 tournament wins, which would be an incredible achievement.

Ian added a bit of life and colour to a wonderful period for European and British golf with Seve Ballesteros and Nick Faldo dominating in the 1980s, but with the likes of Bernhard Langer, Jose Maria Olazabal and Sandy Lyle not too far behind. They came to the fore at just the right time and not only did they win major tournaments on their own but they also played a huge part in stopping the Ryder Cup rot and turning up the heat on the Americans.

I've had some great times with Ian, and I always try to get along to the Masters with him, but unfortunately it doesn't look like I will in 2010 because it is on at the same time we're planning on doing my 25th charity walk. I say unfortunately, but in Woosie's case I know he'll have a smile on because it means he won't have to do it.

This year's Masters trip though was something very special for me personally. To go to the Masters at any time is a great honour, but to go with Woosie as a former champion is a trip of a lifetime. We go along and I get to sit with him in the champions' locker room and have the full-breakfast experience. As we are sitting there all these legends of the game whom I respect and admire are in and out of there. To a man, they all stop and have a little word with Ian because he is a much-loved player. Even the recent winners like Trevor Immelman and Zach Johnson stop to say hello to this little Welshman because they respect him. Tiger Woods breezes in and says hello and I'm like a kid in a toy store just marvelling at some of the best golfers the game has ever seen.

I've sat there with Woosie before and it is truly special, but this year there was an extra buzz about my week because for the first time he invited me to play a round at the Augusta National with him on the Sunday before the tournament began. We played right off the back of the tee so the course played as long as it possibly could have and thanks to Woosie's advice I was very proud of my 93 the first time round. To do that was a truly wonderful experience and to share it with an old friend like Woosie was something I'll never forget. During the week we stayed in a rented house, picked up our barbeque supplies on the way home each day and spent the evenings chatting about golf and all sorts over a glass of wine.

This time around having played on the course with him I could actually have an experience of my own to bring to life just what an incredible achievement it was for him to win the Masters. In particular, when we talked about his tee shot on the 18th in the final round you got an idea just how special a drive it was to take out the left-hand-side bunkers and avoid driving into the trees like Tom Watson did.

I can remember that tournament becoming a bit of preserve for European and British golf with Sandy Lyle kicking things off in 1988, before Nick Faldo won back-to-back Masters green jackets. By the time Woosie got himself into the final pairing with Watson there was only one golfer the crowd wanted to win and it wasn't a Welshman, that's for sure. Ian tells me he got some awful stick that day as the public galleries cheered on their own man, but he kept his nerve. Jose Maria in the group ahead was in with a shout until he found one of those fairway bunkers, leaving Woosie and Tom to fight it out on the last being tied for the lead.

The hole has a dog-leg-right which suggests a fade would work well as long as you don't overcook it so when Tom shoved his right into the trees Woosie had the jacket at his mercy. A monster drive thanks to those enormous forearms of his took him past the bunkers into the members practice area to leave a cheeky eight iron onto the green. Two putts and the jacket was his, and the British dominance continued for a fourth consecutive year. Woosie was on top of the world and he had the number one ranking to prove it too.

Here was this cheeky little man from Wales, who loved a glass of wine like me, but who could strike a golf ball like Thor and claimed one of the four majors all to himself. It showed the world just how good a player he was. He had won plenty of European tour events and had topped the Order of Merit twice, but a 'major' is what really mattered to him and he had it.

IAN WOOSNAM

Knowing what a good all-round game Ian has I think it is a bit of a shame that he hasn't yet managed to win more majors. His talent really does deserve it, because he plays the game so authentically. He is such an instinctive player and striker of a golf ball that his ability deserves another one. To that point when he made a magnificent charge for the 2001 British Open, fully ten years after his Masters success, we had to witness one of the saddest things I've ever seen in sport when his caddie Miles Byrne put an extra club in his bag so that he had 15 rather than the 14 permitted. It meant a two-stroke penalty in an Open that I believe was his for the taking.

I've always felt that he would win the Open because he is such a good links player, but if that was his chance it was a cruel way for it to be taken away from him. Only a couple of months earlier he had parted company with his long-standing caddy Phil Morbey so that he could try to find more lucrative work and it is fair to say Morbey wouldn't have made such a simple mistake.

Usually when Woosie plays Royal St Lytham he only carries one wood and that is his driver before taking an iron. So it was a bad mistake to make. He just drills the ball straight and true and to my mind he is one of the best ball strikers with a long iron that we have ever seen in the game. He is a lovely touch player around the greens too, with chips and short iron jabs to rival some of the greats, but his nemesis is the putter and it has been for a few years now. He is such a good player though and despite his travails with the putter he can still play the game pretty well, as he has shown on the Seniors Tour with two wins so far.

We try to spend as much time together as possible, especially when we're both in the Caribbean. He spends half the year at his place in Barbados now so whenever England are touring in that part of the world we make sure we have a good catch-up with a few rounds. He still tries to give me little tips to help my game and even though the ball regularly flies off into the trees off my club he still perseveres. He also has a few photos around of one of the most fantastic pieces of leadership I have ever seen in any sport. Ian's captaincy of the European team in the Ryder Cup in 2006 was nothing short of perfection.

MY SPORTING HEROES

I felt very proud of him, the way he conducted himself in the job, because public speaking is not something that comes very naturally to him, but he worked so hard on getting his opening speech right and getting the finer details of his team correct that he took the captaincy to a new level.

Let's not forget that he was following in the footsteps of two sensational captains in Sam Torrance and Bernhard Langer, who both won the cup in emphatic style. Langer had actually set the record for the largest European win of all time in 2004, so Woosie's task to live up to those high standards was almost an impossible one. The fact that he was also hit with some unkind words from Thomas Bjorn in the run-up to the event could have knocked him sideways. I know that he was pretty stunned at what Thomas had said about him being a 'pathetic captain' but he pulled his team in closer and got on with the job and that is a sign of the man he is.

I only saw a little bit of him during the actual competition as I left him to his own devices, as well as his workload, but he invited me over to the team hotel and we had a quick drink one evening. We had rather more during the team celebrations though!

On the course I actually had a magnum of champagne waiting for him and as soon as the win had been announced he got soaked by his own players, and he thought that was it. He went around the corner to do an interview on television so I had to run round a match referee to get to him and I let him have it. All I heard was 'Beefy, Nooooo!' but that was drowned out by the champagne that soaked him even more, but he deserved it for such a tremendous week of leadership and tactical awareness.

I hope he gets another chance to do it because I thought he did so well and the players really responded to his style of captaincy. He's a thinking player and he worked very hard on the admin and homework involved in being Ryder Cup captain. He took a lot of time over his pairings and ordering of matches and also on how the team conducted themselves.

To my mind, he went a long way to winning the cup before they'd even teed off on the first day. I can remember that the days before the event were so bad weather-wise, a typical Irish season of wet and windy, then brief periods of sunshine, before wet and windy again. Yet the Irish crowd, in the way only they know how, stood out there in the atrocious weather waiting for the teams to go out and practise. The Europeans went out to practise and they teed off properly and the crowd loved it. I actually went out, got soaked and then went back in because it was so miserable.

The Americans then walked out and with the crowd all gathered by the tee they decided not to bother with the big shot; instead they went down the fairway about 100 yards from the green and just hit a few wedges instead. That was the end of the Ryder Cup for them and any small piece of support they might get from the neutrals. Ian had out-thought them and outwitted them to cement his place as one of my true old-school sporting heroes.

IAN WOOSNAM

I was a natural golfer, but I didn't really have much time to play it when I was a youngster because from the age of 11 to 16 I was working on my dad's farm and so could only play once or twice a week.

It wasn't until I turned professional that I could really start learning my trade and my dad told me to give it five years and treat it as an apprenticeship, which is what I did. I measured myself up against Sandy Lyle who was and is a fantastic golfer and was my junior partner really. I kept going knowing where I wanted to get to, but nearly gave up so many times because it was a difficult road. I didn't though and eventually I came through.

There are different ways I could have tackled it, and what I used to do was get mad and lose my temper quite a bit if things weren't going right. I can remember being on a driving range in Africa and Gordon J. Brand was leading in the tournament despite hitting the ball all over the place. He told me all he was interested in was getting the lowest possible score he could whereas I was trying to hit the ball perfectly all the time. It taught me to accept my bad shots and just do the best I could and that was a real change in my attitude.

I went through a stage of being the best player in the world never to win a major and it is a tough tag to have, but in 1991 I'd just become the World number one ahead of the Masters and I'd also just won a tournament two weeks beforehand, so I had great confidence in my game at that time. Augusta was a course that I felt I could do well on, but it was difficult, especially as I was playing the final two days with one of my heroes, Tom Watson, and the crowd gave me plenty of heckling. But the more they heckled the more I enjoyed it and the better it got for me. The harder it was the more I had to prove that I was good enough to be in the position I was in, and the more I tried the more my shots came off.

'IF' is the biggest word there is and if I hadn't had two drivers in my bag in 2001 maybe it would have been my time to win the Open, but who knows, it's gone and I have to forget about it.

The Ryder Cup though was a great experience – really tough – but I enjoyed captaining the side as much as I enjoyed playing in it. You have to make difficult decisions and when I got abused for leaving certain players out of the team, that hurt a lot. It took a lot out of me, but at the end of the day I proved all the doubters wrong and it gave me great satisfaction to win the cup the way we did.

'Beefy' enjoyed himself that week too and he's been a good friend for a long time now. We catch up all over the world whenever we can and always have a good time, none more so than on our round at the Augusta National. He'd been looking forward to it so much and he played pretty well. He's got a half-decent short game and if you have that then you can do alright there and by shooting under 95 he won a big bet with a mate so that made him even happier!

We both come from similar backgrounds and the way we deal with people is much the same. We keep things simple and treat people how we'd like to be treated and ever since I met him he hasn't changed. Both our families have grown up with each other and it is great to have solid friends like that you can always count on. He's the most down to earth sports star I know and it's always a lot of fun when he's around.

JASON LEONARD
DURABILITY

When England lost the rugby World Cup final to Australia in 1991, I was devastated. I'd watched their progress through the tournament and there is no question they were the best on show, so to see them lose the final to the 'Old Enemy' was heartbreaking. So when Martin Johnson lifted the trophy in 2003 the sense of achievement felt even better to me as a fan, and to have Jason Leonard provide the link between the two games twelve years apart made him a rugby hero above all others.

'Jase' had been there before; he had tasted the bitterest pill there is in sport and yet through his iron-clad will – and ability to play the toughest sport around for more than a decade – he was able to drink the honeyed nectar that comes with World Cup glory. To me his participation in the 2003 World Cup triumph eased the pain for all those great players he played with in 1991. Having Jase on the pitch when that final whistle went provided the perfect nod to the past as well as accepting where English rugby had gone.

He had been a great England rugby player throughout the early 1990s, but having survived the biggest shift the game has ever seen and gone on to become a World Cup winner he epitomised everything good about English rugby. By the time he retired following the 2004 Six Nations, he had more than earned his retirement. He had been trudging, galloping and gambolling around international rugby pitches for 14 years and with 119 caps under his belt, enough was enough.

MY SPORTING HEROES

Jason Leonard was my kind of rugby player. He was as ferocious as they came on the pitch, never giving an inch to the opposition and at the coal face in the front row he knew nothing else would do. Yet off the field he is full of fun and is one of the gentlest men you'll ever meet. It is a bit of quirk with rugby that the meanest men at game time are the calmest and most genteel men when the match is over. England have been blessed with quite a few of them over the years and Jason is a great example of that.

I remember first meeting him at a Five Nations post-match dinner that I'd been invited along to by my old friend Micky Skinner and in those days of amateur rugby the game was almost a side show to the real party afterwards. We had some fantastic times, but invariably the mood in the evening was always that bit better when England had won and the players felt the beers had been well and truly earned. That was Jason's philosophy and we soon hit it off as he held court around the dining table and made everyone have a drink with him.

Not a lot had changed when I later got to know him properly on a charity golf weekend in Spain. When I arrived I found Jason sat in this corner of the bar chatting to a friend of his. Jason said, 'Ah Beefy, come and join me in my corner.' I thought that seemed straightforward enough; however, when I finally left 'Jason's Corner' my world had been turned upside down, literally, as I rolled out of the seat and onto the floor. That was to be my first experience of 'Jason's Corner' and since then I've had a few encounters all around the world as other people get snared in the same way, unaware just what 'Jason's Corner' has them in for. It is part and parcel of his gregarious nature, he has time for everybody whether they are sportsmen and women or members of the public and he is just an exceptionally generous guy.

However, the reason he makes it onto my list has nothing to do with his personality; it is to do with the hard yards he put in for England on the rugby pitch over such a long time.

When Jason made his debut for England back in 1990, rugby union could still be an extremely violent game. I remember clashes between England and France in particular being white-hot contests in which the forwards set the tone for each side. And with the likes of Jase, Wade Dooley, Dean Richards and Micky

JASON LEONARD

Skinner there was no way England would be taking a backward step in the opening exchanges. I remember 1993 being particularly brutal as almost every scrum descended into a load of handbags at dawn between the front rows and Jase never shied away from defending his team-mates and giving as good as he got.

He was a mobile prop who got around the park making his tackles and doing the hard graft for the side, and as he became a real totem in the forward pack so England's fortunes began to improve.

From the dark days of the 1980s when England struggled to win a lineout let alone a game of rugby, Geoff Cooke as manager, Will Carling as captain and the likes of Jason Leonard in the side turned things around.

Nineteen ninety would have been their first Grand Slam as a new team if it hadn't been for a group of Scottish diehards who wrenched the Calcutta Cup – and also won their own Grand Slam – from their grasp. However, from then on England were dominant in their success with back-to-back Grand Slams in 1991 and 1992, and Jason was very much at the heart of that as the forwards provided the platform.

When the game went professional in 1995, there were a number of players who were to fall by the wayside, and knowing how much Jason loved life, there was a real danger he might have been one of them. The change to professional rugby meant he would have to do things differently, but this is where I really respected him.

He did change, he did start taking his training and diet and fitness a lot more seriously, but he didn't change who he was in the process. He remained as fierce a competitor and became an even more impressive prop-forward, but he didn't stop enjoying himself and being one of the lads. No matter how hard you train and how hard you play, you must never forget why you play the sport in the first place. You must never lose your love of the game, nor should you lose your lust for life and Jase most certainly didn't. The modern professional game made greater demands on players than ever before, but Jase was up to the task and when in 1996 he was asked to captain England against Argentina in the absence of Phil de Glanville I think it heralded the start of the second half of his career.

MY SPORTING HEROES

He was considered to be a safe pair of hands for the job because he was always going to be one of the first names down on the team sheet and he commanded the respect of those around him. And on that particular day I was at Twickenham, as he took charge of a side including Martin Johnson, Will Carling and Lawrence Dallaglio, not only did he make sure England continued their unbeaten record against the Argentinians in a close-fought 20–18 victory, he also scored his one and only test try for his country. The stadium erupted at the sight of Jase rumbling over the line, and his celebration was just as big. After six years of 'grunt' work he'd finally got his point-scoring reward.

From then on and into the Sir Clive Woodward era Jase remained a key part of England's forward pack. Other props came and went such as Victor Ubogu and Darren Garforth, who were decent players in their own right, but Jase stood firm. He was 'Mr Reliable' on either side of the scrum which in itself is not an easy thing to do, but his strength, skill and versatility meant he was always a part of England's plans.

Of course he was a British Lion too, going on tour to New Zealand (1993), on the winning South African tour (1997) and dramatic defeat to Australia (2001), and to my mind I can think of no better Lions tourist. Jason will work hard on the training ground – giving his all even if not selected for the test side – and will work just as hard in the bar afterwards, but most importantly he will make the other players around him enjoy their touring experience. And it is this selfless kind of attitude that not only means no one has a bad word to say about Jason, but it is also why he continued to be a part of England rugby for so long.

When his career started winding down and two young props by the names of Phil Vickery and Trevor Woodman became the first-choice front-row men, Jason didn't throw the towel in and give up now that someone else had taken his place. He continued to give his all for their benefit and for the side's benefit too. If he could keep putting pressure on them for their places then they would have to play out of their skins to keep them and that is what they did.

By the time England got to the World Cup final in 2003, Jason already had well over 100 caps to his name, but his finest hour was still to come. As I sat in a Sri Lankan hotel bar watching the final I grew more and more angry at the inability of the referee to spot how the Australian front row were refusing to scrummage, and as he continued to penalise England's front row the game grew tighter and tighter. Who did Clive Woodward call for? Jase of course. And the big man didn't let him down – steadying the ship in the face of some shocking refereeing. It was a huge triumph for English rugby, but 12 years on from his darkest moment, Jase got to enjoy sport's greatest feeling and he deserved it.

When he retired from the game Jason was not only England's most capped player of all time, but he held the world record too until Australia's scrum-half George Gregan surpassed it. He is still top of the English charts though and as a prop I find that truly remarkable. Life as a prop is so hard and brings such great risk of injury that his record may never be broken. Before Jase came along the most matches any prop had played for England was 38 which tells you something about the nature of his achievement. He is an England legend.

JASON LEONARD

As Beefy testifies, my career involved a lot of luck to a certain degree. Luck in the sense that I didn't get seriously injured too many times in my career. I did get injuries and knocks and niggles, but nothing too serious that it kept me out of action for too long.

I ruptured a disc in my neck and had to have a piece of bone taken from my pelvis for it, but that was done during the summer and my rehab was over quickly enough that I could come back and play without missing any games for England. To be fair I don't remember too many guys being totally and 100 per cent fit; we all used to play with a bit of a knock somewhere along the way in our careers – it's a tough game.

The other reason I lasted as long as I did was down to enjoyment. I enjoyed my rugby from start to finish, I loved training and I loved the camaraderie of the game with the other players. I used to enjoy putting myself through the physical mincer in order to perform at the highest level.

MY SPORTING HEROES

Even in my final season I'd be the first one out on the training ground and I'd be the last one back in, and in between I'd have some fun, trying to pass the ball further than the scrum-halves and trying to drop longer goals than the backs.

When the game went professional, my then hobby became my job. Someone started offering me serious money to do my hobby and I grabbed the chance with both hands. To me I felt like the luckiest guy in the world, but I knew with this change came a certain amount of responsibility and I had to start acting like a professional as well. That was pretty tough, but I had to do it. I had to bite the bullet and change my attitude, my fitness and my game. Yet I never lost that enjoyment for it and I never stopped having fun.

In 1991 I played in a World Cup final that we were good enough to win, but the record books show we lost and that will always be one of the most disappointing days of my life. The lovely counter to that was that 12 years later I managed to face the same opposition in their back yard for the World Cup and win. That really was the icing on the cake for me!

I first met Beefy at an after-match dinner and I can remember a certain Micky Skinner drinking with him and it was like watching the Cold War develop on the table as two superpowers went head to head. I do love spending time with Beefy, because not only is he a hero of British sport himself, but he is the most genuine bloke to go with it and a true patriot.

JOE CALZAGHE
DETERMINATION

As a starting point I have to say that any boxer that steps into the ring to fight professionally has my respect. Whether they are a journeyman or one of the all-time greats I believe the courage it takes to step into that arena in the first place makes them worthy of respect. What earns my complete admiration beyond that and what makes a boxer a sporting hero of mine is the way they conduct themselves, the way they fight and the success they have. In all three boxes there is a huge tick next to Joe Calzaghe. Our undefeated boxing hero and the greatest fighter to come out of the British Isles bar none. No other fighter from these shores has won every single professional fight they've had – against quality opponents – and that puts him out on his own in my book.

I'm sure there are boxing pundits out there who will tell me I can't just look at a fighter's record to find out how good they are. I'm sure there have been better punchers, guys who could take a punch better or even guys who won more fights, but I will stand up for a man who has stepped into the heat of battle 46 times in his life and walked away in glory 46 times.

His record says it all and to enjoy that kind of record you've got to have some unbelievable determination. As a super middleweight Joe Calzaghe was unstoppable and although he finished as a light heavyweight it all added up to the same perfect record so that when he retired in 2009 there was nothing left for him to conquer.

To retire undefeated is as good as it gets and I think at that kind of weight too it makes it even more special. As far as I'm aware the heavier the boxer the greater the chance of an upset, because the power coming through an almighty 'haymaker' from a heavy athlete can knock a fighter out with one blow. Of course it can happen in lighter divisions where guys with glass chins can go down from one solid hit, but it seems to be a rarer occurrence – though Ricky Hatton might disagree with me!

It means that in every fight there is a chance that the favourite, the 'champ', the undefeated star can be laid low with a lucky punch. It is what makes heavyweight boxing in particular so exciting. Just look at what happened with Lennox Lewis against Oliver McCall. One punch got through Lewis' defences and one of the greatest fighters the world has seen was left sparked out on the canvas. The fact that that never happened to Joe Calzaghe just adds to his status.

I've never met Joe, so I don't know what makes him tick and I don't know what it took from him personally to reach the heights that he did, but as an outsider – a fan – looking in he strikes me as being the epitome of what is good about boxing and what is good about boxers. I'm very keen to meet him and pick his brains on a few things.

I want to know about his big fights. I want to know the full details about his career-defining encounters with Chris Eubank, Jeff Lacy, Mikkel Kessler, Bernard Hopkins and Roy Jones Junior. Eubank apart, whom Joe beat in 1997, these were the big names that he craved almost his entire career and it was only towards what turned out to be the end that he got the fights he should have done.

I want to know what drove him on to keep working and training and retaining his world titles even though he didn't seem to get the same level of recognition as the likes of Nigel Benn, Steve Collins and Eubank in their pomp.

I want to know how he never seemed to get ahead of himself and chase the limelight, how he kept his feet on the ground with his dad as his trainer and the hard terrain he ran daily around the valleys of Newport – basically his own personal gym. It just strikes me as being a fantastic story about a bloke who had a bit of talent, a good work ethic and an absolute stack of guts and determination to succeed that brought about a consistent career to be proud of.

Boxers are fascinating sportsmen because of the raw nature of their work. It really strips each fighter down to the bone, because once you step into the ring it is all down to you to out-think, outpunch and outmanoeuvre your opponent and no one else can help you. A boxing ring is not the place for the faint-hearted. It is a war zone that requires the fighters to go to places that the rest of us would struggle to.

Sometimes when you're playing a sport like rugby, football or cricket there are times when it becomes very animalistic, whether you are facing a terrifying fast bowler, a rampaging number eight or a wide-eyed terrier of a midfielder and at those times you have to dig deep into your reserves of strength and character to come out on top. But a boxer has to do that every time he steps into the ring; even if it is a technical fight rather than a brawl, you still have to go there and that takes some doing.

For Joe, he looked to me to be the kind of fighter who would prefer to outbox his opponents, but if push came to shove he would get stuck in a street fight like the best of them. Yet no matter how well he did and who he vanquished he didn't seem to receive the accolades his ability or his record deserved. Every time I saw a Calzaghe fight or read about a Calzaghe fight it seemed to be at a lower level to every other boxer. It seemed like his fights didn't really get much coverage at all and I could only assume that he wasn't fighting the boxers who merited big attention. He simply wasn't getting the big names to step into the ring with him.

The boxing world is one that I sometimes struggle to understand, because as a top-level sportsman I was always keen to face the best out there and compete with them to see how good I and my team were, and even when you enjoyed some success against the best then you wanted to do it again and again. Boxing seems to be a little bit different.

MY SPORTING HEROES

Every fighter wants to get to the top, but when they do the contenders that they are willing to fight become quite specific. I guess because money and prestige and a capacity to earn more money by being a champion play a big role, so the biggest names might not be willing to face an up-and-coming boxer to risk losing and therefore missing out on their chance to cash in.

I can understand why some fighters turned Joe down as he was making his way, but after eight years as the WBO super middleweight champion Joe still wasn't getting the big names until Jeff Lacy came along. This was the fight Joe had been waiting for and at the age of 33 up against a 28-year-old American who had been hailed as the new Mike Tyson the record was emphatically set straight.

I made a point of watching this fight and I was blown away by the sheer class shown by Joe. It was a complete dismantlement of Lacy and to be honest I was a bit disappointed by what he put up. Joe took him apart in every department and my only surprise was that he didn't actually knock him out cold.

After a big fight I always look to see what my old friend and fellow *Daily Mirror* columnist Barry McGuigan has to say about it because he is usually spot on and he knows his stuff better than most. He wrote:

> What a fight, what a fighter . . . I raised eyebrows in Saturday's column claiming Calzaghe was arguably Britain's greatest champion. There won't be many who disagree now. Lacy started favourite with the bookies and most experts yet Joe made him look like a cab rank fighter. I had forgotten Calzaghe could box like that. There will be the inevitable temptation to re-evaluate Lacy's credentials after this. That would be an insult to Joe.

That says it all really. Joe proved that you don't have to come from America to be a great boxer and you don't have to chase the limelight to get your just deserts. His win over Lacy was a triumph for perseverance, dedication and hard work.

Everything about Joe Calzaghe I like. Sometimes you get showmen, other times you get solid professionals and on the rarest of occasions you get both and that is the ultimate for me. Joe was that ultimate fighter; he got on with his job, he kept his head down and worked hard, but then when it came to fight time he turned it on. When did you ever see Joe in the papers for anything other than his boxing? A man who had both feet planted firmly on the ground who had a clear vision of what he wanted to achieve and went out and did it. That is why I admire him.

From one career-defining fight to another, Joe was now on a bit of a run and Mikkel Kessler gave him the chance to unify the super middleweight division and I think it was here that he secured his status in the hearts and minds of the British public. It was as if Joe Calzaghe had suddenly become a boxer worth following, when actually he had been getting on with the business of winning fights and knocking out boxers on a regular basis for nearly a decade.

I do wonder sometimes what we're looking for in our champions. You had a guy like Joe shunning the celebrity lifestyle but getting on with what he needed to do to pay his dues, and working his way up – then a young boxer like Amir Khan comes along and by virtue of timing and luck, his silver medal as an amateur at the Athens Olympics makes him a seemingly bigger name than Calzaghe – how does that work?

In the end I think the British public redeemed themselves in 2007 when Joe was rightly named BBC Sports Personality of the Year, ahead of Lewis Hamilton and Ricky Hatton. It showed that they do know what makes a true champion and it showed that Joe's efforts had finally received the universal acclaim they deserved.

Now that he's retired he can focus on his family life with his two boys and he's walked away at the top of the tree – I like that. He simply decided enough was enough and he had nothing left to prove. Effectively he told the rest of the boxing world, 'I've given you 46 chances to beat me and none of you could do it, tough luck!'

There has been no better British fighter.

JOHN FRANCOME
HUMOUR

It is one thing to put your trust in a horse going in a straight line running as it can, it is quite another to put it into one that every now and again must leap up to six feet in the air before carrying on as if nothing has happened. You've got to have some real balls to be able to do that and to do it with enough skill and flexibility that you don't fall off and if you do you don't get seriously hurt. As far as jump jockeys go, John Francome was just about as good as it got. Certainly during the time when I was beginning to take a real interest in horses, Johnny was the man to beat and more often than not it was pretty hard to do that.

As a seven-time champion hunt jockey and winner of some of the biggest races out there including the Cheltenham Gold Cup in 1978, John Francome was one of the finest jockeys this country has ever produced and certainly the best Swindon has ever thrown up! His triumph in the Gold Cup on Midnight Court was Johnny at his very best and it propelled him to the attention of the wider public. Just like me he was in his pomp during the early '80s and up until his retirement in 1985.

I think horse racing jump jockeys are some of the bravest men and women ever to be put on this earth. To go galloping around on a horse and you're getting up to 35–40 m.p.h. and you're lurching over these high fences and dropping onto the firm turf where you may, or may not, stay on your mount takes some sort of death wish if you ask me. It is just terrifying, yet they do it without a second thought.

I don't know if you've ever seen the racecourse at Aintree where they hold the Grand National but some of those jumps are just incredible. I've taken a walk around the course and had a good look at Beecher's Brook and The Chair – two of the more famous jumps – and I've had palpitations just looking at the things let alone careering over them at the speed of the wind.

I think it is an amazing sport and the people involved are just incredible characters. Within the racing fraternity the jump jockeys are the ones that everybody else takes their hat off to. I don't think it is possible to be a jump jockey without some kind of loyalty card with your local surgeon since broken bones are as common as a Member of Parliament with a second home.

In only his second race Johnny actually broke his wrist so he knew all about the rough and tumble of hunt racing right from the word go. It must have been a far cry from his first foray into the equine world as a showjumper! He actually was quite good, winning the European Championships with Great Britain before switching his attention to a more lucrative pastime. The fact is that John pulled himself up in horse racing by his boot straps. He had no family ties with horses or any natural way into that world apart from showing his talent for handling the rides he was on.

His big break came when he was accepted as an apprentice under trainer Fred Winter at Lambourn and it was only a matter of time before he was getting the better rides on the better horses. His fearlessness was well known around the racecourses both on and off his horses.

Johnny is a passionate guy and a very forthright bloke too. One thing you can always say about him is that if he believes in something or feels that something is wrong then he will speak out over it and to hell with the consequences. He is a principled man and no one can take that away from him. He will stand up for what he believes in whether it is to do with racing, the people within racing or even just matters of common decency and behaviour – he won't shy away from it.

MY SPORTING HEROES

He is also a real stickler for old-fashioned virtues like honour and ethical behaviour never demonstrated more sportingly than in 1982 when he ended his season early after drawing level on winners with Peter Scudamore. Peter had been leading the way and looked certain to claim the Champion Jockey title until he suffered a broken arm, allowing Johnny to carry on riding and catch up with him. He could have gone on to claim the title for himself but showed some real compassion and decided to share it with his rival.

It was a great example of how some great champions are so secure in the knowledge of their greatness that they can look beyond the pure statistics of winning. Johnny knew how good he was that season and he also knew how hard Peter Scudamore had worked to get where he had. I think there was probably a part of him that thought Peter might never get another chance to win the title so with three titles already in his back pocket he honourably decided to share one. As it turned out Peter went on to get another seven of his own!

The fact is though that he was a very talented and brave rider who time and again showed his class with 1,038 winners throughout his career. It is not easy being a jockey when you're trying to keep your weight down and Johnny likes his food so I know it would have been tough for him. He's not really a drinker so that wouldn't have been an issue, but he likes to have a good time and he likes enjoying people's company so I think he needed to really work hard to keep the weight off at times.

I first met John during an episode of *Superstars* when we were up against some of the fittest men ever to compete for Great Britain at anything. We had Brian Jacks, the judo champion, who was 'Mr Gym Test', Danny Nightingale who was the modern pentathlon champion of England, and Daley Thompson, the then current Olympic decathlon champion. Now it wasn't going to take a rocket scientist to work out where Johnny and I were likely to finish in this episode, so we decided pretty early on that we'd enjoy ourselves and make the most of the trip to London.

It was filmed over a few days and we were staying in a nice hotel by the Thames and thought we'd see what London had to offer after dark. We went out on some great nights during that time, and of course during the day we struggled somewhat with the competition. I sank my canoe during the rowing race, Johnny managed about three dips in the gym test and when it came to the 800-metre run we enjoyed our crowning glory.

Johnny took one look at the track, spotted the steeplechase hurdle and said, 'I don't mind going round and round a track and getting over those as long as I'm on a horse!' I must admit I agreed. We knew neither of us had a chance of doing anything other than coming last so when it came to the race we all lined up at the start and once the gun went off we started haring round the track, but just after we got round the first corner Johnny and I jumped off into the crowd and discreetly worked our way back to the home stretch. Once Daley and the others had gone past, out we popped and finished the race to much cheering and laughing. I don't know what the organisers had against such ingenuity but they decided to disqualify us anyway and that was that.

I must admit I enjoyed spending time with John and he had a great way with words when he was describing life as a jockey and how determined he was to keep pushing himself. It sounded like a fascinating world to me and as I took a keener interest in horses and started to part-own some horses myself I always remembered the way John talked about the weighing rooms and the jockeys' areas. It sounded a lot like a cricket changing-room at the end of a hard-fought game, lots of banter, even though you were all riding against each other.

When he decided to retire I thought he would make a great trainer, but he only went down that road for a couple of years and soon found himself on television as a pundit. I knew John would make a great go of it, having spoken so richly and eloquently about racing to me. He's a good-looking bloke too, not like most of the guys in the cricket commentary box or even some of the tipsters he works alongside, so he became a bit of a housewives' favourite and I'm sure he'd have found that quite funny.

He always comes across well on the TV, because he not only knows what he is talking about but keeps his opinions simple and succinct which I think helps ordinary people understand what can be a complicated world. I think he really was a student of horse racing even as a jockey, and perhaps that helped him out when it came to getting the best out of his horses. He has a real understanding of the grounds and the courses – just ask him about how Cheltenham is set up and he could explain away for hours with you getting bored.

Following his successful racing career, I'm really impressed by the way he has got into writing in a big way, churning out novels à la Dick Francis, and doing pretty well with them too. I've got to be honest and confess that I'm not a big reader of John Francome books, but I see them in the shops and always have a little chuckle about our *Superstars* adventure together.

He was a tremendous jockey who used skill as well as bravery to become a serial winner in a sport that challenges you physically, mentally and emotionally because you know you're taking your life in your hands when you get out on the course.

John Francome dealt with it all like a champion and as long as he was on the back of a horse you knew it had a chance.

JONATHAN DAVIES
DETERMINATION

Whenever I watch different sports the people who stand out for me are the all-rounders – I guess for obvious reasons! They are the people who have everything that you need to play their particular sport, whether it is great hand–eye coordination and power for tennis, or speed and skill for football. In the case of Jonathan Davies he had absolutely everything you could want in a rugby player and that is why he was such a huge success in not just one code, but two. And if there was a new code of rugby invented tomorrow that no one has ever heard of, 'Jiffy', as we call him, would be the captain of that side within three months.

He had everything as a rugby player; he had strength, he had pace, he had vision, he had skill with both hands and feet, and his versatility was extraordinary. But perhaps beyond all of those physical attributes that entertained crowds on the pitch, it is the stuff between the ears that impressed me even more. His determination to overcome the barriers between rugby union and rugby league turned him from a great in one sport to a great in two and that is no mean feat.

As the golden boy of Welsh rugby union in the mid-'80s, Jiffy took such a huge risk by switching codes and it is one that a lot of people wanted to blow up in his face. There was still a lot of bitterness between the two codes and without question Jonathan was the highest-profile player to move from the amateur game of union to the professional game of league and it could have gone so wrong.

He copped so much abuse from all sides when he moved across the codes that you could have forgiven him if he'd just walked away and hadn't put up with it, but that is not Jiffy's style. He is the most determined and competitive little bugger you're ever likely to meet and if you've got something to throw at him, he'll just use it to his advantage and prove you wrong. If you tell him he can't cross codes he'll do it. If you tell him he's too small to play rugby league he'll prove you wrong, and if you have a bet with him on the golf course then you'd better reach into your wallet at the same time!

I don't think I know a man with a tougher rod of steel running through him than Jonathan Davies, and his career in both rugby codes bears that out. When he left union to go to league, Welsh rugby fans were heartbroken at the loss of their favourite son. And he was their favourite because he was the very best. Yet considering how hard he had to work to win league followers over they then were equally heartbroken to see him go back to union for the tail end of his career. That says it all.

I don't think you'll find any player, coach or rugby community around the world that would not have ultimate respect for Jonathan Davies in either code. Everybody thinks that crossing codes from rugby union to rugby league and vice versa is as easy as pie; well I can tell you it isn't and having seen my own son Liam do it, I've witnessed close up just how tough it is. The only reason people think it is easy is because Jiffy made it look so easy.

The first part of his career as a dashing fly-half for Wales was full of performances to stir the heart. I can remember watching him play in the pivotal number 10 jersey that means so much to the Welsh people and I can pay him no greater compliment than to say he was a fitting talent to follow in the footsteps of Barry John and Phil Bennett.

I'm as patriotic as the next man, but when I see talented sportsmen playing for the opposition I don't begrudge them their glory. I actually want to see them play as well as they can and add to the whole spectacle of what I'm watching before England go on to win, of course! And that is exactly how I felt about Jiffy. He could spot a gap before anyone else and by the time those around him had cottoned on he was already through it. In many respects he was a bit like the other great rugby convert, Jason Robinson, who in my opinion is the only other man to have been as much of a success in both codes.

Times have changed since he took the decision to move to Widnes in 1988 from Llanelli. He was the Wales captain at the time and had just suffered a shock defeat to Romania so you can imagine that his stock was at an all-time low when he announced the switch. But it was something he felt he had to do. Rugby union was still an amateur sport and he knew he had the talent and the ability to earn his just deserts financially in rugby league.

I can remember the furore it caused and a lot of people were against him, to the point where I told my old friend Gareth Edwards that he'd better know what he was doing because too many people were ready to bury him if he failed. Nowadays players move between the codes without the media, or fans themselves, batting an eyelid, but in 1988, Jonathan was given a torrid time of it. How did he respond? In the manner of a champion, that's how.

He was a slip of a lad in union and so he knew he had to bulk up to compete with the bigger, stronger and faster men in league. That is not the case now that both games are professional, but back then he would have been thrown around like a rag doll if he hadn't done something about it. He went to the gym and turned himself into a pocket battleship where he could match those bigger than him for physicality, and then he could outclass his opponents with his skill.

I first met Jonathan when he was just a young lad bursting onto the international scene and I just so happened to be at his Wales debut against England when he put in the first of many man-of-the-match displays. It was a couple of years after that when I actually met him, very briefly, having a post-match drink with my old Welsh rugby mates Gareth Edwards and Max Boyce.

Like so many of my friends in sport it was only after Jiffy had appeared on *A Question of Sport* alongside me that I really got the chance to meet him properly and get to know him. Whenever we filmed the episodes we'd always take the contestants out for a spot of lunch before recording just to put them at ease. And we were always given the same old warnings about not drinking too much before the show.

I knew I would like Jiffy when he came out with Bill Beaumont and me and immediately got stuck into the red wine. He knew Bill reasonably well through rugby and they both knew the score – you played sport hard on the pitch and you enjoyed life off it and that is what we did, so if you get the chance to have a look at some of the old *QoS* tapes you'll notice that Bill's and my own cheeks were always a little bit redder when Jiffy was on the show!

We talked a lot about sport and about how tough things were for him when he went across the codes, but he always made it clear that being a target for the league players and taking a lot of abuse from the fans was all part of the challenge and it was a challenge he relished. That made him all the more impressive in my eyes. For want of a better phrase he got bullied and picked on and he knew he would be, but by the force of his performances he stood up to them and earned their respect the hard way. He also did it by going to the school of hardest knocks in Australia, where he played a couple of seasons in their domestic competition. It doesn't get much tougher than that, but he loved it. Another challenge dealt with.

That was the determination of the guy to succeed. You can have all the ability in the world but if you don't want it, and you don't work hard at it, then you'll fail just as easily as the man with no talent at all.

He not only made it into the Great Britain side as a rugby league convert, but he excelled at full-back, scoring some of the game's greatest tries, and each time I watched him play he seemed to get better and better. To emphasise the impact he made on this code, he even managed to win the RFL's Man of Steel Award in the 1993–94 season.

It is why when he eventually left to go back to union he had done enough to make rugby league miss him just as much as union originally had. It was after his move back to Wales and to union that he had to deal with probably the toughest challenge of all as his first wife Karen faced and ultimately lost a battle with cancer. Jiffy dealt with it in the only way he knew how and took it head on, continuing to bring up his three kids with the great love and affection only a father can show.

For a time when he ran riot in a Welsh jersey in the '80s it seemed as though everything would fall into place as easily as one of his passes or chips over the defence, but life is not like that and he's certainly seen the tough side of things too.

Having got to know him well over the years, he has continued to impress me as a bloke as well as a sportsman and that is what truly separates someone from the pack and makes them a hero in my eyes.

He is one of these guys that you can sit down and have dinner with and 90 per cent of the chat is about sport. Not just rugby and cricket, but soccer, golf, tennis, ten-pin bowling, it doesn't really matter, he is just completely in love with sporting competition wherever you find it. We spent the 1997 Ryder Cup together in Valderrama in Spain and he just couldn't get enough of it. He was the first man up to go tramping around the course and the last man to bed after enjoying the hospitality. I didn't think someone so small could stay the course so long, but he did it every day, matching me drink for drink – that took some determination!

Now as a television pundit on both codes he is excellent, bringing the same passion he had as a player on the field to his insight off it.

He turns up to support my charity walks and I think he hates being my mate because he knows I will make him power those little of legs of his up hill and down dale! Even though he'll have a moan, he always turns up and does his bit and always ends up with a smile after we've done it. That is Jiffy, he will never let you down and if he says he will help out at a charity golf day or event, not only will he turn up and give you his time, he will go beyond the call of duty until he has given absolutely everything he can. There are no half measures with him; his commitment to whatever he is doing is as strong now as his commitment to rugby was in his playing days. It is just his nature, and I love him for it.

MY SPORTING HEROES

JONATHAN DAVIES

Moving codes was a very tough transition for me. I'd never done weights before to a serious degree – I'd only used them briefly when recovering from a niggle or an injury – but when I went across to league I had to use them all the time.

I did it because the other players did it and it was a professional sport. It meant the players were bigger and stronger for their size than in union so I had to make sure that I punched above my own weight too. I actually did a lot of training and a lot of weights for protection as much as anything else. My game had always been based on pace and skill, I was never going to smash anyone so I had to work hard to keep my pace up and improve it, but also to make sure that when I got caught it was as difficult as possible for the opposition.

The training itself wasn't too bad; once I got into it I found it OK. The hard part was the fear of failure and the fact that I was a target for league teams and players. Mentally that was very difficult for me to get over. I took a lot of verbal and physical abuse as a player, I was constantly taunted by opposition and by fans, and I had to take it on the chin and let my rugby do the talking for me. The only way to shut people up was to go out and beat them on the field and slowly my hard work paid off. It really came down to a bit of grit and determination to prove people wrong and to show everyone what I could do and how I could help my teams become successful.

I've known Beefy for a long time since we both held our drink better than most when we were doing *A Question of Sport* and I think he quite liked having someone who could have a good lunch and then still be sharp enough to help him win on the programme. He was an icon of British sport when I met him and like most people who are right at the top he was a lovely bloke with it and he made me feel welcome from the start. Since then we've become good friends and I can remember being on holiday in South Africa once while a cricket tour was on and meeting up with him for an afternoon. We were by the side of a pool in Cape Town and things got a little competitive as they usually do and Beefy decided he was going to throw me in. He's twice the size of me and I knew

I would struggle, so I thought if I'm going in then he's coming with me, and so just when he was about to throw me, I sunk my teeth into his shoulder which allowed me to drop him into the pool too! So I can tell you he didn't win that battle!

JONNY WILKINSON
DEDICATION

Jonny Wilkinson is a freak. He is arguably the best rugby player England have ever produced, and the only reason I say arguably is because his career has been ravaged by so many injuries.

Up until 2003 he had turned himself into the perfect specimen of a professional rugby union international and as a result his match-winning drop goal in the World Cup final against Australia isn't something that should be looked at in wonder or surprise or excitement. It should be viewed as something completely and utterly expected, because Jonny Wilkinson does not leave things to chance.

He is without question the most dedicated man I've ever met in any walk of life let alone sport. He is so focused and so committed to rugby that it is actually quite scary and a little disconcerting.

I've read and heard that he has changed quite a bit since I last saw him, but I'm not sure how much I believe that. It would take a change of DNA to get Jonny Wilkinson to become anything other than England's most dedicated rugby player and I'm not sure how much we should want him to change since his outlook on the game from the day he started to play rugby took him and England to the top of the world.

Jonny is another sportsman whose career you have to split into two parts because of how his body and injuries have conspired against him since 2003. However, he makes my list of sporting heroes because of what he did before and on that magical day in November 2003.

As a young precocious talent Jonny was destined for great things and having been persuaded to learn his trade up at Newcastle under Rob Andrew it was all part of the process that he should be picked for England at the age of just 18.

I've always believed in the mantra 'if you're good enough then you're old enough' and Jonny was certainly good enough for two reasons. Firstly, he had ability. He had been playing the game for as long as he could walk and had a real feel for it. He could run, he could pass, he could tackle, no wait, make that he could tackle like no other fly-half before or since, and he could kick, boy could he kick.

Secondly, together with that talent he drove himself to train and practise harder than was really necessary. I've known some voracious trainers in my time; the likes of Geoff Boycott and Graham Gooch spring to mind. But Jonny was something else and even if now he claims to be able to walk off the practice field at the same time as everyone else, that certainly wasn't always the case.

I know his training regime and his dedication to practice has been well documented in the past, but having my son Liam playing for Newcastle and training with Jonny gave me a genuine insight into what his intense rugby world was like. The pair of them had actually shared a room together on an England tour of South Africa during the summer of 2000 where Jonny had been ill for a few days in the run-up to the Test match. Liam was set to play a part in that game, but unfortunately caught Jonny's bug and while Jonny went off and played, Liam was laid up in the hotel room.

In fact I think Liam got himself a little bit too wrapped up with Jonny during that period in Newcastle and if you ask him now he would say that he trained too hard. Liam and Jonny got on very well and formed a firm friendship because they had a similar outlook on life up to a point.

Jonny never wanted to be in a game and have a situation that he couldn't deal with. He never wanted people to say that he had a weakness with a certain aspect of his game. If he made a mistake one week he would do whatever he could in training to make sure he didn't make it again the next week. He was a perfectionist, driven to the edge by that desire to prove he was good enough to be there and prove to himself that he could become as good as he could be.

In Liam's case he simply didn't want anyone to suggest that he had got anywhere on the back of his surname. Even though he had left cricket behind and was forging a life in rugby, he never wanted anyone to level an accusation that his name had given him a chance rather than his talent, so he trained harder and harder. In each other they found a willing accomplice for their extra work.

That though is where the similarities end because whereas Liam was always interested in other things and has always been a sociable guy, Jonny simply never turned off from rugby. There are stories of him going out, on the very rare occasion when he did go out, and rather than enjoying mixing with people and finding out different things he would talk about nothing but rugby. A pretty girl might want to see what he's got to say for himself and rather than music, films or current affairs, Jonny would talk about the flight of different rugby balls and how the European ball is different to the English one! He was just wrapped up in his own rugby world and it was hard for anyone to break through. He kept himself to himself and certainly didn't court a glamorous lifestyle; rugby was what mattered and it showed on the field.

You can't change a guy like that and if you try to then you're taking away a crucial part of who he is. He was often told not to make big tackles, but that was a part of his game and he wasn't going to stop. As a result everyone at Newcastle and with England respected him for what he was. He was at the top of his game and was the world's best fly-half for a long time.

It was a far cry from his initial taste of international rugby in 1998 when he went on the 'Tour of Hell' to Australia and New Zealand, where England were not just beaten, they were brutally ripped apart. Having been through an experience like that it can either shape you as a man or break you. There were a lot of players who went on that trip who were never seen again, but in the likes of Wilkinson, Josh Lewsey, Matt Dawson and Phil Vickery, Sir Clive Woodward found some gems who would all play a big part in the 2003 World Cup success.

Perhaps it was that tour that pushed Jonny into a whole new level of training and physical preparation, perhaps the scars of that trip ran deeper than any of us could imagine, or perhaps Jonny just loves rugby. From there he got better and better with England and inevitably he enjoyed selection for the British and Irish Lions in 2001 who played some scintillating rugby in Australia despite losing 2–1. And in that season for England he helped fire a back line that really caught the imagination.

What I've always really enjoyed about watching Jonny, and this is up at Newcastle or with England, is his total commitment to whatever it is he is doing. If it is a tackle he's making it has to be a crunching one, and I've seen many a bigger player get off the floor gingerly having felt like they were hit by a dump truck. If Jonny were to be an animal he'd be the dung beetle – no, seriously, it can shift up to 50 times its own body weight. You'll never see Jonny Wilkinson shy away from anything physical. He is ferocious and when he is at his peak he has to be pound-for-pound the strongest tackler in the game.

The other thing I've always admired about Jonny is his ability to put mistakes to the back of his mind during a game. Liam would tell me about how caught up Jonny would get in the mistakes he made and how it would eat away at him during the week. But whenever I was up in the stands he always managed to forget what had happened and do something positive, whether it was a kick at goal or a tackle or a pass. And that is why his performance in the World Cup final didn't surprise me in the slightest.

In the build-up to that World Cup everybody knew he was a special player who made the rest of the team tick. He pulled the strings, he kicked the goals and he made that side function like a well-oiled machine. He became a targeted player in much the same way as the likes of Gareth Edwards, George Best and Bobby Charlton were in their day. He was the guy the opposition targeted because they were scared. Whenever an opposition try to nullify you it is because they are worried about what you can do to them and in a funny way that is a sign of respect.

I can also remember how the Australian media tried to target him and suggest that England were a boring one-man team. 'Is that all you've got?' asked one headline next to a picture of Jonny. It had echoes of the 1991 World Cup where David Campese and the like goaded England by saying we couldn't play expansive rugby. This time it was aimed at Jonny and some say he nearly cracked, but he kept on plugging away and in the end the final was the perfect reward for all the hard work he had put in over a career. He'd missed a couple of attempts before the one that really mattered, but that's the point. When it came to the crunch, he delivered, and so you could say all those extra hours on the training pitch and all those nights in paid off.

Subsequently though his career has been in freefall thanks to injury after injury and so as well as being one of the most talented players to be in the game he must also be one of the most frustrated too because he must wonder 'why me?' far more than any player should have to. The catalogue of injuries just about every different part of the body you can imagine is astonishing to and I just wonder whether when all is said and done he might look back on his career and think, 'Maybe I should have had some more rest and relaxation.'

Maybe he needed something else in his life to help him get a better balance to things. I know he took up the guitar and decided to learn new languages, but he had to make himself do those things. It was never a case of giving up a bit of rugby time for them.

His catalogue of injuries are just a crying shame for a player of such enormous talent and maybe he needed six months' total rest after the World Cup to let the body heal properly, but that is not Jonny Wilkinson. He wants to play as much as he can.

With the benefit of hindsight someone should have told him to bugger off for the rest of that season and let his body recover completely, and then in the long term he might have played more rugby. His talent and ability wouldn't have deserted him because he is that good; however, his body might have appreciated the rest!

JONNY WILKINSON

I'm not a doctor or a physio but I understand that sporting bodies take a lot of punishment and you have to listen to them sometimes rather than telling them what to do. And maybe Jonny's body is telling him just how much it has been hurt over the years.

Each time he gets injured I keep hearing that it is a completely new injury that has no connection with the previous one and it is just unlucky; well I can't quite swallow that. It seems like too much of a coincidence that the player who throws himself around a rugby pitch more than any other and who trains harder than any other and who was playing professional rugby for Newcastle and for England earlier than any other is just unlucky with injuries.

When he started playing, the game had only just turned professional, but along with the likes of David Flatman and Alex Sanderson he began playing Premiership rugby week in week out. David subsequently had three years out of the game with injury while Alex had to retire from the game through injury – is it all a coincidence?

I don't see him coming back to his best until he has a sabbatical. By that I don't mean time out because he is injured; I mean time away from rugby grounds, from rehabilitation and from training – a complete switch-off.

That will probably never happen because of the time he has spent on the sidelines over the last few years; however, each time he has been working towards an immediate comeback. Remember how he'd hardly played any rugby and then in a bid to be fit for the Lions tour his first game back in 2005 was against Argentina as a Lions warm-up. Every time he has been injured he has come back as soon as possible. I am still advocating a complete rest and I think he still has enough time on his side to do that.

He has now made a move away from Newcastle where he had become a part of the fabric although not necessarily on the pitch in recent years. His move to Toulon in France is a bold one and one that will give him a much wider perspective on life as well as rugby. Just to be able to do things differently and experience something new at this stage in his career will be great for him and I wish him every success there.

MY SPORTING HEROES

Even if he never hits the same heights as he did in the past, nothing can take away the bare facts. He's a top-class rugby player who made himself better than everyone else and won the ultimate prize. He is a genuine, 24-carat sporting hero.

JONNY WILKINSON

I have always had that constant desire and ambition to find the best possible performance that I can produce. I have never been happy to accept 'off' days or just shrug my shoulders and accept less than what I am capable of. That feeling within me has dominated my thinking in the past and while I'm not entirely free of it, I would suggest it is now a more healthily obsessive side to my nature and it is something I can control a lot more.

To follow your dreams takes huge sacrifice and an incredible amount of hard work and some people find that either physically or mentally too demanding – I just wanted to keep pushing myself until I reached my peak. The only thing is that my peak seemed to keep rising in front of me.

I started with rugby at a very young age and found that it was the ideal game for me because it is about collective responsibility. The idea is that you have to work together as a team and you have to rely on each other, but individually you have to do your bit at every session and in every game. It reminds me of being in a family and as you grow up you have to look after the people around you and with a core set of values, to me, there is nothing better than pulling together in a common cause.

There have been accusations levelled at me for being too obsessed with training, and with wisdom and experience I can say that it has taken me a bit of time to get the right balance in life which should bring out my best. I feel I'm training smarter now rather than longer and everything is in sync so I'm not fighting with myself as much – I think there is more composure about me now.

Did I have to be the way I was to win the World Cup? No I didn't, but did I have to be the way I was to win the World Cup in that way? Yes, absolutely. I don't for one minute think that the way I got myself to that point was the only way to do it, but the best way to describe it is to say that my rugby career is like a brick wall and each of the training sessions and gym sessions and extra kicking sessions is one of those bricks. If you take one of them away you don't know which one is going to make the wall fall down.

My injuries have been well documented, but 95 per cent of them have been in contact which could happen to anyone at any time. Why they happened to me I'm not sure, but I think that my constant state of worry and stress over my performances might have left me run down, much like anyone after a period of stress, and perhaps it made me more susceptible to injuries. I don't have that worry any more.

I've always been a sports fanatic and when I was a lad I used to have a lot of sports videos, including plenty of Ian Botham, and I used to watch the '81 Ashes quite a lot. My dad actually turned down a chance to play for Somerset in favour of work. I got on hugely with Liam and we had some great times up at Newcastle – I really liked his outlook on life and personal development. It was the perfect attitude for a professional sportsman, and he is also a top man with it. Having his dad come and watch us was always good and I enjoyed getting to know him a little bit after games; he always had a good story to tell and it was clear he was a guy with total faith in his ability. He could just accept he was that good and let loose.

KEN BARRINGTON
PASSION

Ken Barrington epitomised everything good about cricket and what England is capable of producing, and if there was one man I tried to emulate as a cricketer it was him. He was a childhood hero of mine, the player I looked up to and whose footsteps I wanted to follow in more than any other. People think that I must have longed to be the next Garry Sobers or the next Fred Trueman, and yes I certainly admired those players too, but when push came to shove there was only one cricketer for me – Ken Barrington.

As a kid I used to watch him take on the world with that determined style of his that just screamed 'beat me if you can', but it was so rare that anyone did, and when you look at his record it is easy to understand just how good a batsman he was.

I was always so proud that I shared a birthday with him and whenever he went out to bat I would tell anyone who cared to listen – as well as plenty who didn't! – that we were somehow scoring runs together because of our joint birthdays. It is funny what you come up with as a child, but that just showed the immense affection and admiration I had for him back in the 1960s when he was in his pomp.

Whenever I watched him play I got a real sense of his dedication to batting and his determination not to get out. He also had bravery in spades as he took on the world's fast bowlers with apparent ease, but as I then got to know him in later life when I began playing for England and he was a part of the management the trait that really sticks in my mind is passion.

A passion for the game and for England, which endeared him to me even more because that is what I was all about, and in Kenny I had someone to talk to and respect who had made such a great success of his career with the same kind of enthusiasm that I had. His batting was technically sound to the point of almost perfection. When he hit a cover drive or a thunderous pull you knew in your mind that this was the way the shot should be played. He had wonderful timing and a defence that needed a stick of dynamite to be broken. As a result Ken earned a reputation for being a practical batsman rather than an entertainer, but I would ask you how many of his team-mates would rather have him in the side than out and the answer is every single one.

Rather unfairly, I think he would often be referred to as a dour cricketer, the stone-wall extraordinaire before Geoff Boycott took patient batting to a new level! But that is not how I remember him at all. In fact one of my favourite stories about him growing up was how in 1968 on a tour of the West Indies he not only stood up to the might of the great Wes Hall and Charlie Griffith, but he popped Wes back over his head for six to bring up his hundred in Trinidad. Now you don't do that if you're not a special batsman.

His career record remains astonishing even today and I know he was incredibly proud of what he'd achieved in scoring hundreds wherever he went in all the Test-playing countries of the time. In 82 Test matches he scored 6,806 runs at an average of 58.67; now that is remarkable. When you consider how much tougher life was for batsmen in the 1960s on uncovered pitches and with bats no more than slightly thicker sticks compared to what players have now, you can appreciate just how good he was. I have no doubt in my mind that if Kenny was playing today he would easily be averaging in the mid-'60s if not higher, and the fact that he still remains sixth on the all-time list of averages tells you something.

What I loved about Kenny Barrington is that he wore his heart on his sleeve and the Union Jack across his chest with such pride. He was the ultimate 'British Bulldog'. With that jutting jaw of his and that fierce look on his face, he went out to bat meaning business and that is the sort of toughness I love to see in cricket. The game meant everything to him and he passed on the joy and knowledge he had on it with such passion that it was hard not to be inspired by him.

Unfortunately for Kenny his career was cut slightly short by a heart attack when he was 37, leaving him with plenty of time left to forge another career in business. But cricket was his love and it was great when he took an active role with the England side as a coach and assistant manager. The respect that he had earned as a player remained with him as a coach and he built on it thanks to his easy nature. The impression he gave as a batsman was one of total toughness and hunger for the fight, but off the field I can tell you he was the most gentle, warm and kind man I've ever known in the game.

By the time I became England captain and took the side to the West Indies in 1980–81 he was the perfect senior statesman to have in your dressing-room and as an inexperienced skipper I leaned on him quite a bit. I went to him for advice on all sorts of things and whether it was captaincy, man-management or even just some technical batting pointers he was always on hand to help. In fact I can remember a crucial chat we had about my batting on an earlier tour to Australia where I found myself getting out lbw quite a bit and I couldn't understand why because I thought I had everything lined up correctly. Kenny had spotted that I was getting my front pad too far across the stumps when I played, so when I thought the ball was drifting down the leg-side it was actually hitting me in line. Kenny said to me, 'What do you think about taking a leg-stump guard?'

And this was always Kenny's way, he never said 'do this' or 'do that', he would ask you what you thought and then let you make up your own mind whether or not you wanted to do it. As it was I did start taking a leg-stump guard and did so for the rest of my career. That was one of the great things about Kenny as a coach; no matter how well or badly you did, not once did he ever throw the past at you and simply tell you how to do things.

I never heard him utter the words 'in my day' or 'that's not how we used to do it'. He never harped back to his career and what he achieved which he had every right to do with such a fantastic record behind him. Ken was about the 'here and now' and about helping people get the most out of themselves. If you'll excuse the analogy, he wasn't there to wipe your backside for you, he was there merely to point you to the toilet and let you get on with it!

In fact, we heard so little about his career from him that I had to cajole and persuade him to talk about old matches and what he had achieved. He didn't really like talking about what he had done in the past and at my age now I can understand it and I agree that the present is about those playing now. But still I thought it was a bit of a shame that a lot of the guys didn't know how good a player he was until they actually sat down and looked at the history books.

Still, you didn't need history books to know what a wonderful bloke Kenny was, and it is why 14 March will be a day that I will always remember with deep sadness and also affection because it was the day he was taken away from us far too early. You have emotional days in cricket, but when I got a phone call at 7.30 in the morning to tell me that Kenny had died of a heart attack earlier that night in Barbados I was torn apart.

We were in the middle of the third Test against the West Indies in Barbados and after hearing the news I just did not want to go out and play cricket. Everyone in the team took it hard too because Kenny was loved so much and the game came close to being postponed, but deep down we all knew that Kenny was the sort of bloke that would have wanted the game to keep going.

It was one of the most emotional days – not just of my career but of my life – and how we got through it I'll never know, but perhaps there was a bit of that bulldog spirit in all of us thanks to Kenny which puffed out the chest, kept the upper lip stiff and got on with the job.

Both teams were lined up before play after the news and I can tell you there were some hard men in the England dressing-room and some even harder men in the West Indian side, but there was not a dry eye between us all. Everybody had so much respect and admiration for the 'Colonel', as he was known, that it hit us all hard. He was such a fine ambassador for the game and he was welcomed with open arms wherever he went.

MY SPORTING HEROES

He has been sorely missed ever since and my mind regularly casts back to him, not least on our birthday, and I wonder just how good a coach and administrator he would have been. He would have been the sort of bloke who would have prevented arguments and squabbling within the game yet he would have got things done too.

I also sometimes wonder just whether he might have been the calming influence I might have needed at times during the 1980s when my life was more roller coaster than Orient Express. Either way, it would have just been great to have him around longer than we did. He was simply one of the finest sportsmen England has ever produced and I consider myself lucky to have followed ever so slightly in his passionate footsteps.

LAWRENCE DALLAGLIO
LEADERSHIP

Until you actually stand next to Lawrence Nero Dallaglio you don't understand just how big a man he is. He is a monster – an enormous grinning monster who never fails to have you laughing with him, but once he crossed the white line and a game of rugby was under way he turned into something altogether much more frightening.

On the pitch he was the epitome of a rugby warrior. He was England's gladiator-in-chief, urging, cajoling and inspiring his team to greater heights and at the same time making life a complete and utter nightmare for the opposition. He managed to grab games in those huge paws of his and bend them whichever way he wanted, whether it was for his beloved London Wasps, England or the British and Irish Lions – he was a totem around which the rest of the team could function.

And he did it despite having some of the other great rugby leaders around him. Having Martin Johnson as his captain for a time, and then the likes of Jason Leonard, Richard Hill, Simon Shaw and Neil Back alongside him, didn't diminish his contribution as a leader of men; if anything it made him lead by example even more.

Some men are born to lead and there is no doubt that Lawrence Dallaglio falls into this category. From the moment he burst onto the scene as a fresh-faced Wasps player who took the World Cup sevens by storm in 1993, to the day he hung up his boots as his name echoed around Twickenham in 2008, he has led from the front. He knew no other way, and that is a trait I love in a sportsman.

The thrill and excitement of sporting competition just courses through the veins of the very best and they love nothing more than to give of their all and jump right into the thick of it. Whether it is rugby, cricket or football, they just want to be involved in the action and that is what Lawrence was all about. And because of his standing in the game and the respect that he earned from everyone around him, his fellow team-mates wanted to be right behind him as he charged into the fray. It is the same sort of effect that Martin Johnson had (and I talk about him later on in this book), so to have two men like that in England's line-up could only have been a good thing and the proof was in the pudding in 2003.

It was the 2003 World Cup that provided 'Lol' with the ultimate reward for all of his hard work; however, his excellence as a rugby player and as a leader at his peak was about more than just that one match in November. In my eyes Lawrence Dallaglio confirmed his position at the very top table of English rugby, not just by winning that World Cup, but by being the only man to play in every minute of every game of that campaign, and then by coming home and somehow refocusing his own mind on becoming England captain for the second time, and then in the perfect finish, leading Wasps to not only their second successive Premiership title but their first ever European Cup. All this in the space of seven incredible months!

It was the period of Dallaglio's career that summed him up for me. No task was too big, no challenge too great. If he thought he could achieve something on the rugby field he went out and proved himself right.

When it came to the nuts and bolts of the game, Lawrence was a master. He also changed and adapted his game as he got older and wiser, which reveals a real rugby brain. When I was a young all-rounder I used to tear in a bowl at a decent lick, but as I got older and had to deal with injuries I got a bit cleverer and used swing and seam movement to make up for the gentle decline in pace. In much the same way, Lawrence was as quick over the park as any back-rower I can remember and he was incredibly powerful with it – who can forget that leg-pumping try he scored against Wales? – but then as injuries took their toll and his body changed he adapted his game with it to become a clever disrupter of oppositions right on the edge of the game, while also becoming a greater threat around the fringes.

Together with Back and Hill they became the 'Holy Trinity' of English rugby, remaining true to the classic mould of an English forward, yet also evolving into a canny and creative link to the backs that provided the lifeblood to some memorable tries and victories.

I've always enjoyed Lawrence's company; he is a really passionate supporter of English sport, not just rugby, and we've had some great fun together and he is just enormous. He once gave me a golf glove to wear that Nike had made especially for him, and I could get not one but both of my hands into it, it was that big!

Perhaps it is his menacing size that made sure Sir Clive Woodward didn't take him off the field during the World Cup! In truth I think Clive knew that Lawrence was the sort of man he could trust to remain on the pitch and make sure the big games such as the quarter-final against Wales or the semi-final against France were won. However, he would also make sure that the smaller sides like Samoa, who gave England a fright, would also be dealt with. Clive clearly trusted Lawrence and so did the rest of the team and that says something about him.

Despite the low points of his career, such as losing the captaincy over a newspaper sting in 1999, he still had so much ability and character that he remained an inspiration. Whenever Lawrence speaks, others listen. I've seen it at various events when he's just having a laugh, but I'm assured it happened in the changing-room too.

Throughout the 2003 World Cup, Lawrence was a reassuring influence on those around him. I remember watching some of the tournament at home and then going to Sri Lanka for an England cricket tour where I watched the final, and to me he just got better and better. It was fitting that the only try England scored in the final came courtesy of some wonderful link play between Lawrence, Jonny Wilkinson and Jason Robinson, who scored in the corner. Again it was Lawrence at his best.

When he got home from the tournament, like so many other players he could have switched off. Sometimes it is hard to get yourself up for your sport when you've just reached the pinnacle. I've been hearing about Olympic athletes who've really struggled to deal with the comedown from Beijing after winning a gold medal – and that would have been the same for England's World Cup winners.

Some retired, some got injured as their bodies said 'no more!' Some enjoyed their new-found adulation, others just struggled to find any form back at their clubs. But Dallaglio was ready to answer the call yet again, as Martin Johnson's successor as England captain. There were also no excuses as England finished third in the following Six Nations Championship. Dallaglio had standards and a post-World Cup lull was no reason to let them drop – I liked that.

As the season drew to a close, Dallaglio was still going strong. Having won the Premiership the year before he was ready to take another step up, this time in the Heineken Cup, and thanks to some brilliance from Rob Howley right at the death he lifted his sixth major trophy for his club, which a week later was replicated with the seventh. With two of the finest rugby coaches behind him in Warren Gatland and Shaun Edwards, it was easy to see how he'd kept going.

Having taken on the England captaincy, he was never going to back down from a challenge, but in hindsight, maybe he should have given the summer tour a swerve that year, because by the time England had been thrashed by New Zealand twice and by Australia he was running on empty. He called time on his international career too, which many people thought was too early, but if he thought it was time to go then so be it. The last thing left for him was the Lions tour to New Zealand in 2005, which would have been the perfect finish to his international career. He had some work to do though. Having had an operation in the summer it took him a while to get going for his club, but by the time the Lions squad was announced and he'd picked up yet another trophy for Wasps, he was back to his best again.

I believe that some players carry the rest of a team along with them and in the case of the 2005 Lions, Lawrence was that man. The best rugby they played on that tour was the first 20 minutes of the opening game, but when Lawrence suffered a career-threatening broken ankle things blew up for him and the team. That shows how vital he was. I know Brian O'Driscoll was up-ended in the first Test and that in itself was a massive loss, but I think Lawrence's injury cast a far bigger shadow over that tour than anything else as he was the heartbeat of that squad.

With his perfect finish ruined, it was great to see him un-retire himself and then play a role – maybe not a starring one, more as an 'impact replacement' – in England's return to the World Cup final in 2007 where they just couldn't squeeze past South Africa. Having Lawrence within the squad as a wise old head to help out would have been crucial to their success and it was perhaps a more fitting end to such unstinting service for England.

Clearly the death of his sister Francesca in the *Marchioness* disaster of 1989 shook him to the core, as it would any devoted younger brother. I've known Lawrence for a little while now through some charity events that we both take part in, and occasionally I've heard him mention her, always talking about her in the most glowing terms. He refers to her as the talented one in his family since she was a magnificent dancer with a big future ahead of her when she sadly died. From that point Lawrence drove himself with such purpose and a relentless pursuit it is no small wonder that he enjoyed the rugby career he did.

When he finally finished with a fifth and final Premiership crown tucked under his arm, he did so with the entire Twickenham crowd chanting his name, both Wasps and Leicester fans alike. Now, I've seen him shed a tear during national anthems so he is not afraid to show his emotions, but how he managed to keep it together as he said goodbye on that stage must have taken a huge effort – it was spine-tingling. To top it off he spent most of his post-match interview on TV saluting BBC radio rugby commentator – and no mean England player himself – Alastair Hignell, who is fighting valiantly against multiple sclerosis and was retiring from radio after that very match.

Luckily I've never had to take on the game-face Dallaglio because he is always a charm off the field, but that isn't the same for everyone. I remember being at an event for the Caravan charity down in Spain which is a greengrocers' charity; Lawrence is involved with it and tries to come along whenever he can.

It is great fun and everyone looks forward to it – one year we all got down there and had a big dinner and a great time was had by all. The next morning we were due on the tee nice and early but just before we set off there was still no sign of Lawrence. It was obvious that he had overslept thanks to the night before, but we couldn't start the day without him so we had to go and find him. We sent Allan Lamb to go and wake him up and get him down to the course.

Now, the door was locked but 'Lamby' could hear Lawrence snoring. He knocked on the door a few times, but there was no reply and the big man just kept on snoozing. Just then a hotel maid was walking past and Lamby told her he'd been locked out of his room and would she be kind enough to open the door for him. She did and Lamby was now faced with this big bear of a man fast asleep and out like a light.

Lamby nudged him, shouted at him and prodded him to make him stir but nothing was working. Lamby has always been an innovative man and so thought one thing that would wake him up would be some cold water. But he also knew that waking an 18-stone England rugby player out of his sleep with cold water would not endear him to said giant. So he grabbed a bowl of water from the bathroom and no sooner had he thrown the bowl in the air he was out of the door. Lawrence awoke very suddenly and with a huge growl came tearing after Lamby, whose little legs were moving just about as quickly as they'd ever carried him. By the time he got back to us he was almost completely out of breath, but had just enough to say, 'Help me! He's going to kill me!'

Lawrence admitted that for a split second after he woke up Lamby would have been a goner, but by that evening we were all laughing and joking about it and Lawrence promised that Lamby was safe again – until the next time!

LAWRENCE DALLAGLIO

First and foremost you never win anything in rugby on your own and I've been fortunate enough to play with good players in good teams and make the most of the opportunities we've been presented with. My rugby career and my life have been underpinned with core values that have made a difference, things like honesty, hard work and respect. With those sort of values at your core, they shape your personality and what you're about, and they have an impact on how people look at you, what they say about you and how they react to you.

There is no doubt my parents had a huge positive impact on me and in many ways following my sister's death me and my career gave them something to help with that sense of injustice.

I always felt that true champions are people who cannot stand losing and I've always had that disdain for losing. Certain people find it acceptable to lose, but that was never my way of thinking. Of course you're going to have setbacks and short-term failure, but they are a necessity to achieve that long-term success you're after.

With regard to leadership, I've always felt that rugby was about collective responsibility. It is about doing your job well and allowing others to do theirs. In a team game you've got to make sure you do your bit in order to make the whole machine work properly and you have to allow players to flourish in order for them to do that.

I've always tried to instil that into the teams I've played for and make it clear to the players alongside me that everything they do on the pitch is a reflection of themselves as human beings. And when you get picked for England that shirt is not yours. It is being loaned to you for the duration of the game and it carries the hopes and dreams of a nation, so you must reflect that. That year of 2003–04 was a pretty special one for me and my team-mates and in many ways it sums up what life is about – taking opportunities.

As a captain or a leader you have to be prepared to go as far if not further than anyone else. You can't ask people to do things you are not prepared to do yourself. I think there is something in people that makes them good leaders, but you get better at it with time and experience as you earn the respect of your peers through your performances.

I found the game emotional at times and I embraced that because rugby is tribal, it is brutal, it is aggressive and it can be a street-fight at times between you and the opposition. Of course the game contains huge elements of skill and not every match is the same; however, at times it could be quite raw and you have to have all the tools to cope with it.

I think 'Beefy' took a similar attitude towards his cricket, getting stuck in whenever and wherever he could with bat and ball. He was a real hero of mine growing up. Guys like him and Daley Thompson were the people who enthused me, they were a bit different and they were winners. Beefy had a bit about him, and I was always excited when he walked to the crease or was given the ball because he could do something a bit special. I've been lucky enough to meet him a few times since then and I also played a fair bit of rugby against his son Liam, who is equally if not more talented than his dad because he played three sports professionally.

Beefy's charity work has been an inspiration to an entire nation and in particular to a whole generation of sportsmen who use their position to raise money and awareness for various causes, and for that as much as anything he is a very special man.

LESTER PIGGOTT
DURABILITY

There aren't many sports that boys of 12 and men of 57 can both be successful in and even fewer where that success can belong to the same man. Perhaps chess or tiddlywinks or maybe even at a push crown green bowls! But something as active as horse racing?! Surely not. Yet that is what the greatest flat-racing jockey I've ever seen did and it will never be surpassed.

Lester Piggott sat astride horses as if to the manner born, in fact that is exactly what he was born to do with a family entrenched in the horse world long before he came along.

Being five feet eight he literally stood taller than almost any other jockey, but regardless of size he simply dominated the sport like a goliath and was revered for it.

His success in numbers is quite eye-watering when you consider that he enjoyed 4,493 winners in a career spanning forty-seven years and six decades. He even won 20 races over the hurdles, which just goes to show his versatility. He was the Champion Jockey eleven times and he won the Epsom Derby nine times out of the thirty-six starts he had – a quarter. And he won a record 30 English classics, something no one has ever come close to equalling; even the legendary Sir Gordon Richards only won 14 of them.

On those statistics alone you get an idea of how good a rider Lester was, but he was about more than just numbers, he was about winning and what it took to win. He struck fear and loathing in other jockeys because he had no time for reputations – or more to the point their reputations – and he would do whatever he had to in order to win.

The stories of him in his pomp are legendary, as if he used to treat racing and the course as though they were his personal property to do with as he pleased.

If he needed to cut someone up to win, so be it. If he needed to give a horse more whipping than others though, necessary he'd do it and if he happened to lose his own whip he'd think nothing of snatching one out of the hand of a fellow rider mid-race to give his horse a nudge and get on with winning.

All these antics would get him into a variety of trouble with the race stewards and officials but as far as he was concerned it was what he had to do to win. I admire that trait in sportsmen, that bloody-minded win-at-all-costs attitude because it shows that they are giving it everything they've got. There are no half measures involved, just a streak of determination running through the middle.

The other thing it says about Lester is that he had a touch of arrogance that only comes with being the very best at what you do. Only some sportsmen and women have it and even fewer can back it up with their performances. I'm thinking about the likes of Sir Viv Richards, Zinedine Zidane, David Campese and Sir Nick Faldo, who all had that touch of aloofness about them but it didn't matter one jot because they went out and backed it up time and time again. For me, as far as jockeys go, he is the man that sits on top of all others. He was the very best in the game and I don't think there would be many to disagree with that. If you talk to owners, trainers and people who raced against him, he is the first name that comes out every time and for good reason.

Lester was born into horse racing stock with both his father and his grandfather enjoying successful racing careers as jockeys and trainers, but it was the youngster who was to prove the jewel in the family crown. He won his first Derby at the age of just 18 in 1954 and from there he never looked back, riding for some of the best trainers and owners in the world because they all knew he was the best.

LESTER PIGGOTT

As befitting the best, Lester enjoyed some of the most magical sporting moments the British public can ever have enjoyed, winning some incredible races on some of the most magnificent horses. He is perhaps best remembered for his association with Nijinsky – a Canadian thoroughbred horse that he won the Triple Crown with. That is to say the 2,000 Guineas, the Derby and the St Leger. Together with Lester on board they made the perfect horse–jockey combination, knowing each other's strengths and weaknesses and getting the very best out of each other.

The relationship between a jockey and a horse can be so complicated since it requires a bit of understanding on both parts. A jockey that pushes a horse too much will get nothing out of it, while a jockey that asks for little will get little, so it is a delicate balancing act between the two and Lester had it quite superbly with Nijinsky, on which he won his fifth Derby. Unfortunately I was too young to take advantage of such a potent partnership but plenty of the Great British public did and in the 1970s you either backed a horse with Lester or Willie Carson on board.

Just as important as the jockey–horse combination was the jockey–trainer axis and Lester enjoyed the greatest partnership of them all with the late Vincent O'Brien. Between the two of them they rode and trained four Derby winners and eleven other classic winners – it was a match made in racing heaven.

But even when Lester was a freelance jockey booking his own rides he was still a master, continuing to be Champion Jockey without a full-time agreement with a yard. These guys are hired guns and Lester was the deadliest of the lot. If you had a horse with half a chance get Lester on the back of it and watch it romp home.

It was under Vincent O'Brien though that Lester cemented his place as the pre-eminent jockey of his generation and with football pools heir Robert Sangster they had the financial backing to do some damage. Once his association with O'Brien wound down he then found himself with another legendary trainer and enjoyed more success with Henry Cecil.

The fact that he continued to win under a variety of trainers and on top of so many different horses suggests to me that the role of the jockey really is crucial and he was making the most of his talents.

He was of course a royal jockey too, but not just any old royal jockey because he gave the Queen her very first classic winner in 1957 on Carozza in the Oaks. Admittedly it was only five years after she had ascended to the throne but to be the first to do anything is a real thrill. He continued to ride for Her Majesty on and off for the rest of his career; however, the OBE he deservedly received from her for his services to racing was taken away in 1988 as his world crumbled around him for tax evasion.

Lester had already retired from racing in 1985 to take up training and was doing just fine when the taxman started digging around looking for VAT irregularities. As it turned out he had to serve a year in jail for the crime, leaving him as low as anyone could be. How do you get over something like that when you are used to the highest of high lives around the aristocracy that flock to racing? I've got no doubt it would have been embarrassing and more than a little annoying, but he got on with his time inside without fuss and the year was soon over.

His training yard was no longer what it once was as several owners deserted him, so the question again is what do you do? You go back to what you do best and in Lester's case that was riding horses. At the ripe old age of fifty-four he decided to return to racing and he showed that he had lost none of his edge despite having five years out of the saddle. A win in the Breeders Cup mile proved the point, but until he'd claimed another English classic, people would suggest he'd lost the magic touch. That was never to be the case though and with Rodrigo de Triano he claimed his 30th and final English classic win in the 2000 Guineas and it was the sign of a true champion.

He had come through one of the toughest episodes of his life and survived not only to tell the tale but to then be a winner once more, and that is the hallmark of greatness. No matter who you are you're going to get some rough patches along the way, and I know that better than most, but it is how you deal with them on the other side that marks you out. You can give up and go home or you can stand up tall and try again and that is what being a sporting hero is all about in my book.

LESTER PIGGOTT

I do wish I'd been able to get him on one of my horses that I part-owned back in the 1980s, but truth be told I didn't have horses at that end of the table and these guys were always fully booked anyway riding for a yard or a specific trainer, so it was always rare to find someone like Lester free and without a ride. Even when he made his comeback after retiring, he was never going to struggle for a competent horse to get on the back of and he showed why.

To think that I can remember watching Lester winning races when I was a kid and then after I'd retired from cricket myself he was still there churning out the winners. He is a truly remarkable man who set new standards for other jockeys to follow.

The fact that the annual awards for jockeys are now called the 'Lesters' is a deserved tribute to him that sums up his contribution to racing. Between him and Vincent O'Brien – who sadly died at the age of 92 on 1 June this year – they had everything covered and when it comes to horse racing he was untouchable.

LEWIS HAMILTON
COMPOSURE

Is it the car or is it the driver? Those in the know will tell you it takes both to make a Formula 1 world champion and as long as he's got a half-decent car Lewis Hamilton will be right in the mix. He is an unbelievable talent who to me looks like he makes the car just an extension of his own body. He has total control over the machinery and is turning fast driving back into the art form it once was.

I'm not stupid enough to suggest that the best driver in the world can win with a poor car, that simply doesn't happen in the high-tech world of Formula 1. What I've seen and heard of Lewis Hamilton, however, tells me that this kid is something special.

I've got some good friends in Formula 1. Eddie Irvine, who used to race for Ferrari, is a good pal of mine and we've talked about the sport all over the world when we've been together – although I'd suggest avoiding skiing with Eddie unless you have a death wish! When I saw him on the golf course about two years ago I did ask him straight out, 'How good is Lewis Hamilton?'

He told me, 'Beefy, I think that boy will be the best of all time,' and there was a glint in Eddie's eye that told me how excited he was about him. He told me he'd watched him as a youngster and from the moment he saw him driving in a go-kart he thought he had something.

He intrigues me and has raised my interest in a sport that had stopped capturing the imagination of the British public. From afar I think of him as 'Mr Cool' because of the way he handled his first season at the highest level of the sport, and then managed to put the disappointment of defeat behind him to win the world title at the second time of asking.

Following that, he struggled to keep pace at the start of the 2009 season and got himself embroiled in a messy business over misleading race stewards, before returning to form in 2010 to lead the drivers' standings in one of the most interesting seasons for British motorsport fans. Together with Jenson Button, we have two hometown heroes battling it out for supremacy, and in my opinion Lewis Hamilton could prove himself to be the best racing driver to come out of these shores in a generation. This lad could go on to be the very best of the best and break every record in the sport – a big call, I know, but he looks like the sort of person to make a big call about.

I've never met Lewis, but I would love to spend a bit of time in his company, because to me he looks special – hence he gets the nod and is amongst illustrious company in this book. I'm not sure what it is with him, but I'd like to have the chance to find out. What I struggle to get my head around is just how dedicated and professional he has been from such an early age. The story goes that he met Ron Dennis at the age of ten and while asking for an autograph he also told the McLaren boss that he would one day drive for his team. 'Come back and see me in nine years,' said Dennis. As it was he signed him up at 12 after seeing his early potential in karting where he first won the UK championships in his class in 1995.

As a father and a grandfather I've seen my fair share of ten-year-olds and at that age kids want to be all sorts of things, from astronauts to train drivers to actors to racing drivers, and most of them change their mind every other week. For Lewis to have made up his mind, then stuck with it for his teenage years, and not deviated away from his plan reveals something about his character. It shows his commitment and loyalty both to the sport and to McLaren, plus it also shows how focused and dedicated he is about what he is doing – very similar you might say to our tennis prodigy Andy Murray.

MY SPORTING HEROES

As I've said before elsewhere in this book, these sportsmen and women are not one-dimensional people who only have a part of the package, they are the best of the best and they have everything. Lewis Hamilton is one of those and I think he is showing us more of what he is capable of all the time.

Having been signed up on a development contract by McLaren he has had to put in the hard work and the hard graft to make sure he didn't waste his opportunity. I'm sure there were plenty of racing drivers out there who had to find another way of making it to Formula 1 and there is probably a lot of jealousy flying his way for having been in a privileged position at such a fine team, but that does not diminish his effort at all. If he hadn't stepped up to the mark in every way for the team there is no way they would have kept ploughing money into him.

I understand it cost them around £5 million to turn him from karting protégé to Formula 1 world champion and he didn't let them down. Just because you are provided with the best doesn't always mean you will become the best. There are scores of young players who don't make it at Manchester United, but does that mean the ones that do are soft? Of course not – being groomed in any given sport from a young age still requires a lot of talent and hard work on that person's part and Lewis has done that.

Having won lower-class titles throughout his career and a GP2 title in 2006, he was finally given the chance to realise his dream of driving in a Formula 1 car in proper competition and what a way to start. Nine podium finishes in his first nine races certainly announced him to the world and then to win his first race at just the sixth attempt was astonishing. Formula 1 is supposed to take a bit of time to bed into, but not for Lewis.

What I most admired was the way he just went about his business, remaining calm and unflustered even though his team-mate Fernando Alonso was creating a fuss in the media about what was or wasn't being done vis-à-vis their respective cars within the team. Alonso's behaviour really surprised me, because it showed that he was too easily distracted. Here was a double world champion getting annoyed and upstaged by a rookie and it got to him. Alonso should have been the bigger man in all of this, allowing his driving to do the talking, but instead he got himself bogged down and it cost them both in the end.

As a result of their spat Lewis is hardly a popular man in Spain, but the racist element of the abuse he has had to endure out there sickens me. With his Caribbean heritage on his dad's side, Lewis is something of a trailblazer in more ways than one, and that does bring a certain amount of extra pressure with it, even though the colour of your skin makes not one iota of difference to who you are or what you're capable of. If anything though it should be seen as a positive, with Lewis becoming a role model for children of all colours. For someone so young he handled that nasty element in Spain with a maturity beyond his years, which again showed his mental toughness to go alongside his undoubted skill as a driver.

Lewis should have been the first driver in the history of Formula 1 to win the world title in their debut season; he had shown the skill, tenacity and ability to be champion, but when it mattered he and his team faltered. In fact he had plenty more to distract him off the grid when his team were caught up in a spying affair and found guilty of using Ferrari information to further their own car. It was an episode that could easily have knocked the wind out his sails, but despite that and the removal of constructors' championship points, he was still able to focus on his job. The picture being painted, even by then, was of a very calm, unflustered and professional young man.

Even when midway through the season he had a 150 m.p.h. crash at the Nurburgring in Germany to remind him of the dangers of the sport, he didn't budge in his quest for glory. Poor tyre choices in the penultimate race in China caused Lewis to retire for the first time in his career, but it still meant he would have a four-point lead over Alonso and seven points over Kimi Raikkonen. In Brazil his destiny was in his own hands, with a third place finish or better guaranteeing him the world title. As it turned out a gearbox problem and a stunning drive from Raikkonen ended with him finishing seventh and losing the title to the Finn.

It meant his next season in 2008–09 would be full of new pressures that would be hard enough for a veteran like David Coulthard to handle let alone someone in just their second season, but he was equal to it.

A topsy-turvy season between Lewis and Felipe Massa, plus the drama of the year before, brought Formula 1 back into a spotlight that I think it had missed during the predictable Schumacher years. It was a genuine contest between two great teams and two fine drivers. With the previous season's failure so fresh and so raw in Lewis' mind, I can only imagine what he must have felt like going into the final race knowing that it was his to lose again.

This time he needed to finish fifth in order to secure victory and with just one lap to go he was down in sixth having been passed by Sebastian Vettel, with Massa leading the way home. Now depending on your point of view you will either say that last lap was the luckiest piece of motor sport history or the most calculated. Due to a rain storm that had soaked the track, the tyre choices were crucial for the drivers and the man in fifth, Timo Glock, was on the wrong set. According to McLaren, Hamilton knew he had the speed to catch him and could have risked overtaking him before the final dramatic bend. However, such was his composure and focus he knew the best chance lay in doing so at that final bend, and therefore with just one chance to make his own piece of history, he bided his time and took it.

Never mind that Massa, his Ferrari team-mates, his family and all of Brazil were celebrating their first world champion since Ayrton Senna, Hamilton had done it. Such complete and utter concentration when it mattered and when it counted earned Lewis his title. It was like David Beckham's free-kick against Greece, or Jonny Wilkinson's drop-goal against Australia. He did it when it mattered and that is the complete definition of a Botham sporting hero.

Now he is a world champion and his dream has been realised so with that come even greater demands and expectations. He found it difficult to deal with in 2009 and got himself into situations he shouldn't have, but another year on and he is flourishing again at McLaren with the current world champion Button pushing him all the way. With experience, I think Lewis has developed into an even better driver and his drive to second place at the 2010 British Grand Prix was an example of his phenomenal talent. He had no right to be that close to the Red Bull of Mark Webber, but he held his nerve to grab as many points as possible and finish on the podium in front of the home fans. His driving is doing the talking now and that won't tell any lies.

LIAM BOTHAM
BRAVERY

In choosing people for this book I've thought long and hard about why they deserve a place. Each one of them has shown various characteristics that go into making a sportsman or woman of the highest class. For nearly all of them, their achievements on the field have said more than enough about them. For others I have seen something in them that I identify with. Whether it is the style they've competed with, or the uniqueness of their achievement, or because I have been lucky enough to get to know them and have seen what goes on behind the scenes and what makes them tick.

In the case of my son Liam, 've watched him grow up from a boy to a man and having seen what he has put himself through to try and reach the top of his chosen sports I couldn't be more proud. However, if I can take my rose-tinted glasses off for a second and look at him objectively, his achievement in being the only man I can think of to have played three sports professionally in this day and age is something that should get an impressive raise of the eyebrow full stop. He played first-class cricket, top-flight rugby union and rugby league and if it wasn't for a twist of fate he came within a whisker of full international honours with union.

Nine of the best-known sporting clubs and counties in Britain across three sports have parted with money so that Liam could play for them. And considering eight of them are in a sport I've got no association with whatsoever, accusations of nepotism or being carried by the surname are blown out of the water straight away.

However, I know what some of you are thinking. Martin Johnson, Sir Nick Faldo, Liam Botham? Doesn't exactly roll off the tongue with most sports fans, but then again I'm not most people. This book is about people that have impressed me and people who inspire admiration from me and Liam certainly does that.

Unless you are the offspring of someone famous I'm not sure it is easy to understand the kind of pressure you are put under from such a young age. It is why so many kids born to high-achieving people in the public eye tend to move away from the career of their parents and seek something out for themselves. Of course some follow the same path and make just as much of a success; however those occurrences are fairly rare. I can think of Graham and Damon Hill, or Dick and Will Greenwood who have done it particularly well, but it is such a hard thing to do.

Liam went both ways and I think he can be pretty satisfied the way things worked out even if he was so cruelly denied a full England rugby union cap by a stomach bug given to him by a certain Jonny Willkinson!

As a professional sportsman you miss a lot of your children growing up and so I have actually seen a lot more of my grandchildren growing up than I did of my children. Even though I tried to get Kath and the kids out on tour as much as I could there was just so much time spent away from the family that it was bound to have an impact.

I was always proud of what Liam was doing, like any father would be, but I couldn't take as active a part as others might due to my career. It is partly selfish because you want to achieve the very best that you can, and it is partly selfless, because you're also trying to provide for your family and give them the best that you can. Hopefully you end up falling somewhere in the middle and luckily for me I now have a fantastic relationship with Liam and it has worked out.

One thing I knew about Liam from an early age was that he

was a very talented sportsman in his own right; I just didn't know what he would end up doing. I certainly didn't want to push him into cricket because it was something that he had to decide for himself, but when he told me that he wanted to give it a try with Hampshire I was delighted. I told him there would be a lot of eyes on him and the pressure would be huge, but if that is what he wanted to do then I'd support him all the way. In truth it came as no surprise to me to see him make the grade in the way he did and secretly I wondered just how good a cricketer he was going to be.

I remember Liam's first game of first-class cricket for Hampshire against Middlesex and he got 5–67 (including a certain ex-England captain), and the next morning the headlines were 'chip off the old block', 'following in the footsteps' and 'like father like son'. This is not exactly an easy set of expectations to wake up to and I think that might have got to him a little bit in the sense that he was asking himself, 'What do I have to do to make my own mark?' That was Liam out there playing the game and taking those wickets, not me, but unfortunately people didn't want to see that for themselves.

I left Liam to his own devices and didn't actually go down to watch his first game. Instead Kath and I were 'watching' it unfold on teletext over a pub lunch and each time the page refreshed it seemed like he had got another wicket. It wasn't too long though before his heart was being pulled in another direction with the rugby.

He was a very good rugby player and so when he came to me after a season of cricket and said he was going to give rugby a go professionally I thought that those headlines couldn't have helped. I wondered whether the pressure of the name had got to him, but I soon realised that Liam wasn't running away from anything, he was actually running towards something that he felt he could be successful in. I think if he'd stuck with cricket he could have gone quite a long way in the game. How far, we'll never know and it doesn't really matter at this stage, but he had the ability to swing the ball at a good pace and could get good batsmen out.

David Lloyd is a decent judge of a cricketer and when Liam was playing for Lancashire youth sides I know 'Bumble' was very keen to get him to sign for them. He decided to go to Hampshire to get away from the close home environment that he'd grown up with and wanted to spread his wings a bit, which was understandable. He had a half decent time of it with them and I know that when he made his mind up to play rugby, they were very reluctant to let him go – I think they held onto his registration just in case he changed his mind, but he didn't.

He started at West Hartlepool and did quite well there, but when he then went to Cardiff things really took off for him. He had a fantastic time there and I think his try-scoring record of 42 in 72 matches is one of the best ratios they've had at the club.

He was a powerful athlete on the rugby pitch. He wasn't Jason Robinson electric quick but he glided up to top speed and once he was motoring it took an awful lot to stop him. He scored some sensational tries in his time at Cardiff and he really knew how to finish. I don't think that is something you learn; it is an instinctive thing and Liam had it. Whenever I spoke to former players at the club they were really excited by what he was doing and believed he would march into the Wales team under Graham Henry after completing his three-year qualification period.

It was at that point that things started to unravel for him. He had played representative rugby for England at under-21 level and was on the radar of the coach Clive Woodward, but he was told that he'd be better off playing in the English Premiership if he wanted to be an England player. He'd already done enough with Cardiff to make it onto the 2000 England tour of South Africa, but decided to take that advice and up sticks to Newcastle to play with their exciting young back line that included Jonny, Tom May and Jamie Noon.

It was on the tour to South Africa that he came within a 'dicky' tummy of playing for England, as the bug that had laid low room-mate Jonny had jumped across to Liam leaving him bedridden while a fit-again Wilko went and did what he did best. It was one of those things and I guess it just wasn't meant to be for him.

His move to Newcastle was not a happy one and I think it is fair to say that his experiences there sapped his love of the game. He became very disillusioned up there and his career went nowhere fast. He should never have left Cardiff and who knows, if he had stayed there he might still be running in tries now. He really didn't enjoy the final throes of his Newcastle days; he'd had some injury problems with his neck and he needed a complete change of scene, so when he turned his hand to rugby league I thought he was being braver than even I expected, but it was another challenge to get stuck into.

When he went to league I noticed a return of the fire in his eyes and the motivation to play. He thoroughly enjoyed his time in league and relished the involvement he was having in games at Leeds and then at Wigan until he suffered a second neck injury which cut things short. He saw two neurosurgeons who said, 'We can repair you, but is it worth it, considering the damage you're doing and could do again?'

Liam accepted that he'd had ten years of professional sport and even though he was very settled at Wigan by that stage he realised there is more to life than sport. When you think of the risk he'd have been putting himself at by playing on, I think he made the right decision. When you're talking about neck injuries and the tragedies that we've seen from that part of the body it wasn't worth pushing on unnecessarily.

The day he called it quits I can remember being sad for him in the sense that I knew how much of a wrench it would be to give up the passion in his life, but with his wife and kids behind him he knew it was the right thing and from that point of view I was happy for him. We get to spend far more time together now than we ever did and our shared interests in fishing, shooting and a whole host of outdoor activities keep us both entertained. We have a proper relationship now and when I look at him I can't help but be impressed by the man he has become. Of course I have to lay most of the credit for that at Kath's feet because she has been such a wonderful mother to him and our other two children, Becky and Sarah.

I know he doesn't have the medals or the trophies to go toe-to-toe with some of the other people in this book, but if anyone asks me who my sporting heroes are, Liam's name is somewhere near the top and that's the way it is. Who knows, if he hadn't had the surname Botham he may well have made it as a top-class international cricketer.

MY SPORTING HEROES

LIAM BOTHAM

I never ever wanted to be in a situation where anybody could say to me you're only here because of your surname. I had that a couple of times as a kid and I can remember playing for Yorkshire under-10s in my first game and there were five cameras there. As soon as I'd faced my first over and scored my first runs they all left because they only wanted to see this nine-year-old get a duck in his first game.

I've been lucky in the way that I've had the press around my whole life so I've grown up knowing how to deal with it all, but I still never wanted anyone to turn around and say I was only ever doing something because of my name.

That is why when I went to rugby I was one of the hardest trainers around to prove that point. I was always one of the first to turn up and one of the last to leave in whatever sport I did and actually I think it was part of my downfall as a rugby player because I sometimes trained too hard in practice and left some of it in the training room rather than take it out on the pitch with me. That is one of the things I regret about my career, but that is me and I can't change who I am.

Cricket had always been my first passion, and from the word go that was all I wanted to do and so when I signed for Hampshire at 15 it was what I had always wanted. I had no real inkling that I was going to play rugby at that stage. It was something I enjoyed and played for fun to keep me fit during the off-season, so when I'd played a little bit of cricket for Hampshire I was surprised to be offered a contract at West Hartlepool, but very excited by it too. Dad just said he'd back me whatever I decided and that was it.

The pressure had been there on me from the beginning and the name has never bothered me so that certainly wasn't the reason why I left cricket for rugby. It was a situation where I was leaving rugby before the end of the season to go back for pre-season cricket training and not wanting to go, and then when it came to the end of the summer I was just itching to get back to rugby so the passion was there.

The biggest mistake I ever made was leaving Cardiff. I think people didn't want to see me playing for Wales and so I went

LIAM BOTHAM

back to English rugby and to the Falcons where I ended up with Rob Andrew, who was without doubt in my opinion the worst coach I ever played under.

When I moved to league I just loved it. I had got disillusioned with union under Rob and Jonathan Davies suggested I give league a go. I learnt my trade at Bradford and then Leeds came in for me with a dual contract and I jumped at it.

Hand on heart I loved my time in all three sports. Who knows what I might have done in cricket, but I'm not one for ifs, buts and maybes. I made some great friends during my career and I had a great time.

It was always good to have Dad up in the stands when I was playing and I think he was proud of what I was doing. It was the same buzz any player has when their parents watch them. The fact is I didn't really get to know him properly until I was 16 or 17 when he retired from cricket and since then we've had a fantastic relationship. I respected what he did as cricketer hugely and that has never changed, but I also respect him a great deal as a father and a grandfather to my kids and that means everything.

MARTIN JOHNSON
LEADERSHIP

England's rugby World Cup-winning captain would get into most people's top 50 sporting heroes and I'm no exception. He won everything there was to win for club, country and the Lions, but such is the measure of the man, he once told me that people had somehow forgotten about the times he lost which he thought were just as important as the wins.

I like Martin. He is great company and knows a little bit about wine so that is always a bonus in my book, but I like the fact that he didn't bring Martin the rugby player with him whenever I met him, because he would have terrified me!

He was a brute of a player on the pitch and I mean hard. If ever a player knew about the dark arts in the tight forwards it was him and his opponents knew it, but once the battle was over and he was off the pitch amongst friends he was a sharp witty man with a mischievous and dry sense of humour.

'Johnno' made an impact very early as a rugby player and he could have had no deeper-end introduction to international rugby than in 1993 when he was thrown into the bear pit in Paris to meet the French on the back of just one training session.

Having been called up to replace the injured Wade Dooley for his England debut, he barely had time to introduce himself to his team-mates before being thrust into the toughest contest the

Five Nations had to offer. It clearly didn't faze him as England won 16–15 and it became clear that in the great tradition of outstanding second-row forwards our country had produced yet another one.

Except it wasn't just about what our country had produced because Martin had also enjoyed a spell in New Zealand as a teenager, which was to have a lasting effect on him. At 19 he went to play for King County and he was so good back then that he was even picked for the New Zealand U-21 side and donned a junior All Black jersey. It meant when he came back to play in England he had had an experience very few players would have had and it gave him a tiny advantage over his peers. Years later when he came up against New Zealand as an England player it gave him another little advantage in that he knew just what he was up against. He could understand the psyche of a Kiwi rugby player because he had been there, lived it and breathed it. I was lucky enough to play a bit of grade cricket in Melbourne before I broke into the England side and it certainly helped my development.

After a taste of the Aussie game as a kid I always wanted to play a season of Sheffield Shield cricket. It was the Australian state competition of the time and it was where the likes of Dennis Lillee, Ian Chappell and Rodney Marsh learnt their trade. I wanted to know what kind of environment produced these sorts of cricketers and I wanted to sit in their dressing-rooms and soak it up. I knew what the Aussies were about, but I wanted to get a taste of their mindset first hand. In the end I managed to do it when I played for Queensland in 1987, but I was 32 at the time and in many ways I wish I'd experienced it at an earlier stage of my development.

After Martin's debut he began a long and fruitful association with the three pillars of his rugby life, England, the Lions and of course Leicester Tigers, and it is no coincidence that all three of those sides enjoyed more success than ever with him involved. Of course rugby isn't a one-man game and I can't lay all the glory at his feet; however,it is clear to me that any rugby team with Martin Johnson in it and leading it was going to be a better one than without him and I don't think anyone can disagree with me there.

When it comes to captaincy and leadership, there are a few good ones out there who get their teams to succeed by talking and by cajoling, but I don't think that is the best template. For me it is all about doing and showing; that way your side will respect you and that is what I think Martin was all about. Respect, and in his eyes respect had to be earned.

If you look at the side he captained he had people like Lawrence Dallaglio, Neil Back, Jason Leonard and Will Greenwood. He had a team of leaders, but they all wanted to play for him and they all gelled together for the good of the team. It is a simple fact of his England team that they would all do whatever they could for him. I've spoken to players and management involved in that side and it doesn't matter whether they are backs, forwards, masseurs, physios' or even the head coach, the one name that comes up above all others is Martin Johnson. These types of men stand out in sport and what I admire most is their ability to take the game to the opposition and bring everybody with them. It is not a case of looking over his shoulder to see who's there, he doesn't have to look to see who's coming out of the trenches with him because he knows they are all there right behind him and that is real leadership.

He led from the front and never asked a player to do anything he wasn't prepared to do himself, which I think is an absolute must for any captain and it is where so many fail in the eyes of their players. You cannot demand more of your players than you are willing to do yourself. If you need your front row to go that extra yard and put in the biggest scrum of the game because two of your back-row players are in the sin bin then you'd better be ready to do the same. That great Welsh number 8 Scott Quinnell – who played under Johnson during the 1997 and 2001 Lions tours – summed it up perfectly when he said, 'You'd do anything for Johnno, he was that impressive a captain. If he asked you to run through a brick wall you'd do it, but to be honest it wouldn't be much of a problem because there would already be a huge hole in it where he'd gone through first.'

Martin had many a great game for Leicester, England and the Lions, but none stands out for me more than the World Cup final in 2003. An obvious choice, yes, but one that carries so much significance and iconic status that you could have accused me of going mad if I'd chosen another.

MARTIN JOHNSON

For that game I was sat in a Sri Lankan hotel bar and I can remember thinking how ideal it was that I was there because it meant the game started at 3 p.m. on a Saturday afternoon like it should do. I was in the Hilton in Colombo watching the game with the television crew who were covering England's tour that winter. It just so happened that most of the cameramen were Australian so the atmosphere was perfect from the start with plenty of banter flying about. I was actually in the minority because there were a few South Africans there too and the last team they wanted to win was England so I was copping it from all sides. By half-time though the mood had changed as Martin and the boys took a grip on the game and I honestly thought we'd walk it. It didn't quite work out that way, but at least we scraped home.

I'm putting the real credit for the victory at the feet of Martin Johnson for keeping the side going and focused throughout. In the face of some dubious decision making by the referee at the scrum, and a never-say-die performance from the Aussies, who always raise their game to a new level against England, Johnson's leadership made sure the prize never slipped too far from his grasp.

I know Jonny Wilkinson's drop-goal was the dramatic moment that everybody talks about as where the World Cup was won, but I think the true story goes beyond that kick. Don't get me wrong, Wilkinson showed nerves of steel to slot that kick and it was a remarkable moment in English sporting history, but the foundation had been laid well before then and much of that is down to Martin.

And I believe that two particular moments during 2003 showed his leadership in the perfect light. England had gone over to Dublin to compete with Ireland for the Grand Slam and after losing out at the final hurdle for the previous few years nothing was going to stop them this time. So, when Johnno and the boys lined up on the home team's side of the field to meet President Mary McAleese and were then asked to move to the other side, he stood firm. The Irish administrators had no chance in getting him to budge and with the entire world watching, Johnno, with those huge bear-like eyebrows, held his ground and from there England dished out a rugby lesson.

MY SPORTING HEROES

The second pivotal moment for me was in Wellington against the All Blacks during the summer. With both Lawrence Dallaglio and Neil Back in the sin bin and with a five-metre New Zealand scrum bearing down on their own line, Johnson not only provided the ballast in the pack that held them at bay, but his inspirational leadership meant that the rest of the front five pushed like they'd never pushed before to keep the try line defended. I remember Johnno talking about that in the aftermath and when asked what it meant when two forwards left the pitch and the England pack still held firm, in a classic example of his dry wit, with a wry smile he just said, 'It meant that Lawrence and Neil don't push very hard.' He is a colossus of man who refused to give an inch on the field and it seems very straightforward to me that he has gone on to take charge of the national side now.

His greatest challenge is to now convert that following and that inspiration he had as a player into management. The early signs are good with a second-place finish in his first Six Nations, but things have been a bit up and down since then. He has been on the end of some serious beatings from the southern hemisphere sides and his players have struggled to show the sort of flair you need at the highest level. It has led many to question his credentials as a coach, but I wouldn't judge him too soon. If anyone knows what it takes to win international rugby matches it is him and the recent win over Australia Down Under showed that there is some light at the end of the tunnel. The question is whether he can build on that. Ultimately it will take time to make that transformation from player to manager complete and people have to understand that successful teams are not built overnight. You have to work hard to get to the top and even then hard work alone does not make the difference. You have to marry that work ethic with talent and ability, and with the next World Cup in 2011 it will be interesting to see whether Martin will have the same kind of top-class rugby players at his disposal as a manager as he had as a player.

A manager is only as good as the players he works with, but I believe Martin Johnson is the sort of guy you put your faith in and trust to do the best possible job because you know the people around him will give him everything they've got and he should be able to get the best out of them – woe betide them if they don't show it!

MARTIN JOHNSON

The biggest key to my success as a rugby player was honesty. I was honest to myself and I was honest to those around me. I never got carried away with what other people said about my career and the fortunate thing about playing the sport I did and in the position I did was that you cannot really kid yourself because if you try you will get taken down a peg or two.

Having a very sporting mother who ran marathons helped me because there was never any room for self-pity about what I was doing. It never seemed like a sacrifice to me to train hard and I enjoyed doing it. I played the early part of my career as an amateur which meant you had a job to do outside of the game and then you had to fit your work and your training around it which was very normal. When I look back on that now after being a professional you wonder how you did it, but that was the way it was and I was happy to work hard.

I was fortunate enough to grow up near the Leicester Tigers and no matter what you achieved in the game you were never a big fish there. If you played England representative rugby as a youngster, so what? Lots of other players did. If you played for the Midlands, so what? Nearly everyone had done that. Even if you played for England it didn't matter much, as half the team had done that too, and if you reached the pinnacle and played for the British and Irish Lions, then you almost certainly found the coach and the chief executive had done that as well! It was also a club that bred loyalty so I played nearly all my career with the same bunch of guys who were good players and good men. The same goes for England, which had a good crop of players who grew up internationally together, and leading them was a privilege I enjoyed.

We had some great wins together but there were also failures and I think that goes unnoticed at times. For every World Cup I won I lost two others and for every European Cup I won I lost plenty more and that is part of the process and it makes you who you are.

MY SPORTING HEROES

Captaincy is not something I ever really aspired to and actually I think I became captain of the Lions before I became captain of Leicester, and then England last of all. I was happy to be one of the troops and when I did get the job my style was of a low-profile nature because that is the way I liked to do it. Captaincy is a responsibility and it means that you have to think about other people as well as yourself without ever losing sight of the need to be playing well enough to merit your place in the team. I grew into the role the more I did it and by the end of my career it helped improve my game and it felt natural to me, but that comes with experience.

I've met Beefy a few times, most often up at Newcastle after playing against his son Liam, who was a pretty good rugby player and a good lad with it. I actually played a couple of games with him too when he played for the England A team in 2000 as I was coming back from an injury. Whenever I've met Beefy he's been great fun to chat to and he clearly loves his rugby. I've got a few mates who used to play for Leicestershire and I'll catch up with the cricket when I can, but I can't admit to being as big a fan of that game as he is!

SIR MATTHEW PINSENT
COMPOSURE

As children we all have it in front of us to do. We all have our growing up and developing to get through, and usually over time we blossom into the adults we want to become. We step out of the shadows of our parents and our older siblings to make our own way in the world. For some that whole process is easier than others; however in Sir Matthew Pinsent's case he found himself having to step out of the shadow of a solar eclipse in the shape of Sir Steve Redgrave.

Steve was just about the finest rower to have ever sat in a boat, and to the untrained rowing eye like mine I think Matthew will understand what I mean by that. Steve was and is an icon of the sport. Even before he won his fifth and final Olympic gold medal he was a legend; in fact before he and Matthew won their first together in Barcelona he was a legend. When it comes to Olympic rowing, the names Redgrave and Pinsent are etched onto the British psyche like Compton and Edrich for cricket, or Coe and Ovett for running, and it is hard to think of one without the other. So for Matthew to stand tall and reach the peaks that he did in claiming four consecutive gold medals of his own – and not all with Steve – makes him just as impressive a sportsman in my mind and someone that the British public can be truly proud of in his own right.

MY SPORTING HEROES

Steve Redgrave got me interested in rowing as an Olympic sport, but Matthew sustained my interest. I must admit I haven't got to know Matthew as well as Steve but when I've spent time with him it is always enjoyable and he has a fantastic wit. I've met him a few times at the odd golf day and he is an imposing man on the tee box, but my admiration for him stems from his achievements and the way he kept on pushing himself until he was satisfied that he had given everything he could have and had won all he could have.

For the record, Matthew won four Olympic titles, three with Steve and one without, ten World Championship gold medals and two 'Boat Races' for Oxford. If it wasn't for Steve and his pesky fifth Olympic gold it would rank as the greatest rowing record this country has ever seen, but even with Steve's tally, it is still eye-wateringly impressive.

Those medals are the highlights of a wonderful career, but for any sportsman the hard work and dedication begin a lifetime earlier when you find a sport that you love and that you are good at. It is at that stage when all those medals are nothing more than dreams that the hard work begins. I've read that a four-year training regime from Olympics to Olympics involves rowing around 35,000 kilometres on the water and on a rowing machine while the extra weights and cardio training you do means that for each stroke in an Olympic final you have put in about 15 hours beforehand. Just think about that for a moment.

Nothing sums up the sheer dedication to the cause than that statistic, yet it is par for the course as far as rowers are concerned. If you don't put that kind of effort into your training it will cost you since you know full well that your opposition has done it.

The life of a rower is one of the hardest in sport because it involves early starts and punishing regimes seven days a week, come rain, snow or sun. And no matter how good you are or how much you love your sport it takes some motivation to get yourself to the river bank day after day after day.

Matthew would have just moved into his teens when Steve won his first gold medal at the 1984 Los Angeles Olympics. And seeing as it was Britain's first gold medal for 36 years it put him on a pedestal. The fact that he won another in 1988 made him

SIR MATTHEW PINSENT

Britain's superstar on the water, so the first time Matthew got a chance to meet him let alone train with him would have been a thrill. How do you get over that first sense of awe and admiration? The answer is to prove to yourself and to him that you might be able to become his equal. In sport, if you don't believe you can at least match if not beat someone else how can you expect to succeed?

Before Matthew and Steve joined forces they raced against each other, one the Olympic golden boy with experience to burn, the other a 'young buck' trying to prove that he belonged with the big boys. However, once Steve was on the lookout for a new partner following the retirement of Andy Holmes and injury to Simon Berrisford Matthew took his chance. At 19 he teamed up with Steve and their journey together could really begin.

I've spoken to Steve about his training and the atmosphere around rowing crews and he says it is the most competitive environment he's ever known. Even with guys that are on the same team as you, the training takes on a competitive hue that cannot be shaken, and as far as he and Matthew went it was a competition to the end.

Before they began their Olympic odyssey together though Matthew had the small matter of the University Boat Race to take part in and between 1990 and 1991 he found himself in the victorious Oxford crew. The University Boat Race is an event that has always intrigued me, not so much for the level of competition which is fierce and close to international standard, but because on one day of the year it seems like the entire cities of Oxford and Cambridge become rowing fans and descend on the River Thames. For the remaining 364 days of the year I bet they couldn't give a stuff about rowing, but for one day everybody has a straw boater and a glass of Pimms in their hand ready to cheer on the Dark, or Light, Blues.

I suppose rowing in the Olympics is just like that on a much grander scale. It is only every four years, at which point everyone in the entire country becomes a rowing fan – I know because I do too, and that has simply been down to Steve and Matthew.

In 1992 their success in the coxless pairs was a great triumph, but I can remember Steve again taking most of the glory, as befits a man who has just won his third gold medal in a row. But in a pair the simple fact of physics tells you that each rower does half the work and Matthew had not only done all the work that he needed to beforehand, but he did it in the race too. And their clear winning margin showed just how much better they were than the rest of the world.

I can't quite remember much about what happened after Barcelona, but I do remember there being a lot of hype surrounding them going into the 1996 games in Atlanta, largely because Steve was going for an unheard-of fourth gold medal. All I can say is thank goodness for the pair of them otherwise we would have left those games without a single gold.

After eight years together Matthew had earned himself two gold medals, which in itself – to be a double Olympic champion – is something quite remarkable. With Steve deciding to retire following his famous line 'if anybody sees me near a boat, they have my permission to shoot me,' the road was clear for Matthew to forge ahead with his own career without the hero/father/older brother/team-mate/competitor figure standing over him. Yet incredibly Steve chose to carry on.

I wonder how Matthew must have felt about that deep down, to know that even though the next four years would be tough, when it came to their potential moment of glory in Sydney, the focus would again be on this superman going for five gold medals rather than shared equally with his partner who was doing half the work.

This is where I think we see some of Matthew's down-to-earth and essentially good-natured team-man ethos shine through. He is obviously a competitive animal and he clearly would have wanted to shine as brightly as Steve, but he knew that Steve was the main man that not only deserved his time in the spotlight, but who would make the boat better and faster by virtue of being in it.

I think the relationship between the two men is both as simple as it could be and extremely complex and I think it goes deeper than just being team-mates. I can't quite explain it because I've never been in that same situation, but I think there is a bond that comes from shared pain, which the training schedule ensures you both have. I think there is a willingness to help each other out because one man's success cannot occur without the other, yet you have to constantly look to test and beat each other to actually push to reach greater heights. It is a fascinating situation, but ultimately one that worked well for British rowing as they triumphed together yet again in 2000 in Sydney with the help of Tim Foster and James Cracknell. Watching the documentary that recorded the four men training prior to the Olympics was enthralling – that saw Steve even passing out in a monitored race on the rowing machine as he was pushing himself so hard.

Finally, after three Olympic Games together Matthew was free of Steve, and this is where he could have faltered. This is where his already deserved reputation in British rowing could have been blown out of the water if he'd failed. He was no longer the 19-year-old kid rowing with his hero, he was now the senior statesman in a four-man boat having to prove himself all over again.

Perhaps that is too simplistic a way of putting it, because to my mind I just wanted to see him win that fourth gold of his own in Athens as I'm sure the rest of the country did too. If he didn't manage it, then of course everyone would have said he could only win with Steve Redgrave alongside him. It would have been unfair, but we all know it is what a lot of people would have thought.

His race was the most hotly anticipated event of the whole games for me as a British fan. I knew that there had been some late reshuffling with Alex Partridge dropping out with a punctured lung, which brought Ed Coode into the boat, but if I'm honest I was tuning in for one thing. To see if Matthew could do it. To see whether all his hard work would pay off or not and to see whether we really were lucky enough to produce two once-in-a-generation rowers in more or less the same generation.

I always marvel at how lucky Australia were to have Shane Warne and Glenn McGrath in the same cricket side for 13 years, together with the likes of Adam Gilchrist and Ricky Ponting coming along too, but then I look at what we produced in rowing terms with Steve, Matthew, James Cracknell and Steve Williams and I see how it can be done!

That 2004 coxless fours final was one of the most dramatic races I have ever seen in any sport anywhere and when all was said and done I knew I had witnessed one of the greatest sportsmen the world has ever seen give one of the greatest performances of all time. In the tightest possible finish against the Canadians he appeared to pull the British boat over the line by himself by digging so deep into his reserves that the well had not only run dry but had been carved that little bit deeper. It was a heroic performance and one that ended any debate about just how good he was.

Of course his tears on the podium told their own story and if ever a man has been laid bare to his very soul that was it, yet through the tears and the raw emotion we saw what a true champion looks like. It was entirely fitting that he received a knighthood for his achievements in sport which I believe transcended just rowing to make him a role model and an inspiration to us all. Sir Steve might be sat at the head of the top table, but Sir Matthew is sat right alongside him.

MATTHEW PINSENT

I didn't really think I could make a career out of rowing until I came out of the junior ranks. While I was club rowing I could see what the gap was like between me and the rowers that were coming back from the Seoul Olympics and I thought if, as an 18 year old, I wasn't too far away from that standard then it might be something I could do – however it wasn't a planned career move. My idea was to go to university and then join the rat race like everybody else, maybe as an accountant or something like that, but luckily while I was at Oxford, rowing took over.

Pairing with Steve meant that I got a decent sponsorship package and it meant I could afford to continue rowing so that after 1992 in Barcelona we made the conscious decision to defend our title in Atlanta. I never thought I could make a lot of money out of rowing, I just thought I could survive, which allowed me to pursue the idea of winning.

I don't think I changed my character to suit my sport, I think the sport tapped into characteristics that I had. I was always competitive and driven so together with the sport and being in close proximity to Steve they were magnified and turned into the building blocks for success. You have to be motivated, determined and willing to put stuff to one side in order to succeed. It was only in the pursuit of gold medals that I thought this could be a lifestyle and I didn't struggle with that, but I had an ability to switch it on and off so that when I went home from training those same character traits weren't necessarily at the fore.

I can't really pick out one gold medal above the others because they were all special for different reasons. However, Athens was a big career moment for me. I couldn't overplay it in my mind, I had to have confidence in my own ability. It was good for me though because it was without Steve and I had to prove to myself and everyone else that I could win without him. That has made a massive difference to me long term, that I can be respected in my own right and not just as Steve's sidekick.

In all honesty, it would have been impossible for me to carry on without Steve in the first part of my career because there wasn't anyone like him, but by the time he finished there were lots of mini 'Steve Redgraves' who were willing to do what was necessary, so that made rowing without him a little easier.

Steve's attitude to rowing and winning put him on his own when I first joined the British team and ten years later everyone had followed his lead. We've gone from also rans to being dominant and that is down to Steve's example.

I'd like to show Ian that I can win at golf as well, but having played a few rounds with him, whatever his official handicap is, I'm not sure it is enough! It is always great fun though spending a bit of time with Ian and I think we can all reflect on our sporting lives with a smile.

MIKE GIBSON
SKILL

To find sport at its best you nearly always have to have two competitors or teams at the top of their game bringing out the highest standards of each other. Think Watson and Nicklaus, Federer and Roddick at the recent Wimbledon final, or South Africa and the British and Irish Lions in 2009. Sometimes though the best players are in the same squad and must therefore outdo each other to get into the team and there is no better example of that than in rugby and Lions rugby in particular. And that is why I found Irishman Mike Gibson's ability not only to break up the Welsh back line in the 1970s, but to shine within it a real triumph of cream rising to the top no matter what the circumstances.

In order for the British and Irish Lions to be successful they must have every player vying for a position to be putting more and more pressure on their opponent or team-mate so that when the Test side is announced you know that you've got the absolute best 15 players possible on the pitch. In recent memory I can think of Neil Back and Richard Hill going hammer and tongs for a spot in the 1997 Test XV, constantly raising the bar week after week.

In 1971 it would have been easy to fill the Lions back line with Welshmen because they were that good. They had won the Five Nations Grand Slam and when you think of the likes of J.P.R. Williams, Barry John, Gareth Edwards and John Dawes you're talking about some of the greatest players to have ever played the game. But to that list you simply must add Mike Gibson. He was a dreamy centre with all the skills and more to outshine some of the Welsh greats in that era. And there is no exaggeration involved when I tell you that the Lions' success in New Zealand in 1971 and South Africa in 1974 could have faltered without him.

In fact the first Test match on the 1971 tour contained a back line made up entirely of Welshmen bar Mike. Even though he was a classy player with two Lions tours already under his belt he still had to oust the Welsh centre Arthur Lewis who was also on the trip. Having been a part of that year's Grand Slam success Lewis would have had an eye on a Lions test shirt, but Mike rose to the challenge and made sure he was the only man to spoil the Welsh dominance. It changed in the second Test onwards when England's David Duckham joined him, but I think the point was already made.

With Barry John and John Dawes on either side of him, Mike was able to showcase his full range of talents in the Lions midfield and his reading of the game was second to none. Having played plenty of rugby as a fly-half he knew how to manage a game, how to time a pass and how to thread a kick, but he still had to get on the park and do it.

He stood out in a great era for rugby and it is down to him and others around that time that my love of the game grew and by the time he retired with a record 69 Irish caps his position as a rugby great was secure. The fact it took 26 years for his record to be broken by Malcolm O'Kelly, in an era where a lot more international matches get played, speaks for itself.

I had been a stalwart soccer fan throughout my school days and into my teens, but guys like Mike Gibson converted me to rugby. The more I watched the more I loved it. The way they played the game, how tough they were and how hard they were, yet they'd pick each other up and have a drink in the bar afterwards. It was my kind of game.

It is probably just as well that I didn't discover rugby before I turned professional at cricket as I may well have had a go and would have been playing for Buckler's Mead Old Boys 4th XV rather than being the cricketer that I was. Rugby is a game I love with real passion and Mike Gibson was one of the men I specifically remember getting me into it.

When I later got a chance to meet him and become friends with him my respect for him grew because he is such a decent, intelligent and sharp man, the sort of man who does the game of rugby proud. I know that was the amateur days for rugby and everyone had to get back to their normal job in between, but for Mike to be in a tough and demanding line of work like being a solicitor spoke volumes for his commitment both to his career and to the game. And with his own legal practice he became a tremendously successful solicitor too, not just one in name. He is a bright, clever and passionate man and also a bit of a perfectionist so it comes as no surprise that he made a success of his business.

I'm sure his working career rubbed off on his rugby and vice versa, but he had that rare thing which only the very best have – time. His reading of the game meant that he had a split second longer than others and that is why he was such a devastating player who made the sport look effortless. Even though he had some decent players around him for Ireland like Willie John McBride I don't think they had the depth of quality to be successful. Ireland had players full of passion but they didn't have the complete list of players that they've got now. Plus they were up against a magical era of Welsh rugby. I think that is why Mike stands out in my mind, because he managed to raise himself above mediocrity rather than be sucked down by it.

I look at the recent Irish Grand Slam winners of 2009 and I can see some fine similarities between Brian O'Driscoll and Mike Gibson. Fantastic leaders who set high standards for themselves and for those around them, but also astonishingly talented players in their own right. O'Driscoll is doing for centre play what Mike did 40 years ago.

They're gutsy, tough players who take a lot of bangs. Mike was a marked man when he played, but he ran through it all and kept going even when people were using fair means or foul to try and stop him. His discipline was exceptional, but I suppose that is to be expected from a man who has his own legal firm.

It has to be remembered though that Ireland was going through a grizzly time with the Troubles during the 1970s and actually their participation in the Five Nations Championship was restricted due to some teams refusing to go and play in Ireland. Being a Belfast boy Mike felt that period perhaps more acutely than most and that is why when I went over to play in a charity match in 1986 he was particularly appreciative.

It was during a spell when I was banned from playing cricket, but rather than sit on my backside waiting for the old boys at the TCCB to let me play again I did a few bits and pieces to keep busy. When Mike called me up and asked if I could come over to Belfast and play a game of cricket on the Falls Road during the Troubles, I was only too happy to help and he told me he thought it was one of the best things I could possibly have done for Belfast at the time. With Barry McGuigan fighting under the banner of peace, it was clear that sport can have a role in bringing people together despite huge differences. There was a big crowd and a real party atmosphere and he said it blew him away. Much like the work I now do with the Laureus Sport for Good Foundation it showed that sport can break down barriers and it does bring people together regardless of creed, colour or religion.

Since that day we've become good friends and I've seen first hand just how competitive a bloke he is. I actually feel rather sorry for some of the players who came up against him because he would have given them nothing. Like most of the people in this book his competitive streak is fierce and like me it hasn't waned despite the advancing years so when I invited him to my house a while back for a barbeque it came as no surprise to our respective other halves to see us scrumming down with neither of us willing to concede an inch of ground. I can't quite remember how we got to that stage but needless to say a glass of wine might have been involved!

It is always good fun to spend time with Mike and I know that he made the perfect Lions tourist. Whole-hearted commitment on the field and a good craic off it, which is what you need in that environment. The fact he went on a record five Lions tours between 1966 and 1977 tells you what he brought to the party.

He's not stupid though and he knows when to call it a night. Many times I have been to Ireland for a game and I promise you

MY SPORTING HEROES

the best place to go and watch rugby has always been Dublin. I get there, check into my hotel, dump my bags and meet Mike and a few others. He has introduced me to fantastic friendly people over the years and the weekend tends to get a bit hazy, but every night he manages to make it home before too late and then join up with me again in the morning looking bright and breezy. Somehow he evades my attempts to get him to stay, as if I were a rogue New Zealand tackler that he has slipped by.

The thing that stands out for me though is that Mike was a classy player who looked regal on the pitch. Everything he did was done with precision and class and even though there were more thrilling players and more edge-of-your-seat performers, I just admired his perfection. I don't think anyone has filled the position of centre with more accomplishment that him and that is why he is out on his own.

SIR NICK FALDO
DETERMINATION

Nick Faldo is the best British golfer we've ever had and I would go so far as to call him the best European golfer we've ever seen this side of the Atlantic. To win one 'Major' is a phenomenal achievement and it can never be underestimated just how tough that is, but to win six is the mark of true greatness, and he got there with complete and utter single-minded determination.

Golf is often described as a competition between you and the course and simply a case of shooting the lowest number you can in the conditions you face, and yes, to an extent that is true. However, put two golfers together on the last day of a Major tournament and the game takes on a whole new dimension – you're no longer just playing the course, you are playing your opponent. By playing the course over three days you earn the right to face a rival head on from where it becomes a battle of skill, nerve and determination.

And that is where Faldo was a master. He was one of the first golfers to have a strategy for each opponent, like an army general, and whoever he came up against on the last day of a tournament would have their mettle tested to the last.

I can remember walking around the course watching him during the final round at Muirfield in 1987 as he took on Paul Azinger for the British Open. And on that day he actually just went round paring every hole because he knew what he needed to do to win, not to try and break course records but to win, and that is what golf was and is all about to Nick Faldo.

He just stuck to his game plan and beat the player opposite him, not the course, and as I walked alongside I could see just what he was trying to do; he was trying to wear Azinger down and suffocate his ability to play and that is what happened. Nick though was just a picture of determined concentration throughout. He looked up every now and again and we caught each other's eye a few times, but even though he flickered a brief nod of recognition there was nothing and no one who was going to shake him out of his zone.

Once he'd won the 'Claret Jug' I saw him and his then wife Gill and he was as happy as I've ever seen anyone. He was steadily closing in on his dream of being the best golfer this country had ever produced and that is what made him happy. I said to him that I thought he looked in a trance out there, he seemed so focused, but if there was any doubt over whether he'd noticed what was going on around him it was dispelled when he gave me a bit of a ribbing for not walking round the whole course with him!

I told him nothing could be further from the truth and that I'd been there every step of the way, but he still carried on winding me up about not walking the whole course with him. I told him I could have any number of people vouch for me that I'd been there right to the end. 'Ah yes,' he said, 'but tell me, which England cricketer did I see being ferried around on the back of a golf buggy?'

Well, I was stuffed, because at one point the crowds were so big following him around it was quite difficult to get from one green to the next tee, so when I spotted a Japanese film crew with a buggy heading up the course I jumped on the back for a little lift. It was only a little one and it was just so that I could see more of his title-winning round – but he wasn't having any of it!

I first came across Nick Faldo when he was just a teenager playing at Welwyn Garden City golf club. I was doing a charity event there and he was busy practising so we didn't actually speak to each other. I was told by the pro at the club that he was one to look out for, because of his ability not only to play the game out on the course, but also to play the game off the course. His commitment to practising was legendary and is certainly not a route I chose to go down! I think he was the assistant to the golf pro at the time and although we didn't actually meet, I remembered the name because it wasn't too long before it became the only name in British golf.

It wasn't until a few years later that we met properly when he, myself and Bob Willis all went out for dinner during an Ashes tour in Australia and we became firm friends from then on. He has helped out on my charity walks and I've played alongside him on a number of golf days when he's great company because he isn't in competition mode. He can just be himself and not worry about having to win all the time. In fact this is the side of Nick that has started to come to the fore more and more now that he is enjoying a successful second career as a commentator. Some people who came up against him during his heyday in the 1980s can't believe it is the same man on the TV who would have done whatever he could to get one up on his opponents.

Nick's reputation as a somewhat surly golfer back then is probably a fair call because when he was on the golf course it wasn't his job to make friends with people. As an individual game it also paid dividends for him not to be too friendly with his competitors off it and how right he was as he won tournament after tournament. But to the rest of us who have got to know him over the years he is a decent human being who, at times, has gone out of his way to help out or fulfil a commitment you wouldn't expect him to.

When I retired from cricket in 1993 I had a big dinner at the Cafe Royal hosted by some businessmen to celebrate the end of my career and as the dinner approached Nick was busy representing Europe in the Ryder Cup up in the Midlands at the Belfry.

It just so happened that Nick decided to fly down to London and landed at Heathrow at about 5 p.m. the same evening as the dinner, and after losing to the Americans – despite Faldo's half with his old foe Paul Azinger – there was no way I was expecting him to come. But instead of going home, he got straight into a car and made his way over to town, pulled on his dinner jacket in the back of the car and arrived just in time as the night began. I told him just how grateful I was that he would come and show his face, even just for an hour or two, to help add some extra star quality to the evening.

As the night wore on I saw Nick mingling with a few people and I thought he was hiding the disappointment of the defeat well. Another hour passed and still Nick was there holding court on what had happened in the Ryder Cup. By midnight I thought there must be something wrong with him, so I went over to see if he was alright and he just laughed and said, 'Don't think you're going to get rid of me before I try some of your red wine!'

Along with golf, red wine is a passion the two of us share and he didn't need to say it twice, so by two in the morning the pair of us were just about the only ones left in the Cafe Royal chatting over a bottle of red, as he told me exactly how the Ryder Cup had been lost that year and how much it hurt him. The hard-nosed golfer that Nick Faldo became still had a gentler side which felt the pain of defeat just as keenly as a Sam Torrance or an Ian Woosnam but that was a side he rarely showed.

Nick wasn't a golfing Ferrari, he wasn't a sexy shot maker like Seve Ballesteros, he was the reliable Volvo that always starts and just keeps on going, or a Jack Russell that keeps nipping away at your ankles and no matter how much you try to shake him off, he'll just run right back up and bite some more.

Just look at what happened to Greg Norman on the last day at Augusta in 1996 at the Masters. Faldo's nagging ability to just do enough to stay in contention had every great golfer in the world looking over their shoulder at one time or another while he played at his best and in the case of Norman it provided the perfect subplot to the greatest choke in golf history.

They say you should never take your foot off the pedal, but perhaps that's what Greg did at the Masters, going out for the final round with a six-stroke lead. The 'Green Jacket' was as good as his, until Faldo started biting at his ankles. By the end of the round he had not only overtaken him but went on to win by five clear strokes, a fine example of never-say-die determination that epitomised his career.

Nick had this single-minded attitude to his golf where he

would let nothing get in the way of what he was doing on the course and it is a trait that worked wonders for him as a player. He turned himself into a great golfer with that outlook, but you can't always translate what works for you into success for others as the Ryder Cup defeat under his captaincy in 2008 proved. The single-minded determination that had poured through his being as a player got in the way of his dream to win the Ryder Cup as a captain.

For some, that trait can work in their favour, such as Nasser Hussain and the England cricket team. He turned his determination to succeed into a positive for his team, but Nick failed to make it gel over in Kentucky and lost the trophy. Despite that defeat, Nick's record as a golfer is outstanding and should be celebrated. I have nothing but respect for what he achieved in the game and also for the way he went about it. He made no apologies for wanting to be the best and why should he?

Until recently I've never felt that Nick Faldo has received the complete respect that he deserves for his achievements. For all that he has done for the game of golf in Britain and for all his success there is still an element of resentment that follows him around and I don't think that is fair. I don't think that a man who has made golf his life and has given absolutely every fibre of his being to the game with a return of six Majors should be treated as anything but a hero and a national treasure.

Yet the clear eagerness with which he was attacked by some quarters before and during the Ryder Cup, until they could revel in his misery at having lost the trophy, was deeply saddening and makes me wonder why successful British sportsmen and women are not judged solely on their merits. I believe a lot of Nick's reputation is based on an old-fashioned disease called jealousy. He has had a lot of tags thrown his way, and although he is not completely blameless – and he will be the first to admit that he has brought some of it on himself – far too much of it has been a result of jealousy.

His recent elevation to a knighthood though shows that HM can cut through the nonsense and see a true champion for what he is. I was absolutely delighted to hear that Sir Nick had become just the second British golfer to be awarded such an honour and it is completely deserved. Having experienced the feeling of such a recognition I know it will mean a huge amount to Nick and he will wear the title with a huge amount of pride and satisfaction for the rest of his life.

I know the current crop of British golfers look up to him for what he did and if some of them can follow ever so slightly in his footsteps with a Major or two then his service to British sport will have grown another notch too.

SIR NICK FALDO

I guess I was fortunate enough to have the determination and the work ethic – that was just me. One of the key elements to it all though was my parents' trust in me. They let me head to the practice ground from the age of 16, where I was more than happy to work away virtually every minute of every day building my game. I just had the passion and a love for the game of golf.

I've been fortunate because I've loved every minute of practice and I still do; at times I've been frustrated, but I've never been bored with it. It was a game where I had to build my self-belief through hitting hundreds of thousands – if not millions – of golf balls, which gave me that inner self-belief . . . I'd done it so many times I knew I could do it when I needed to. Golf is a long process of climbing a ladder and very few golfers have ever had overnight success and there is a good reason for that.

All the hard work paid off with my proudest achievements being my Major wins. I'm also very proud of having had that period of time for a couple of years when I was the best player in the world. I had a different mindset at that time and I was going into the Majors with the knowledge that I could genuinely win them rather than just bowling up and thinking 'maybe this will be the week' – that was a great period of time.

As for the Ryder Cup, it is something I've loved every minute of, going back to my first involvement in 1977. It has given me some great competitive memories and it was a great honour for me to be Captain – which was a great experience in Valhalla.

Ian and I met right at the beginning of our careers when we were both young and inexperienced sportsmen and then off we went in our different directions. Ian forced himself into a position where he was the greatest all-rounder we had and I remember, in that era, with the style of cricket that he played, it sometimes felt as though he used to take on the Australians single-handedly. He took passion and strength in that era of cricket to another level and it's been good to know him throughout.

NIGEL MANSELL

INSTINCT

Throughout this book I've looked at some of the greatest sportsmen and women to have ever crossed the whitewash and even though some of them have been stronger in some areas than others in terms of skill, natural talent or leadership qualities, the one thing that runs really high through all of them is their competitiveness. That will to win and to beat the person standing opposite them is so great in all of these champions that I've found it hard to say whether one gold medallist is more competitive than another world champion. Well that is until now. There is competitive and then there is Nigel Mansell.

This guy is like no other when it comes to wanting to win. He would walk across hot coals if it meant a two and one win on the golf course against you and whenever I play golf with him it is nothing short of a war. If you were six up with six to play he would still think that he could win. He won't have worked out that he could only draw, he is that hell-bent on winning.

He is so ruthlessly competitive it comes as no surprise to me that he won the Formula 1 World Championship. The only surprise is that he didn't win more than one world title, but that had less to do with him and more to do with the conditions around him.

Nigel drove his cars like a man possessed. Not in a devilish way, but in one that spoke of his inner determination to do well and to show people just how good a driver he was. After all, he got to the top the hard way and he had a lot of false dawns and frustrations to overcome before he actually reached the peak of his personal Everest.

He was 39 when he finally won the World Championship with Williams in 1992 and it came after years of close shaves and near misses and even a retirement from the sport. Thankfully he was cajoled back into racing after leaving Ferrari in 1991 and in his second spell with Williams he was given everything he needed to become champion and he didn't waste it.

It was one of the most dominant performances in sporting history with nine wins out of sixteen, and fourteen pole positions. He had it all wrapped up by the 11th race and there was no question who was the best driver at that time. He was just relentless and it went to show just how good he had been all along, except a mixture of bad luck, bad timing and bad cars had previously conspired to deny him – comparisons with Jenson Button perhaps?

I do think that Nigel's story as a racing driver is one of the most inspiring tales our nation has produced because it has everything. Hard work, joy, heartache, success, failure, anger, compassion and above all else a hero who overcame every obstacle put in his way to become the very, very best.

Unlike Lewis Hamilton who has had the full backing of McLaren from such a young age, Nigel had to back himself and it was a huge risk he was taking. As a seasoned go-karter and then Formula Ford and Formula 3 driver Nigel was moving up the ranks towards his dream of Formula 1 but he had to pay for it himself. He is so down-to-earth though that as a humble 'Brummie' he was able to take the plunge by scraping together just enough money to keep him going until all the sacrifices made by him and his wife Roseanne paid off when he was spotted by Colin Chapman and became the test driver for Lotus.

That was the big break for him, but I subsequently discovered that Nigel's initial drive in the Lotus car before he was offered a contract came hot on the heels of an accident where he'd suffered a broken back! Despite the obvious agony he was in, he still went and test drove for the team owner and did enough to secure the deal. It proved that if you want something badly enough and you're prepared to go the extra mile to get it then it can be yours.

He is a guy we should be incredibly proud of because of that attitude which came through in his racing. Everything that he got in his career he had to earn. Nothing was handed to him on a plate so not only does it show things like his dedication and commitment of the highest order, it also means that when success does come along it is appreciated that bit more readily.

I didn't really follow Nigel's career too much while he was at Lotus and to be fair to him he languished near the back of the grid for much of that time. It was only when he moved to Williams in 1985 that I really stood up and took note of what he was doing, and boy was it impressive. Bearing in mind that he had joined former World Champion Keke Rosberg's team, he had to prove himself to his new team-mate and to the mechanics and engineers behind him which is no easy thing. I've spoken to Nigel about this many a time and he assures me that the amount of hours put in behind the scenes by the back-up staff is astonishing and it is just as important to the end result as what the driver does with the car when he gets it. Having experienced several different teams throughout his career he knows the difference between having a group right behind you and not, and it can be the difference between winning and losing.

So much is dependent on the mechanics of the cars that even the slightest mishap or poor-quality work on it can have it conking out before a race is in full flow and Nigel experienced the full range of good days and bad days as far as that went.

In 1985 though he managed to win his first Grand Prix and he did it at home at Brands Hatch, although it was the European and not the British race. It must have been a dream come true to have finally won at the highest level after 72 attempts, and to do it in front of his own fans would have made it even sweeter. I do think though that it is always tougher to get success away from home because the conditions and the environment are much more alien to you and so it is a bit more of a challenge. Nigel soon put that right by winning the next race in South Africa to make it two from two and announce himself to the world as a proper Formula 1 challenger.

NIGEL MANSELL

I watched a bit of that season on television and read a bit about Nigel in the newspapers but I took a bit of a keener interest in the 1986 Championship and it was clear to me that Nigel was the best of the lot in an incredible field of drivers. We're talking about an era that had him battling it out with Alain Prost, Ayrton Senna and Nelson Piquet for the title – all great drivers.

Having won two of the last three races the year before, Nigel would have been keyed up for a big start to 1986 when team boss Frank Williams found himself fighting for his life following an accident that left him without the use of his legs. That would have been hard to take, but racing drivers are used to dealing with serious accidents because of the nature of their job and so Nigel was still fully focused on what he had to do that year.

He showed just how much by winning five Grand Prix races, including of course the British, to give himself a six-point cushion going into the final race in Adelaide. All he needed was to finish third and the World Championship would be his. He was cruising along doing just that in third place when his left rear tyre blew and ended both his race and his title hopes. Nigel had actually wanted to come into the pits for new tyres but was told to stay out on the track and it cost him, as Prost took the chequered flag and the title for the second successive year.

I was gutted for him because I had met him at a couple of charity functions that year when he was giving it everything and he was a fascinating bloke to talk to. He got a lot of unfair stick in the media from people who called him dour and boring but I enjoyed talking to him about what he was doing and we also both shared a passion for golf, so we talked a bit about that as well. He was trying to tell me about the mechanics of the car and how well it was handling, but he also warned that because the cars were right on the edge it wouldn't take much for things to go wrong. How prophetic those words proved to be.

I wondered just how badly he would deal with such a cruel and heart-wrenching loss, and the following season proved what a great champion he would prove to be. He got over his disappointment to win another six Grand Prix races, but again fell short of the title as more mechanical failures cost him at least three victories.

MY SPORTING HEROES

He was a fearless driver who kept pushing himself and his cars to the edge and I like to think that is why the great Enzo Ferrari chose him to drive for the famous 'Prancing Horse'. As it turned out Nigel was the last driver to be chosen by Enzo and he would have surely brought the title back to the Italian stables had it not been for a fall-out with his great rival Alain Prost. Nigel drove so well for Ferrari he was nicknamed 'Il Leone' – 'The Lion' – which was so appropriate for the way in which he drove. He was exciting, brave and whole-hearted in his style of driving, which centred around braking later than other drivers and using the pace through a corner rather than slowing into it and accelerating out. It was a high-risk style, but one that ultimately made him faster in his cars and like most fans I loved him for that.

The skill factors and the fear factor involved in racing at that level is just frightening and to be that good takes something not everyone has in their make-up. Nigel had it and his competitors knew it, but they also knew that he could get easily agitated. So much of sport comes down to mind games and Formula 1 is no different with drivers looking to get an edge both on and off the track. Senna and Piquet were masters of it, but perhaps not as much as Prost, who managed to make Nigel's life a misery while they were 'team-mates' at Ferrari, by getting the mechanics to back his car more than Nigel's.

It was only when Nigel made sure he had the number one drive for Williams that his results completely backed up both his talent and the quality of the car. I can remember being in Australia during the 1992 World Cup when the season got underway and watching highlights of his first two wins and thinking this could be a great year for British sport. I thought we'd win the World Cup, he'd win the driver's World Championship and Nick Faldo would win the Open. As it turned out only Nick and 'Nige' did the business that year so I suppose two out of three ain't bad!

Having won the title I thought it was outrageous that he wasn't given more of the same red-carpet treatment the next year, but instead of retaining his title he left Formula 1 altogether rather than be a team-mate with Prost again.

What I like about Nigel is that he is outspoken and forthright in what he believes in. He won't accept mediocrity because that competitive streak in him won't allow it and so with his head held high he went over to Indycar in America – racing for Paul Newman's team – and won that instead. It was a fantastic way to stick two fingers up to the Formula 1 blockheads who didn't have enough faith in him and it cemented his place in British sporting folklore. He was a brilliant driver who got the job done. He wasn't a flamboyant James Hunt, but he didn't need to be and that doesn't make him any less of a champion. With his 31 Grand Prix wins he is simply one of the all-time greats.

PADRAIG HARRINGTON
COMPOSURE

Golf is a hard game to play. It should be easy; the ball doesn't move when you try to hit it, the hole doesn't move when you putt the ball and there is no one around who can knock you, kick you, punch you or do anything to ruin what you're doing. Even the crowd keeps quiet when you address the ball to hit it. It should be easy, but it is anything but. And having spent a lifetime playing the game and spending time with the very best players the world has ever seen, I can say with total and utter confidence that Padraig Harrington is a very special sportsman.

The softly spoken Irishman has confirmed his place at the very top table of golf by winning three of the toughest prizes in sport to date. I say to date because I'm certain there will be more, but for now his three Majors of two Open Championships and a PGA Championship put him up with the very best there has ever been.

Only seven British and Irish men have won more Majors than Padraig, but only one of them has done so since 1913 – Nick Faldo, of course! The bare fact is that Padraig is the best European golfer in a decade and he is now leading the way where the rest of our golfers must follow.

With three out of the four Majors played in the USA there has long been a heavy leaning to the number of Majors won by American golfers, but Europe did have a proud tradition of upsetting the applecart on a fairly regular basis. Up until Padraig came along and won the 2007 Open the apples were resting a little too comfortably for my liking. Not since Scot Paul Lawrie won the title in 1999 had a European bothered the engravers until on the same Carnoustie course Padraig broke through the glass ceiling.

I think anyone who has watched him closely over the years knew that he had at least one Major in him, and it opened the floodgates for him to go and win another two soon after.

To retain the Open in 2008 and then go on to take the PGA in the same year was astonishing and spoke volumes for his character and his dedication. He was not happy enough to win and relax; he wanted more of the same like all the very best sportsmen do, and that is what marks him out as something special.

He has moved into another bracket of sportsmen in my eyes and he is now the sort of golfer that you have to take seriously for any tournament he is entered in on any continent in any conditions. He is the sort of golfer that Tiger Woods needs to look out for too. Who knows where he may end up, because he has a lot on his side in terms of hunger, age, ability and desire and there is every chance he could challenge Nick Faldo's record of six Majors.

I first met Padraig in a pro-am tournament at the Oxfordshire golf course. I was playing my round alongside Lee Westwood, but he'd been having a bit of trouble with his foot and it was getting quite sore as we went around the course.

I usually love playing with Lee because he is such a good golfer and such good fun, but on that day his golf was a bit off due to the pain he was in and his usual banter was virtually non-existent because his foot was making him grumpy. After playing the ninth hole he couldn't carry on so he spotted Padraig on the driving range and asked him whether he minded stepping in for him and playing the back nine.

He jumped in and on the tenth hole he drove down the hill true and straight and then his approach into the green hit the pin. Well, I was won over right there and then! Since that day I've paid close attention to his career and it has been a real joy to see how he has done and how he has grown into an all-time great golfer.

He is a dedicated sportsman who trains and practises very hard to achieve his goals. By doing that he has crossed not just one but two hurdles in winning both his first Major and then retaining it and winning a second in the same year. To me that is a magnificent standard to have achieved and I believe there is so much more to come.

He is a bit of a quiet man and a family man who keeps himself to himself, but his passion for golf shines through. He isn't demonstrative, loud or arrogant, he is an absolute delight and golf is the priority in his life.

What impressed me most about Padraig is the way he finished those Majors off and in terms of composure I don't think you'll find a better example than when he won his first Major, and it was in such a contrast to the way Sergio Garcia arguably lost it.

Beginning the final round six shots behind Garcia he knew he had to play well to give himself a chance of winning the 'Claret Jug' and perhaps earn a slice of luck too. Going out in three-under was a good start for him, but it was his eagle at the 14th which put him in the driving seat. At nine-under for the tournament and with Garcia struggling to keep up, Padraig had a one-shot lead on the 18th tee and for those of you who can remember the drama of the 1999 Open with Jean van der Velde standing in the Barry Burn it looked like happening again. Padraig put his ball right into the burn not once but twice! To everyone it looked like his chance had gone, but this is where his composure came to the fore. He made sure that his approach and putt were spot on and even though he took a double-bogey he posted a clubhouse total that required Sergio to at least par the 18th to win.

Sergio would have sunk that par putt a thousand times before, but this time it had the Open riding on it and he missed, giving Padraig the play-off chance he hoped for. Both golfers had to clear their minds for the four-hole play-off, but it proved too much for Sergio, who at his shot saw Major glory cruelly pass by again as he bogeyed the first extra hole and Padraig birdied it. Game, set and match to the Irishman and to me it showed what a mentally strong golfer he is.

The following year he was the returning champion at Royal Birkdale and the pressure on him would have been nothing like he'd faced before. To top it off his wrist was giving him some trouble so he nearly pulled out of the tournament altogether, but he took it all in his stride.

He'd been battling all the way with Greg Norman and in many ways a lot of the crowd were on Norman's side because of the emotion involved in a great player coming back for a last hurrah. There he was, the 'Shark', reliving past glories once again and he'd managed to get himself in that final group on the last day and if he'd won it would have the fairytale finish that the romantics would have loved. But Padraig took all the emotion out of the round to stay focused on what he had to do and that is typical of the man.

The defining moment for me was his second shot at the par five seventeenth. He was two shots ahead and could have been conservative in his approach but instead he hit a five wood about 260 yards to set up an eagle. There would have been a lot of players who would have laid up, chipped on and taken advantage of their lead, but he backed himself and believed in himself to take on the shot and push himself home for the title. Under the circumstances, that second shot was one of the best shots I have ever seen. To me that shot is up there with Ian Woosnam's two iron out of the woods in Augusta or Ernie Els' five iron to win the US Open. It is right up there with the great golf shots I've seen and I thought for Padraig to go for it was mind-blowing and revealed a player full of confidence and at ease with his game. He knew he was good enough to make the shot and went ahead and proved it.

Padraig is a sharp, witty man to go with the calm, reassuring golfer and he is the perfect man to lead Europe's next assault on the Ryder Cup. He is now the man the rest of the team rallies around, like a Seve Ballesteros, a Nick Faldo or a Colin Montgomerie. And Monty would be happy to have a player of his calibre playing at his best at the top of the singles board.

I always remember being at a pro-am at Woburn and as I was being driven away from the course in my wagon of a car with blacked out windows I saw Padraig with J.P. McManus and Eddie Jordan and a few other successful Irish businessmen having a chat in the car park.

MY SPORTING HEROES

As I drove out, I slowed up, pulled alongside them all and wound down the window to say hello. I just said, 'Hi Padraig, how are you?' He turned to me, looked me up and down and said, 'Bejesus! I thought you were a drug dealer!' Which obviously had the rest of the group in stitches.

He is very relaxed off the course; he hardly drinks at all. I can only ever remember seeing him drinking his coke with ice and lemon, but he is great company and is a much loved member of the tour.

The golf world is a strange world and it is not always that easy to cope with. You have to get the balance right. It is an individual sport where you are playing against the course and everyone else, but you're also trying to beat your mates who you play with in the Ryder Cup, and at times it can be a lonely existence.

You're travelling around the world a lot and you're in different parts of the world and in different hotels night after night and even though people think it is incredibly glamorous travelling all the time, it isn't.

When you've got to do it for your career it can become quite tedious and lonely so to keep your focus when you've got long periods away from home and away from the family is tough and that is why I respect international sportsmen so much.

The story is very much the same for international cricketers who are now travelling to different parts of the world so much more than I ever did. It is hard to keep yourself up and motivated as you move from place to place. At least in cricket it is a team game so as part of a squad if someone isn't feeling too hot or happy, there is usually someone else in the dressing-room to help you out of it and get you going again. For a golfer it is down to you and you alone to make sure everything is as it should be. It takes some real focus and steeliness to make sure you perform in those circumstances and Padraig definitely has that running through him.

How many more Major honours he will pick up, I'm not sure. What I am sure of is there will be more.

PADRAIG HARRINGTON

I would say that my main strength would definitely be more on the mental side of the game, establishing what I need to do and going about it pretty doggedly. In addition, I have an ability to put my mind to something, figure it out and keep working until I have success at it. I have never really minded failing as long as it is in the process of getting better and it was always about getting better for me. I was never satisfied with where I was and always wanted to improve, even if that was at the cost of some short-term goals. I was always looking at the long term with a view to getting better and better. Again, it is not solely about talent for me, but more about the hard work and the mental side of figuring out what needs to be done.

I would say that dealing with big-pressure tournament golf never came easy to me. I always had to figure it out and was one of those guys who always lost before winning and given that the losses were painful enough they made me sit back and learn. The fact that I went back into battle always meant that I was prepared to put my neck on the line and whilst it did get chopped off at times, I always came back and quite enjoyed the accomplishment of succeeding after failure.

It was never easy but at each level I got myself to the top, as a junior, as an Irish amateur and as a European Tour professional, so it has always been a case of slow steps but definitely plenty of hard days. I have been second about 30 times as a professional now but every time you lose you learn; you very rarely learn anything from when you win. Winning is a good habit but it is not something you learn a great deal from.

Obviously my standout memories right now would be my three Majors, but to be honest I have others. Just being a European Tour professional was a big deal for me. I really thought I had achieved just by getting out on the Tour, then winning my first event after ten weeks was a real spike. I have played three Walker Cups and five Ryder Cups, there were a lot of milestones, but definitely the three Majors are the proudest, because that is what I will be remembered for.

As Ian has referred to many times already in this book, achieving a major breakthrough only makes you more hungry for more of the same. Obviously the breakthrough from quality professional golfer to a Major winner looks to some people like it happens overnight but to be honest it is a gradual process. I have improved steadily. My curve would be actually quite smooth in an upward trend from fifteen years of age, or even from the age of seven when I really started playing golf. The odd time when people see the results they think it is a spike but in general I made it to the required standard before I actually won at that level, then I progress after that again and it takes me a little bit of time before I am comfortable again.

In the 2006 US Open I had three pars to win and I played lovely golf, well within myself, that week. I came ever so close and you know with hindsight I probably just pushed a little too hard the last couple of holes. Of course everybody else was finding them tough too but when I walked off the golf course having lost I was thinking, 'You know what? I am well capable of winning a Major by just playing my own game.' Up to that point I think I always thought it had to be a really good week with a little bit of fortune for me to win but losing that week convinced me that I could win a Major and just over two years later I had won three.

Despite not being the biggest cricket fans in Ireland we grew up knowing Ian Botham. He was a larger-than-life character but I think that it is reflective of his ability at the crease. I think that is the greatest thing about a sportsman; if you can perform on the pitch without really taking it too seriously off the pitch, it is a tremendous attribute. He did everything he needed to do and looked like he was enjoying the sport, which is obviously the aim of all sportsmen. You want to play well but you obviously need to have a good balance to your life and I think that has to be admired about Ian. He always seemed to be a leader, both on and off the pitch, and generally someone his team-mates seemed to gather around. He seems to be one of those people that team-mates played for and who was well capable of getting the best out of his team. It is very important that they have a person who can lead on and off the pitch.

With regards to the golf I have played with him, obviously like a lot of sportspeople who play golf, he showed that he can certainly hit the golf shots in spots, although obviously the consistency and the ability to move a very high level is what is lacking, but I think most sportspeople find that when they are truly good at one sport, they know that the effort required to put into another sport would need another lifetime. I think Ian has a nice balance with his golf, he likes playing, enjoys it and understands that for the odd moment on the course he can again be a big-time player and a hero, but in general it is just a nice pastime.

PAUL GASCOIGNE
SKILL

They say genius is just one step away from madness, and for the most part Paul Gascoigne's footballing ability was touched with genius. I say for the most part because without question his descent from much-loved football hero to fallen star with drink, drug and mental problems has tarnished his legacy. I only hope that in due course 'Gazza's' lasting picture in people's minds will be for his footballing talent and not for his problems off the field. I know that is what he wants and it is how I intend to look at him. Only he will be able to ultimately overcome his issues.

On the field though is where Gazza became a hero. It is where he made football an art form and it is where he filled a nation with joy. Paul is arguably the most talented footballer England has ever produced, and if it hadn't been for an unlucky knee injury and his subsequent off-field problems, I believe we would be talking about him in the same breath as Pele, Maradona, Zidane and Best.

You would go out of your way to watch Paul Gascoigne play football. Even if you didn't support either team and you turned the TV on and saw he was playing you'd stay and watch it. That is what you call an entertainer and someone special.

In cricket you have plenty of examples of 'bar' players. The cricketers who empty bars when they walk to the crease, men

PAUL GASCOIGNE

like Andrew Flintoff, Brian Lara and Adam Gilchrist. The sort of players who get your pulse racing by watching them do what they do best, and Paul was one of those.

That is why he will always be a sporting hero to my mind. The way you play your sport is important, and in Paul I saw a footballer who was filled with happiness out on the park. He wanted to win, of course, but he also wanted to entertain the crowd as much as he could and that is why he would go on those runs, it is why he would take on those shots. He had the ability to make the crowd love him and he set about doing just that every time he crossed the 'whitewash'. His control of a football was second to none. He could run, he could dribble, he could feint, he could shoot. He had all the tools to be the greatest, but his scriptwriter wasn't as kind to him as he might have been.

There are so many good images of Paul on a football field that spring to mind, from his goal against Scotland in Euro 96, to his goal against Arsenal in the FA Cup semi-final of 1991. There are the dramatic and sad ones too, like his tears in the Italia 90 World Cup after being booked in the semi-final against Germany and knowing that he would not be able to appear in the final if England got there.

However, for me, Gazza's enduring image on a football pitch is in full flow, beating defenders and getting fans off their seats. I can't think of a specific one because there were so many. Whether he was playing for Newcastle, Tottenham Hotspur, Lazio, England, Glasgow Rangers or Everton, he was able to draw you into the game like he drew in defenders and then get you excited by a twist of the hips or a jink of the feet. It was extraordinary.

For some people things come very naturally and Gazza was a prime example of that. There are other people in this book who had to work very hard to do what they did. Geoffrey Boycott, for example, I would never describe as a natural walking talent, but, along with someone like Nick Faldo, made himself into the best. Gazza on the other hand I would call an absolute natural and would say the game came more easily to him than most people.

The fact that he was such a lovely lad with it made me even happier when I watched him play. I met Paul a few times when he would come on *A Question of Sport* and he was such fun to have around. Because of his profile at the time he was almost always on the show and a good thing too because he was hilarious and you never knew what would happen when he turned up.

One day he came along to filming and the producers were desperate to make sure that we didn't drink too much ahead of the episode and Gazza was in determined mood. He wouldn't touch a drop and was on soft drinks all day, except someone might have convinced him that advocaat was a soft drink! It certainly made for a funny and interesting show. Of course no one knew what was in store for him on that front at the time and he was just enjoying himself to the full.

To me he was just a lad who wanted to be loved by everyone and have a laugh with everyone. Life was for living and everything was hunky-dory, but sadly he didn't have anyone to pull the reins in a little bit. After George Best he became the best-known footballer in the British game and as a result you don't always attract the right attention. Some of his so-called 'friends' were anything but as they put themselves before him even though they were riding on his coat-tails. It is a fact of sporting stardom that hangers on are there and they're not always as good for you as you think they are. That is where you need strong support from those closest to you – your family and your tightest friends – and maybe that support wasn't there until it was too late.

It all happened so quickly though. One minute he was at the top of his game and there was no better example of that than in 1996 during the European Championships in England. He was the star of the show, pulling the strings that took us to the semi-finals. His near-miss during extra time against Germany in so many ways summed up his career, so near and yet so far.

From there his descent into drink continued at a pace so that when he was told he would be left out of the World Cup squad to go to 'France 98' he completely trashed the room in front of manager Glenn Hoddle. His career really just drifted away from him after that and his off-field problems with drink and drugs, together with marital problems, took control. It was such a shame and such a waste of great talent.

It was the George Best story happening all over again and yet no one was able to stop it. I do firmly believe that if he'd had Alex Ferguson as his manager we might have seen a lot more of Paul Gascoigne than we did. It may well go down as the biggest mistake of his life that he chose Tottenham Hotspur over Manchester United back in 1988. I know that Sir Alex rues his failure to get Paul to sign for him for what it would have brought both to the club and also to Paul himself. I'm not saying that Sir Alex is the cure for all wayward footballers; however someone of Gazza's brilliant ability would have loved the environment at Manchester United because his love for football is almost as strong as Fergie's.

I would see it time and again when he used to come and watch rugby with me at Newcastle. I mainly got to know Paul over the years through various charity events, but I also knew him through the training he did with my son Liam. Up in the north-east they trained together when Liam was playing for the Newcastle Falcons and Paul was coming back from an injury with Middlesbrough in 2002. They were put together by Steve Black, who is a fitness training legend in that part of the world, but he didn't tell Liam initially who he'd be working with. He just asked, 'Do you fancy training with this new lad for a little while?' to which Liam said yes and then in walked Gazza and off they went.

During that time he often came and watched the rugby with me and he liked it. I was a little surprised how much he loved the sport because he admitted the rules were all a bit confusing for him, but the basic running and tackling he loved. He'd come up into the box with his mate Jimmy for lunch and then watch the game with all the passion you'd expect from a rugby supporter. He might not have known the game inside out, but he knew what good sporting performances looked like and he loved anything involving Newcastle and that shone through.

His passion for football though was always there and I would love talking to him about the game and how he felt most comfortable on a football pitch. The thing that struck Liam was that he was a thoroughly nice guy but without a solid base around him and that is a shame. That sums up Gazza; he would do anything for anybody and was as nice as pie, but he lost his way in life.

All the great memories I have of him are under a dark cloud now because of the concerns over his health. It would be a miserable shame if he couldn't get his life back on track because he'd then be remembered for all the wrong reasons rather than the right one which is his football.

Once, following a rugby match that he'd come to watch we were hanging around waiting to leave and someone had a rugby ball with them and was showing Gazza how to pass it. He struggled a little bit with that, but then he started doing keepy-ups with it and he kept going and going and going. I don't how many he did, but he had this big grin on his face and the ball was dancing to his tune. That is the sort of skill we're talking about. It was only a little muck about, but with a ball on his feet he was magical.

It was a sorry finish to his football career in the end, but by that time he had plenty of bigger battles to fight. I haven't seen much of him lately, but I've seen the odd interview and he seems to be trying to do whatever he can to sort his problems out. I sincerely hope he manages to do that because his ability with a football was something special and if he can beat his demons that is all we'll say about him. Genius.

RYAN GIGGS
DURABILITY

If you were in Dr Frankenstein's lab looking to create the perfect footballer, one that would score you lots of goals, create you lots of goals, dig deep for the good of the team, track back and make tackles, excite you and the fans with his skill and most importantly keep going so you didn't have to keep replacing him, you would end up with Ryan Giggs. Quite simply the finest example of a professional footballer I've ever seen. Whenever he finally decides to call it a day and stop tormenting defenders for fun it will be the day that football will forever be a little bit poorer.

His exploits as a player are astonishing and his list of medals and honours would fill a book all on their own. He is the most decorated player in the history of the English game and when you consider how much hard work goes into winning just one trophy, for him to have won 23 major trophies and counting is mind-boggling.

The ingredients that you need to be successful are plentiful and if you're lucky you get to be part of a successful side that can win a hatful of trophies during a glory period, but such is his durability, Ryan has won trophies in three glory periods and he is still going.

In addition to the number of medals and the length of time he has been winning things as a footballer, the thing that really impresses me about Ryan is the way he has carried himself as a person. He really should have his own category all to himself. What a great example of a professional sportsman and a footballer in particular. You often read and see a lot about footballers that you don't want to read and see. Falling out of nightclubs, papers full of kiss and tells, plus violent acts are some of the stories you hear about and it does the game no favours at all.

But Ryan Giggs is a man who very much keeps himself on the straight and narrow, producing the goods on the pitch season after season. Don't think that he didn't have fun as a young lad because there were one or two stories that I can remember about him and his celebrity lifestyle, but he quickly decided that wasn't for him and that there were more important things to him, like enjoying a long and fruitful career. He found himself a long-term girlfriend who is now his wife and he is now a very happily settled family man and I can think of no better example to set. I would say that if you had to look for a role model for any young footballer or indeed for any youngster growing up then you don't have to look much further than Ryan. He is the ultimate professional who just keeps rolling on and is consistently one of Manchester United's best players. He epitomises professional football for me.

It wasn't that long ago that Ryan burst onto the football scene as a whippet of a left winger who had the sort of silky skills that belonged to George Best, plus the pace and the engine to run all day. Each time I tuned into *Match of the Day*, the main highlight of the programme invariably revolved around Ryan Giggs going on a blistering run, crossing the ball for either Eric Cantona, Andy Cole, Ruud van Nistelrooy or Wayne Rooney to put into the back of the net. I don't think I can remember a time when I've watched that programme and Ryan's not been on it.

He obviously still looks after himself incredibly well and he is still running around at 35 with the enthusiasm and glee of a player half his age and that is so good to see. I've heard he's even taken up yoga to strengthen his core muscles and help his hamstrings!

There are a lot of spectacular moments that belong to Ryan Giggs, but I don't think I have witnessed any more memorable a goal in over 50 years of watching football than his winner in the 1999 FA Cup semi-final against Arsenal. He dribbled past what looked like the entire Arsenal team before thumping the ball emphatically past David Seaman. I was sat at home watching that game, and supporting neither club I was so excited by the goal I made Kath my wife come and watch the replay with me. I just couldn't believe what I had seen; it was a goal of such sublime skill that it deserved to win the trophy there and then. Of course it turned out to be just one of three trophies he picked up that season.

In many ways his career is also a testament to Sir Alex Ferguson because he is not the only one who has survived for such a long time. The likes of Paul Scholes and Gary Neville are also great examples of professional players who have produced the goods for years and have done it in such an understated way. They have all pulled together and got on with the business of winning trophies and it has to be applauded.

I've met Ryan a couple of times, but I couldn't say that I know him that well. The first time I met him was with Bryan Robson when Manchester United were getting some kind of sports team of the year award and 'Robbo' introduced me to him, saying, 'You want to watch this kid, he is going to be something special.' That not only tells you how old I am, but how Ryan has lived up to expectations. He has always been lovely to speak to when I have met him, but I can tell you he is not someone I needed to meet to have this much admiration for him. I believe him to be a real credit to British sport and he deserves every accolade that comes his way as a player or after the day that he hangs up his boots – probably as a 50 year old!

I noticed he recently won the top Professional Footballer's Association 'Player of the Year' award in 2009, which was richly deserved. I can't believe there were some comments made that it was nothing more than a sentimental award for a player who was yet to win it. Well, there are two things that astonish me about those pathetic claims.

Firstly there is nothing sentimental in professional sport and especially not football. It is as competitive an environment as you are likely to find and the idea that the majority of professional players who are competing week in week out would go soft for a rival is barmy. The simple fact is that when the votes were cast

MY SPORTING HEROES

Ryan was again taking the game by storm, scoring and creating important goals for Manchester United. The second thing that I can't quite believe is how he hadn't won it before. Here is a guy who has regularly been at the forefront of Manchester United's success and who has continued to produce wonderful memories for fans and neutrals alike yet had been overlooked for the main individual prize. I guess it goes to show that timing is everything and just like one of his late runs into the box these days or one of his pinpoint crosses from the left wing he has still got it. He added to his long list of accolades by collecting the BBC Sports Personality of the Year award in 2009, which was well deserved for a wonderful career. Again some people thought he hadn't done enough that particular year to merit the award, but the fact is Ryan Giggs struck a chord with the general public and they wanted him to have it. It was almost as though they thought, we're not letting him finish without this acknowledgement, and how could you disagree?

With a record of over 800 appearances for Manchester United there is nothing he hasn't accomplished in the club game, but there are a lot of people who wish that he'd been born on the other side of the Severn Bridge with English parents on both sides. That way the lucky 'Welshies' wouldn't have got him all to themselves once he'd decided to stay loyal to his mum, and good on him for that! But it is a shame that the world didn't get to see him produce his magic on the international stage at the major tournaments. He would have lit up the World Cup or European Championships had he played, but then again maybe the fact that he didn't has got something to do with his longevity. Rather than strain his body over a summer of tournament football every two years he got to have proper rest and recuperation before going into pre-season training and that can't have hurt.

How much longer he will go on for will be interesting to see. Physically he is still in decent shape and although he might have lost a yard or two of pace over the years, his experience and footballing brain are more than making up for it. It wouldn't surprise me if he kept on going for a few more years yet and once he is done the footballing world will be his oyster.

I get the feeling that Ryan is not in the game for anything other than love. He doesn't strike me as a materialistic sort of guy, just someone who wants to do the best he can on a football field and get those around him to do the same. As a result I think he may well go on to become yet another of Fergie's players to go into management and there is every chance he will be the best yet. Why? Simply by playing under Fergie longer than anyone else. His association with Manchester United might just have more than a few chapters left.

RYAN GIGGS

My career and success as a footballer doesn't just come down to one thing, there are a combination of reasons why I've been able to play as long as I have, but I think one of the main ones is my enjoyment of playing. I'm enjoying the game more than ever and that sense of fun and enjoyment makes it easy to put the effort in and to keep pushing myself. I've kept hold of the desire to train hard and to try and better myself and that has paid off in my continued ability to play a part in Manchester United's success.

I've always worked hard at the game, but another key factor is that I don't think you can underestimate just what a difference it makes to have great players around you. I've been lucky to have played at the best club in the world and as such it means I've had some top players to play alongside and I've had the best support system I could possibly have wanted.

Playing football as a 17 year old I can tell you that 35 seems like a million miles away, so what I did was set myself little targets each year. My first aim was to get into the first team and then from there it was to try and stay in the first team so I never really looked beyond each year. I never thought I'd still be playing here at 35 because you just didn't look that far ahead.

A lot of things have worked in my favour, such as the ability to play in a variety of positions, and I've always done that from a young age. I was never just an out-and-out winger, so when I started to lose a bit of pace I was able to adapt into playing a different sort of game and keep on going.

I couldn't say that playing professional football is easy, but there were things in the game that came naturally to me like my pace and running with the ball, but there has been a lot for me to work on, like my tackling, my positional sense and my heading. There were lots of things to work on and that is what I've done over the years in training and it has paid off for me when the games come around. There are a lot of achievements that I'm proud of in the game, but I'd have to say that winning the first league title was incredibly special. Growing up as a United fan and having not won the league for 26 years made it an unbelievable feeling of joy and relief.

One of the great successes of Manchester United is that we've always had a good team spirit and the manager has always brought in characters who haven't rocked the boat and who have bedded in. As one of a few players who have been around for a long time it is up you to pass on the history and traditions of the club to the next generation because I won't always be here.

I've met Sir Ian a couple of times on *A Question of Sport* and the odd charity golf day and he's a legend. I used to watch a lot of cricket when I was younger and in the mid-1980s when I was taking a keen interest he was at the top of his game and I loved watching him. I've always respected him and his achievements, and after meeting him he confirmed what I thought about him, which is that he's a great bloke and a hero of sport himself.

SAM TORRANCE
HUMOUR

Sam Torrance is a great man full stop. He is the life and soul of any room, telling stories and gags as if he'd been asked to do a turn at the Comedy Store. In fact I'm not sure who I'd rather listen to for a laugh, Peter Kay or Sam Torrance . . . who am I kidding? Of course it would be Sam! He has always got a joke to tell you and anywhere around the world that you see him he will have a smile on his face come what may, and that is why he is one of the most loved men in sport – not just in golf.

His ability to take the sting out of any situation and lighten the mood is why he was such a fine Ryder Cup captain in 2002, but before I dwell too much on that I want to make it clear that Sam has made it into this book as much for his ability as a golfer as for anything else.

I know he didn't win a Major, but he won 21 European Tour titles as well as 11 others and if ever someone needed a nerve of steel to go with a superb golf game then it was in 1985 when he sank the winning putt to give Europe their first ever Ryder Cup win after expanding the team from being Great Britain and Ireland, and the first win for this side of the Atlantic for 28 years!

Everyone will point to his success as a great Ryder Cup captain, but that is to forget what a superb player he was. Forty-three professional wins and counting says it all. The reason I love and admire him so dearly is that he has managed to forge such wonderful success as a golfer with a lust for life and genuine humour. It is always fun to be around Sam and he is one of the blokes I most look forward to spending time with.

If you're ever lucky enough to get drawn with Sam Torrance and get the chance to have a round of golf with him I suggest you take it, because it is the experience of a lifetime. I would say he is the best company to have on a golf course bar none and it doesn't matter if you're slicing and dicing your way round or keeping pace with the big guns he will treat you just the same.

Many years ago I was in a round with him and Robin 'Judgey' Smith at a benefit golf day in Birmingham and we had a fantastic time laughing and joking around the course. Judgey had this putter of his that he claimed to have won in another golf day and at the start of the round he told us how it had revolutionised his golf game and how he was now putting better than many of the pros thanks to this new bit of kit. To me it looked like he had just nicked it from a crazy golf course on Blackpool pleasure beach, but he insisted it had this new technology and that new system to help him putt.

As we made our way round, Judgey's putting went from awful to downright criminal and he just couldn't sink a putt all day. Of course I found this all tremendously funny, as did Sam, but being the guy he is he tried to offer Judgey a few golfing tips and pointers along the way. It wasn't working and as we made it to the 12th hole, Sam and I found ourselves walking behind Judgey and his caddy as we strolled past the lake next to the fairway. Sam gave me one look and then quietly pulled the putter from Judgey's bag, took a couple of steps towards the water and said: 'Hey Judgey, I've got one more piece of advice for you and your putting!' after which he hurled the putter with all his might out into the middle of the lake as Judgey screamed, 'Noooo!'

From then on Judgey had to use his sand wedge to putt for the rest of the round and he even managed to putt more balls with that than his favourite sunken putter. After the round Sam told Judgey that he had provided him with one of the funniest rounds of his life and by way of thanks presented him with a proper putter with a pair of goggles attached to it.

SAM TORRANCE

Sam loves to have fun whatever he is doing, but he also has a serious side when he needs it and he was able to strike that balance perfectly as captain of the Ryder Cup team. He was always there to ease the pressure on his players, but if they needed to be serious and talk to him honestly about the game he had that element to him too. I was fortunate to be invited along to that Ryder Cup as Sam's guest and he kindly gave me the title of vice-vice-vice-captain and made me feel like a part of the team in many ways, although some wag thought it was on account of my many vices!

As a diehard European golf supporter I thoroughly enjoyed every moment of it and I saw Sam working away at close range, and I was so impressed by the way he handled things. From the dinners and the speeches off the course, to the team selection and pairings on it, Sam did everything with aplomb and went up even further in my estimation. I had long considered Sam to be a special sporting talent and a good man to have at your side, but watching him over the course of that weekend, he became a true sporting hero in my eyes. Sam took on the job as Ryder Cup captain and did it in his own special way, using his natural humour and charm to put everyone at ease and let the golf do the talking. It was wonderful to watch. I'm in no doubt that his natural knack of dealing with people is what won Europe that trophy. His ability to put his players at ease is what allowed them to flourish so well on the course.

The funny thing about the Ryder Cup is that it comes with unbelievable pressure that many golfers are not used to. Normally a golfer travels the world trying to win tournaments for himself alone. He might feel a little pang to win for his family and his friends who have supported him, but really in truth it is about one man succeeding and the joy or despair it causes him. But when he gets to a Ryder Cup it is not just about the individual. At the very least it is about the eleven other players in his team, but it goes further than that. He is playing for his country and his continent and the level of expectation and support from golf fans across Europe is something that can be hard to cope with.

In addition you've got the entire American golfing public plus a few more wishing you nothing but failure and they will do whatever they can to ensure it. As a player you've got to embrace both sides of the coin and as a captain you have to foster the right sort of environment to help the players do that. In Sam Torrance the European tour had the perfect man who brought the best out of everyone, making it a happy team to be a part of. In fact, several of the players told me that they'd had such a good time playing for Sam that even if they had lost it would have been a Ryder Cup to remember fondly. The fact they won 15.5 points to 12.5 made all that hard work worthwhile.

Once the competition was over and the team had won then it was time for me to move on back to my hotel and let them enjoy their victory. I'm very much of the opinion that when a team is successful it is the team's moment and it is their time to enjoy themselves and reflect on what they've done. In any case I was due on a flight early the next morning and I was being picked up at 6 a.m. so I thought I'd better get a decent night's kip.

Just as I was getting into bed at about 10 p.m. I got a rather angry phone call from a certain Mr Torrance. 'Oi Beefy, where the hell are you?!'

'Oh hello Samuel, I'm just getting a bit of shut-eye before I get my flight tomorrow.' Now Sam is a very happy-go-lucky, cheery sort of bloke, but once or twice I've seen him get a bit angry and when he does his Scottish accent gets broader and broader, so when he said to me, 'Get your arse oot of tha' bed noow and git down here!' I knew he wasn't joking.

'Where is here, Samuel?'

'I want you in the team room nooow!'

I had no choice, so I got dressed and went back out to see the boys and it was one hell of a celebration led by Sam with singing and dancing on tables par for the course.

Eventually I managed to slip out of one of the back doors because I simply had to try and get some sleep before my car came to pick me up. When I got back to my room I was relieved that I had already made sure everything was packed and ready to go for when I woke up, and as I sat on the bed taking my shoes off the phone rang. 'Excuse me, Mr Botham, but your car is ready to take you to the airport.'

'Surely not! I've only just got back.' I hadn't noticed the clock before then and my heart sank as it read 05.55 on the display. Thank you very much Samuel!

We've had some great fun all around the world together, but home is where the heart is for both him and me and some of the best times I've shared with him have been when he and his wife Suzanne are round a dinner table with me and Kath and as many of our kids as we can get along. That sort of environment is where Sam is at his warmest and funniest, and I think it would be fair to say happiest.

One of life's big pleasures for me is the summer barbeque and like most men I enjoy getting behind the grill myself and cooking away for others to enjoy. Well, so does Sam and each Easter wherever possible I find myself having an almighty row with him in America over who is doing the barbeque cooking during the Masters when he's commentating. 'Woosie' (Ian Woosnam) is happy enough tucking into the red wine as Sam and I argue over the tongs. By the end of the night neither of us is quite sure who's done the cooking but it always ends with an arm around the shoulder and another one of Sam's gags.

It is always the way on my charity walks too when he comes along and he usually stays up the front with me for a good little while longer than most. We tend to go at a fair old lick on the walks and I love having him trundle alongside me, although one year he disappeared from my side rather quickly as we were nearing the finish-line in Cornwall. I didn't know where he'd gone until ten minutes later when I got my answer as the support vehicle raced past me and who should I see laid out in the back with a pint of Guinness and a fag, but the cheeky Scot. He had certainly earned it though.

With his infectious humour people often forget just how good a golfer he was in his pomp and how good he still is. He continues to play on an even tougher seniors tour and he enjoys regular success on it which proves his golf game is still in decent shape. Sam is a breath of fresh air, but he is also an emotional man who is liable to have a sob at any moment. He wears his heart on his sleeve and his emotions are always near the surface, which I think is what endears him to so many people and rightly so.

I can remember when I got my knighthood a lot of my friends

phoned up to congratulate me and Sam was one of them. I think though that he was the only one in tears on the phone as we talked through it. He said some special things to me that I will always cherish and they will stay with me until I die and for that I regard him as a true friend and a man I admire hugely.

SAM TORRANCE

For me golf has always been about hard work, fun and a love of the game that has grown and grown. The hard-work ethic was instilled in me by my dad at an early age as was a desire to win, and that has remained with me throughout my golfing life. I must admit I didn't enjoy the practising too much, but the actual playing when it mattered I loved.

Playing top-level sport is all about winning and that was how I went about my business. Yes I enjoyed myself, but everything I did was geared towards winning and it was the greatest feeling I ever experienced on a golf course as a player – winning tournaments. Coming second never felt any good at all to me.

My love for golf has really shone through at the Ryder Cup and in 1985 to sink that winning putt was quite extraordinary. I actually had three putts to win so it wasn't too much of a problem, but the moment was so special as the first team to win in a long time.

When I was asked to become Ryder Cup captain for the 2002 event I knew I had to leave no stone unturned in the search for the win. The key things for me were setting up the course with minor changes like narrow fairways that relied more on the skill which suited us rather than the booming drivers that America had, and also making sure that everyone got on well together. Sir Alex Ferguson told me that in your team you have no superstars and that taught me a lot in bringing up the younger players but not taking down the senior men. The Ryder Cup is a whole different animal to what players are used to and so you have to try and make sure they feel as comfortable and as at ease as possible.

If you three-putt on the last to lose an event you just get in your car and drive home and deal with it, but when you have to walk off the last green and then go in to face your team-mates in the team-room having lost, there is nothing worse, so it makes you try harder and as a captain you have to be there to pick everyone up where needs be and try to foster as good a spirit as you can. Likewise there is nothing better than a win and then everyone can share in the joy.

'Beefy' is an amazing man, and the first time I met him he was an absolute icon of British sport, yet I soon found out he was just like me, a great big bloke with a soft spot and a heart of a lion. Ever since we've had a fantastic relationship and he was as much a part of that Ryder Cup in 2002 as me. There was no way he was slipping away during the celebrations! It was great that I was able to share that with him because we are good friends and without doubt it was the pinnacle of my career by a million miles. Captaining a winning Ryder Cup team is simply the best thing I've ever done in golf and ever will do.

LORD SEBASTIAN COE
DETERMINATION

Sebastian Coe is up there as one of the greatest middle-distance runners the world has ever seen let alone Great Britain and Ireland. A double Olympic champion is hard to find, and certainly at the distance of 1,500 metres the club is extremely small. In fact it consists of just one member – Seb Coe. No man before or after him has ever managed to successfully defend the 1,500 metres gold medal like he did in 1980 and then in 1984 and that tells you something in over 112 years of modern Olympic competition.

Seb was a middle-distance running genius who not only had the talent but also the work ethic and the determination to succeed. He was a ruthless athlete who made the very most of his ability. Together with his father Peter as his coach they worked as a tremendous unit to turn Seb into a British hero of the first order.

His record is quite something having set more world athletics records than any other Briton with nine outdoors and three indoors, and his 800-metre mark that he set in 1979 has still to this day only ever been beaten by one man, Wilson Kipketer. For such a popular distance like that to have only been bettered by one other athlete in 30 years shows Coe's class beyond any question and it shows you that when it comes to something like running you can compare generations perfectly easily and realise that Seb would have been a great whenever he was born.

LORD SEBASTIAN COE

Since his athletics career finished he went on to succeed as a politician, a businessman and a sports administrator until he was given what I believe is the job he is tailor-made for, running the Olympic Games in London.

I first met Seb on *A Question of Sport*, and I thought he would be a ferocious competitor. I thought he would be intense and maybe even a bit moody because I'd heard of his absolute desire to always be the best, but that was only half right. Yes, he was extremely competitive as all the people in this book are, but he was a very captivating bloke too and I can see how he has gone on to achieve the things he has off the track.

Everything he seems to turn his hand to succeeds. He has become a hugely impressive administrator – and in his hands I believe the 2012 Olympic Games in London will not be anything other than a wonderful sporting triumph for the country. Let's face it, if Seb hadn't got involved with the bid it is highly unlikely that we would have got the same happy outcome that we did get. Having Seb on board made the International Olympic Committee sit up and notice us. He was the man who could walk into the sporting corridors of power around the world and get people to listen to what he had to say.

It is not exactly a simple case of show us your medals, but it is something like that and in Seb the London bid had something that no other bid could muster – a giant Olympic middle-distance hero.

We were very lucky during the 1980s when we had a golden generation of middle-distance runners in Steve Ovett, Steve Cram and Seb – all at their peak around the same time, but without being too unfair to the others, I believe Seb was the very best of the bunch. They say you either had to be a Coe or Ovett supporter, such was their rivalry, but I didn't see it like that. I was delighted to see a British winner on the world stage regardless, but writing this book has made me think about it a bit more deeply and there is no question in my mind that Seb was the finest of all time from our shores.

I loved the style with which Seb won his races too, with a tremendous 'kick' towards the end that would take him breezing past the competition when it mattered.

MY SPORTING HEROES

If you watch the way Dame Kelly Holmes went about her work in Athens in 2004, she too hung back a little until right at the death she made her killer move to take the gold in both the 800 metres and 1,500 metres. And I know she laid a great deal of credit at Seb's feet for his inspiration during her formative years.

Middle-distance running is not something that I was particularly interested in until Seb and Steve emerged on the scene but when those two were running, or even just Seb on his own, you wanted to watch and see what they would do. If Seb was running in a race you knew he was probably going to win it and it doesn't matter who you are, I think watching a countryman succeed at sport is one of life's great joys. I will watch sport until the cows come home, but if there is a chance of watching a Brit winning as well then I'll keep watching as the cows go back out and come home again!

To be as good as Seb was at something like running, which is about as straightforward a sporting contest as you will find, you have to have a certain amount of natural ability. The question is what do you do with that ability? There is a great old saying that 'Hard work always beats talent if talent doesn't work hard'. You can have all the natural ability in the world, but if you don't have that drive to be the best you can be and take it as far as you can then you can't be surprised if you fail to achieve.

A lot of the credit for that must be laid at the feet of Seb's father, Peter, and I know just how well they worked together when he was alive. It was a remarkable relationship between father and son, as well as between coach and athlete, but they made it work well despite what you might call a little blip in 1980.

Seb was a versatile athlete who covered all the middle distances with ease, thanks to that extraordinary burst of pace at the end of his races, and at one stage he even held the records for the 800 metres, 1,500 metres and the 'Mile' all at the same time. However, the 800 metres was his favoured event and it was the distance at which he should have claimed his first Olympic gold medal. Seb and Steve Ovett had actually raced each other for the first time as schoolchildren back in 1972 but eight years later it had become a rivalry to whet the appetite of sports fans across the globe. Seb had become so focused and dedicated to beating

LORD SEBASTIAN COE

his countryman in Moscow that he trained twice on Christmas day the year before.

As one of the 20 million viewers who watched that race I could not wait for it to take place. However, when the Olympic final finally arrived Seb had a stinker and calls it 'the worst tactical race of my life', and rather than taking the gold he came a disappointing second to his great rival. He has gone on to say, 'If you want to show a young athlete how not to run a race, show him the video of my performance in that 800-metre final.'

Tactically Seb was usually so astute and strategically clever. The work done off the track is almost a given now as athletes and coaches work out what they have to do at each round before the final and then how they need to race the final depending on who they're facing. There is a lot of information out there now about runners and how they perform, whether they like to hang back, steam ahead and things like that. That sort of attention to detail was something Seb was good at when it wasn't the norm to be good at it, and he usually turned it to his advantage, even though he was outwitted in 1980. It is a skill that I think has served Seb well throughout his life and not just as an athlete. You can see his tactical brain and strategic thinking coming through in his second career.

Having lost out to Steve in a tactical race and been at one of his lowest ebbs this is where the mark of a true champion is revealed. After all the hard work and effort that he had put in, to come up short would have been a devastating blow and even though he had a 1,500-metre final to get ready for his world must have been turned upside down.

But that is why you dedicate yourself to your sport, so that when you get a rare opportunity to do something special you take it. And even if you've already missed out on one, you still have enough about you to take the next one and that is exactly what Seb did. His race in the 1,500 metres final was an emotional triumph of heart, soul, mind and body which put Seb on top of the world with Steve drifting home in third spot.

Having seen Seb raise himself to such heights was as thrilling as the Olympics gets and it showed his character to the world. Over the next few years his career was dogged by illness and it stopped

MY SPORTING HEROES

him from enjoying what could have been the most dominant spell of his career, but after dealing with a viral infection in 1983 he was able to step onto the line for the 1984 Games in Los Angeles and this time there was a young Steve Cram to look out for as well after he had won the 1,500 metres world title.

Again Seb was beaten into silver in the 800 metres as the Brazilian giant Joaquim Cruz won the gold, suggesting that perhaps the illnesses had taken their toll after all. However, he went into the 1,500 metres ready to perform and in a remarkable race in which he and both Steves were in contention for most of the way, his determination brought him the ultimate glory. Steve Ovett was too ill and actually pulled up, but Steve Cram pushed him all the way until the very last when the adrenaline and that famous sprint finish took him to a second Olympic gold.

I was so impressed by that performance to follow up the one four years earlier and told him so the next time I saw him. And even though he never managed to win the 800-metre title that should have been his, he showed that sometimes you have to write your own script when things don't quite work out the way you thought they would.

Since his athletics career finished he has enjoyed a remarkable second career and I've seen him close up in his pin-stripe suit working away with the same kind of dedication he brought to his running. He was a founder member of the Laureus Sport for Good Foundation alongside myself and Daley Thompson and watching him go to work on charitable projects around the world provides a fascinating insight into how he goes about his business.

I'm not sure we'd ever have made a decision about where to help without him. He was always cross-checking, reading between the lines, doing his research to make sure that the money and effort we put into sporting projects around the world was well spent. Before that though his time as a Member of Parliament for Falmouth and Camborne and then later as William Hague's Chief of Staff also gave him the perfect grounding he needed for his new Olympic role.

There couldn't have been a worse time to host the Olympics in terms of the global recession and the economic downturn which has slashed the amount of money both the government and private investors want to plough into the Games. There are financial black holes appearing all over the Games from lottery funding to sponsorship and it is making a tough job even tougher, but I don't think you'd want anyone other than Seb in charge of the project. I would guess there are plenty of countries who missed out on securing the bid who are now thinking, 'Christ, I'm glad they didn't pick us!'

Even though he is facing this huge challenge, Seb is taking it head on and he will get it right, I have no doubt about that.

SHAUN EDWARDS
DEDICATION

For those of a certain age you may remember a 1980s theme tune that went, 'Dedication, dedication, dedication, that's what you need. If you want to be the best and you want to beat the rest, dedication's what you need. If you want to be a record breaker!' As the late Roy Castle sang and tapped his way into the public's hearts as the presenter of *Record Breakers* he could easily have been singing for just one man – Shaun Edwards, the most decorated rugby league player in history and a genuine record breaker.

As far as sporting heroes and rugby legends go he is it. On every scorecard, in every debate, on any criteria you wish to choose, Shaun Edwards comes out on top and for that I have nothing but the utmost respect and admiration for him.

When I think back on his career as a rugby league player first and foremost and now as a rugby union coach, I have to scratch my head and wonder whether it is all true. Can this man have actually been and continue to be that successful? How is it possible that he can win every honour going in rugby league and then switch to a new code and win everything available in that too. It just doesn't make sense, unless you are as gifted, as hard-working and as lucky as Shaun.

I've met Shaun a few times and he is a great man. He comes across as very serious, with serious work to do and I know he has the ability to strike fear into his players and his team-mates, but he is also a lot of fun to be around. He has a laugh and enjoys a social drink so we get on just fine.

The bare truth is that Shaun has put more effort into being the best sportsman that he can be than just about anyone else I know. I have to be fair though and acknowledge that nearly all the people in this book have worked bloody hard at achieving what they have done. And perhaps I shouldn't say that Shaun worked a bit harder than Sir Steve Redgrave, or that Ryan Giggs worked a bit harder than David Beckham. What I know for sure though is that Shaun could not have worked harder to get where he did and the proof was in the pudding.

After joining Wigan as a 17 year old amid a lot of fanfare – even I can remember reading and hearing about this 'wonder kid' they'd signed – he went on to become the game's most successful player in history at the most successful club. Wigan took the game to a whole new level, but in Shaun they had a player who was ready to take his own game to a new level and he wanted those around him to do the same.

He had been training as an athlete from a young age and was good enough to play both rugby league and rugby union for England Schoolboys, but he made his mind up to follow the professional route that meant a better financial life as well as a more structured life that suited his hard-working personality. Having had a rugby league-playing father whose own career was cut short by injury, Shaun knew what he was letting himself in for, but such was his drive and determination to be successful, nothing was going to stand in his way.

As a scrum-half he had such a talent. He had speed, vision and a wonderful set of hands that almost never let him down. Coupled with that was a toughness that goes without saying in rugby league, but still has to be on display in every tackle and every confrontation. I used to watch him make those darting runs of his and look so light and agile, and then bang – in went a crunching tackle that knocked the stuffing out of the opposition and marked his territory on the field.

The Wigan side of the late 1980s and early 1990s was a frightening example of what can be achieved if you have the right ingredients. The players they had from Edwards to Andy Gregory, Martin Offiah, Andy Farrell, Denis Betts and plenty more besides simply tore oppositions apart, and Edwards' ability as a playmaker was absolutely crucial.

The lucky part of Shaun's career is that after a brief spell in the second division he had joined his hometown club which had some serious backing and were prepared to bring the best players to their cathedral at Central Park. As he and other rugby players keep reminding me, it is a team sport and without good players around you, you won't succeed.

Shaun though made sure he succeeded and there is a great story about him in Australia on his first tour with Great Britain where he locked himself in his room, coming out only to train and eat before the second Test. Great Britain went on to win that game and he was the man of the match. That is the kind of total focus and dedication Shaun brought to his game.

As a player he won nine Challenge Cups with Wigan, including eight in a row, he won eight league championships, he won two World Club Challenges including another stunning man-of-the-match display in 1994. Now that pleased me no end because England's cricketers were about to tour Australia that winter and it gave me a bit of ammunition to pile into some of my Aussie mates who think they're the only ones who know how to play rugby league. He also played 36 times for Great Britain and made it to the 1995 World Cup final with England. It was a glittering career that the game had never seen before.

Wigan's dominance throughout that period was called boring by some people, but how can winning be boring? Did Wigan just have to turn up to be handed the trophies? Of course not, they had to work just as hard if not harder year after year to keep winning, and that is what impresses me and is the trait in Shaun that I love. He had no time for second place, he had no interest in taking a training session off because he'd just won his fifth Challenge Cup. As far as he was concerned, winning was all that mattered and he proved it.

There wasn't anything particularly flashy or spectacular about Shaun's rugby; it was just a relentless pursuit of excellence. When I used to watch him play I would often look for something that set him apart from the rest. I would look for that outrageous sidestep like Jason Robinson's, or I'd look for the afterburners like Offiah's and they weren't there. He just did everything as it was supposed to be done and that level of concentration, professionalism and focus is what made him such a remarkable player. Don't get me wrong, he had some serious talent and skill, but it didn't make your jaw drop. He was about doing things right full stop.

If Shaun had retired from the game as he did in 2000, never to be seen again involved in sport then he would have still made this book; however, what he has gone on to achieve in rugby union as a coach puts his position as a sporting hero beyond reproach, and it sums him up better than any words ever could.

His decision to join Wasps as a coach in 2001 was down to two factors. Spending time with his young son James and facing up to a new challenge. He had followed rugby union ever since his schoolboy playing days, but although he knew about fitness, tackling, running and passing a rugby ball, in truth he didn't know too much about the nuances and tactics of the game. Yet under Nigel Melville, then Warren Gatland and now Ian McGeechan he has devoured information, absorbed it like a sponge and has turned himself into one of the pre-eminent rugby union coaches in the game. His dedication to coaching took him to Australia and New Zealand off his own back as he set about turning Wasps from a good club into a great one.

His no-losing philosophy was met with a like-minded Lawrence Dallaglio at Wasps and he brought a similar dynamic that he had had in the Wigan dressing-room to the Wasps dressing-room and it worked. With Shaun at the club they have won four Premiership titles and two European cups, to be the stand-out English rugby union team of the last decade.

It came as no surprise that when Warren Gatland became Wales coach following a dismal World Cup he wanted Shaun to come with him. As soon as the men in charge of England heard that they should have elbowed the 'Welshies' out of the way and said 'hands off!' He is as English as they come and I know he wants to coach his national side at some point, but he also loves his club life and wanted to combine the two. The Welsh said OK and the English let him slip through the net – how short-sighted was that?!

Shaun goes to Wales and surprise, surprise they win the Grand Slam. Some of my Welsh rugby chums have told me just how effective a coach he is and how a period of player power and relaxed attitudes has been replaced with total commitment thanks to a mixture of respect they have for him and Warren, the brilliance of his ideas and a little bit of fear too. You don't mess with Shaun Edwards, that's for sure!

To cap his second career off he has also become a British and Irish Lions coach in 2009. As a player it is the pinnacle and that goes the same for the coaching staff. There are some who claim the Lions coaching party is a bit of a Wasps love-in with four out of five having had an involvement with the club. Well, I don't care if they all came from the same family. If they're the best then they're the best and in Shaun Edwards there is little doubt about that. The tour to South Africa was a brutal and brilliant contest. Two top teams going hammer and tongs at one another. With a little bit of luck the Lions might well have recorded an historic whitewash, but it was not to be. But Shaun acquitted himself well as a coach in the cauldron of top-level international rugby union, helping shape a disparate bunch of world-class players into a formidable defensive unit. A unique achievement.

SHAUN EDWARDS

The influence of my mother and father was enormous. In particular my father's input into my life and career was so important. He had been a professional rugby league player himself before being crippled at 24, and he was the driving force behind me, making me dedicated and making me train hard.

He gave me a lot of constructive criticism as a schoolboy which stood me in good stead for my career and there is no question how important that was to me because at times you had to do things that hurt a little bit and you had to have the strength instilled in you to get past that. Training in the cold, dark, wet evenings is no fun and it is uncomfortable, but you have to do that if you want to achieve things.

SHAUN EDWARDS

When I was 13 I got involved with athletics and started training harder than other players I was up against. It made me one step ahead of the pack because athletics led the way in terms of physical preparation. Anything you want out of sport you have to go out and get. You have to put in the hours and the work and only then will you reap your rewards.

The year-on-year success we had at Wigan was driven by a core group of highly motivated and dedicated professional athletes who just didn't like losing. The financial rewards we received for being successful made it worthwhile, but I think we had a group of players who would do whatever they had to do to win regardless. And the thing about rugby is that unless you've got good players around you then you cannot win, it is impossible. One man certainly doesn't make a team and so the investment made at Wigan to get the best players there was crucial to my success.

As a coach I've always been a willing learner and even though I was a rugby league player I'd always studied both codes. The technical aspects of rugby union took a bit of time for me to grasp, but if you have good teachers and a willing student then you can achieve things. I did a coach education programme and went to spend some time with the great Australian rugby league coach Wayne Bennett and I remember watching the British Lions train while I was there at Ballymore in Brisbane. I looked on with admiration at the whole set-up and it became a long-term goal of mine to get involved.

I had to establish myself as a decent club coach first and thanks to my home away from home at Wasps I was able to do that, but in 2005 after watching the Lions play a couple of games in New Zealand I had the excuse in the back of my head that I wouldn't be able to coach them without any international experience. Luckily, unlike with England, Wales have given me the chance to continue my work with Wasps as well as help coach a national side which has opened the Lions door. It has taken a bit of hard work but that is what the highest level is about.

I've met Beefy a couple of times and I've coached sides to play against his son Liam, who was a good player in his own right. But the last time I spoke to him was one evening in Dublin when I bumped into him with Steve Collins in a hotel. He was having a glass of red wine and I asked him what he was doing the next day and he told me he was flying to northern Scotland from where he would set off and walk to the bottom of England! And that just summed him up as a guy who lives life to the full and has been a hero to so many because he is not a one-dimensional character. He's a top-class sportsman who has made the absolute most of his opportunities.

SIR STEVE REDGRAVE
DEDICATION

Steve Redgrave is the greatest Olympian we've ever produced full stop. He is in the category of the best of the best because no one else can touch him, not only from our shores but worldwide. Five gold medals at five different Games – that makes me tired just thinking about it. He is a true sporting hero for those feats alone; however it is also the way he has dealt with things out of the water that marks him out as a truly special person.

He suffers from dyslexia and colitis, but most disruptive of all was the news in 1997 that he was diabetic and would have to inject himself with insulin every day to keep it at bay. Not many people know that he is a diabetic and he told me that at times, just to balance his body out with all the training he was doing, he had to inject himself with insulin seven times a day. I know what that is like because my daughter has got diabetes and I know how much of a grievance it is and how much frustration it causes her, so for him to do that marks him out in my book.

He thought that his rowing career was over when he found out at the age of 35 and for most sportsmen of that age that would have been true. In fact they wouldn't even need a condition like that to prompt them, but not Steve. Years of careful dedication to his sport and to his body meant that it was just another obstacle to overcome and he set about doing just that.

MY SPORTING HEROES

No one would have minded if he'd kept his promise following the 1996 Olympics when he considered retiring with four gold medals. We all know the famous line about shooting him if he got near a boat, but he knew he had more in him and he wasn't about to let the small matter of diabetes get in the way.

The life and career of a rower is so punishing. You're up at the crack of dawn rowing for miles and miles along the river towards your goal once every four years, and in many ways like running or swimming it is all about the activity you're competing in. If you want to become a better runner, you run and if you want to become a better rower, you row. I don't think I could have done that.

The monotonous nature of it day in day out, getting up and training beyond levels imaginable to most of us is quite remarkable – and let's be honest, rowing is not exactly a sport in which you experience something different each time. You sit in a boat and you row. The water doesn't change; it is still water day after day after day. The oars don't change; they are still heavy in your hands and they require the same action and movement stroke after stroke after stroke. The back of your team-mate's head doesn't change – apart from the odd haircut. But you're still staring at the same bloke doing the same thing day after day after day. Where is the variety? Where is the unpredictability that you get from sports such as football, cricket and rugby where your opponent can do something new to outfox you or you can try something different against them? Where is the new shot that you need to produce in golf if you're in a bunker, or in some rough or behind a tree? Where is the unknown, such as having a live horse underneath you where you have no idea what it is thinking or is going to do next?

Rowing has none of that, which makes the dedication of Steve Redgrave and the rowing community all the more impressive in my opinion. I'm sure there will be rowers galore hurrying along to tell me how wrong I am and how no two races are the same and how every stroke of the oar is different. Maybe, but to my sporting eyes rowing has many great things going for it, but variety is not one of them.

At least with cricket you have the chance to bat, bowl, field, catch, run and stand very, very still! It offers plenty to keep you occupied, but for rowing it is all about rowing. It takes an awful lot of determination and self-discipline and the focus required to maintain that routine is something that I admire.

What always struck me about Steve was that while he was a rower he led a life of denial. He denied himself so much in order to achieve his goals. He rarely drank, he would come along to the odd charity dinner, but he would head off early because training was just around the corner the next morning. But it was a price he was willing to pay and I think everyone is glad that he did.

I'll be honest and admit that rowing is not something that ever really grabbed my attention. Even when Steve won his first gold medal in 1984 I was more interested in what Daley Thompson was up to or Sebastian Coe. When he won again in 1988 I thought he'd obviously done quite well, but it wasn't an earth-moving event. It was only in 1992 when he picked up his third gold medal and his first with Matthew Pinsent that I began to take notice.

Here was this guy winning gold after gold and doing the country proud and it sucked me in. I became interested in what he was doing and started to follow his progress to see whether he could win what would have been an incredible fourth gold. And thank goodness for him in 1996 when he and Matthew became our only British gold medallists of the Games. I'm convinced that the 1996 low point for British sport in the Olympics is part of the reason why there has been such a concerted effort on the part of Olympic sports since then, but we could at least hold our head high that year thanks to him.

By the time 2000 came around his event had become the only one to watch for British supporters. I know we had some fantastic gold medallists throughout those Games, but by virtue of Steve's excellence over such a sustained period, it was all about the rowing for me. When he won, 16 years of Olympic success was completed and it was one of the proudest days in our sporting history.

I had met Steve a few times by then and this thoroughly decent bloke had made all his sacrifices worth it. There was a BBC documentary about his run-up to the Games in Sydney and it showed just how hard he and the rest of the coxless four were training. It showed how early they had to get up and how hard they pushed their bodies – it was frightening. This was just a brief snapshot of what they had been doing, but it made you wonder just how hard Steve must have trained during his lifetime. Since then he has made full use of his position in the public eye and in the public's hearts by raising money for charity and becoming a motivational speaker.

Once he had finally decided to retire for good the next time I bumped into him I noticed such a change. It was as if the shackles were off and you could see a change in him that said, 'Right, what have I been missing out on – I'll have some of that now.' Which is a great reward for all the years of hard work he put into being the best. For years he'd been forgoing those 'treats' and now he could finally relax and enjoy himself. Whenever we go away on charity trips now, no matter what the event he is always now the first one up in the morning and the last one to bed at night. It is as if the blinkers have been taken off and he can now roam free! And what that shows me is how dedicated he was during his rowing career. He supports all my charity walks and events where he can and for that I'm grateful, because after the amount of hard work he has already put in, I wouldn't blame him if he wanted to relax on a beach instead of working harder still.

The one thing that sums Steve up for me is not so much his achievements as a rower, as great as they were. I think Steve's greatest achievement will prove to be the legacy he has left behind in rowing and in the Olympics. Our dominance in rowing is as much down to him as it is to anything because his success paved the way for more funding and more interest in rowing which in itself breeds further success. He is one of the people who has truly woken Britain up to the Olympics and he has turned a sport that not many people get to take part in, into one of the most eagerly anticipated and watched events of the whole Games.

During the Beijing Games in 2008 I found myself glued to the TV watching the coxless fours row themselves to another gold medal and it was one of the events that absolutely everyone was talking about and had watched. The reason for that is down to Steve Redgrave – he has put rowing on the map. When I go and stay with some friends of mine who live near the river in Kent

I'm constantly amazed at how many people are rowing up and down the Thames at six in the morning. I don't remember seeing that in years gone by.

His performances in a boat have helped shape a nation. I suppose we should be good in boats thanks to our island life, but I believe that if it wasn't for Steve Redgrave, rowing would just be something you did with your wife.

DAME TANNI GREY-THOMPSON PASSION

Each and every sportsman and woman has some kind of battle to go through to get to the top. Some find it easier than others to overcome these battles, but every person in this book did just that; they overcame the challenges their sport put in front of them to succeed. In the case of Dame Tanni Grey-Thompson she has overcome more than just a sporting battle, she has faced up to a lifetime challenge and succeeded in such an inspirational way that you can forget about calling her a sporting hero, Tanni is one of my all-time heroes full stop. Being born with spina bifida is something Tanni has learnt to cope with and as a wheelchair Paralympic athlete she has excelled in ways that we can all only dream of. She became our most decorated Paralympic athlete and I gave up counting just how many medals she'd won because it was that many! In doing my research it turns out she's won an incredible eleven Paralympic gold medals for her wheelchair racing over distances from 100 metres to 800 metres, but in addition she has also won the London Marathon six times, which just goes to show how supremely gifted an athlete she is to be as dominant over short distances as she is over long. Just like a cyclist or a sailor, Tanni is able to adapt herself over all sorts of distances and in the end it is her skill, talent and character that bring her out on top.

She first came to my attention following her huge successes at the Barcelona Paralympics where she won four gold medals and added to the golden euphoria surrounding the likes of Sally Gunnell and Linford Christie at the Olympics. As a result she came onto *A Question of Sport* which is where we first met.

If I didn't know how competitive she was before, I certainly knew after that recording. She is just desperate to win, like all champions are, and there is no quarter given. We got on pretty well and remained friends from then on, with her helping me out with my charity walks and with us both doing our bit for the Laureus Sport for Good Foundation.

I also made a point of watching her Paralympic career wherever possible, and as far as I'm concerned she revolutionised the way the Paralympics is viewed, supported, covered and financed.

She has blazed a trail for her sport and for other Paralympic sports and I'm convinced that her success has had such a huge positive impact on the success that our Paralympians have. She is an inspiration to all of us and the way she has battled hard on and off the track for the benefit of so many makes her heroic.

There is no pity or sympathy involved here, simply because like most wheelchair athletes Tanni just doesn't allow it, and even though I've been impressed by her as a person and as a mother since getting to know her, it is her achievements as an athlete that have got her where she is.

Her talent for wheelchair racing was there for all to see at 15 when she won the 100 metres at the junior national wheelchair games, and by the time she was just 19 she had won her first Paralympic bronze medal at Seoul in 1988.

The challenge of dealing with being paralysed from the waist down is more than enough for someone to cope with but the fact that she still had to undergo spinal surgery following those Games highlights just how tough she is. A year away from training and the track clearly took its toll, yet somehow she managed to return to action in time for the 1992 games where she wrote her name into the history books.

To me that showed the sort of grit and determination that any athlete needs to succeed. When you get a knock-back and have to dig even deeper into your reserves, that is when the true character comes out and so it was wonderful to see her do so well.

She trained just as hard if not harder than many able-bodied athletes throughout her career and often with much less recognition. She claims she used her husband Ian as her motivation, since he was a wheelchair athlete too; she was always trying to beat him, which drove her on to greater success against her female opponents.

In 1996 she took home one gold medal and three silvers from Atlanta and there were some who suggested her glory days were over – not that Tanni was about to believe them. Like any true champion that gets beaten, there is only one thing to do, get back to basics, and train harder and longer, to prove just how good you are. That is exactly what Tanni did and her performance at the Sydney Games in 2000 was nothing short of extraordinary. At 31 and with doubts over her ability to take on the rest of the world when it mattered, she shone brighter than ever before to claim another quartet of gold medals in the 100 metres, 200 metres, 400 metres and 800 metres. It was such a huge triumph for hard work and dedication, and she got all the plaudits she deserved.

Her continued success in the Paralympic Games in Atlanta, Sydney and then Athens helped push disability sport to the front of people's consciousness during the Games. Like many able-bodied sports we only really hear about them during the Olympics and it is from that moment of success that things get to improve for the sport. In the same way that track cycling now has a higher profile and is receiving more sponsorship thanks to the efforts of Sir Chris Hoy and co, so too the same can be said for Paralympic sports thanks to Tanni. Her third place in the BBC Sports Personality of the Year awards behind her great friend Sir Steve Redgrave showed just how much the British public admire a winner full stop and that is exactly what she is.

Even though Tanni is incredibly warm and funny with those that know her, I can imagine that she must have had plenty of frustration dealing with idiots who don't really understand just how it all works. She tells a good story about how sometimes people ask her whether she trained at all for her sport! That kind of ignorance is thankfully being steadily eradicated thanks to her and other successful Paralympians.

She is a wonderful person, such a kind and generous soul, but she is as tough as they come. She has as much inner strength and steel as any person I know. She is a gladiator of wheelchair racing and she takes no prisoners.

When you watch the wheelchair races on television it can seem like quite a serene and straightforward sport, but just like the able-bodied races they can be fearsome and tactically ruthless. Chairs clash all the time and you've got to be strong to come out on top. Knowing Tanni like I do, it is no surprise that she came out on top as often as she did.

I've always thought she is one of the gutsiest competitors I've ever seen and there is no better example of that than when I call her up and tell her I've got a charity walk on and she is absolutely hell bent on doing the toughest leg she can do.

She likes to do a Welsh leg because of her heritage and her support for a children's hospital she has been instrumental in raising money for down there, but the first question she will always ask me is, 'Which is the toughest day?' Whichever it might be that is the one she will do with me. That is simply the nature of the beast and that is what makes her an automatic for this book.

I can remember doing a stretch of the walk in south Wales, near Aberfan, and I remember she had her racing wheelchair with her and we made our way up this hill. It wasn't too bad an incline, but it was a 'double-black' run downhill and the same again going up the other side. Now I hate walking downhill; it is really hard work on the legs and the steeper it is the more agony it causes. This hill was a tricky one because as it reached the bottom there was a little chicane before you went over a bridge before beginning the climb up. Tanni turned to me and said, 'I've got to give myself a chance here,' so from the top she launched herself down this slope and she must have hit terminal velocity about halfway down! She was travelling at an almighty speed, probably somewhere near 40 miles an hour, and by the time she got to the bottom, the skill she displayed in manoeuvring the chair through that bend, it was as like Lewis Hamilton negotiating Monte Carlo. I don't know how she did it but she kept a lot of speed going through the turn and it got her through the first quarter of the hill climb and then she started powering those arms of hers to get up the rest.

Near the top she was struggling a bit more so she turned the chair around and pulled herself up the final few yards backwards. Absolutely no one must touch the chair, even if she comes to a complete stop; you leave that chair alone or face the wrath of a very angry woman. The bigger the challenge the more you get out of her.

She got to the top and then so did I, and I was feeling OK having preferred the walk up over the walk down, but seeing how hard she worked to get up I thought she qualified for my medicinal juice. This juice is an orange and tequila concoction that has got me through many a tough section of my walks and I save it for myself and others who deserve it. I give it out when I see people in some real pain and when Tanni got to the top I thought that was a case in point. So I handed her the bottle and she said, 'Oh good, orange juice,' and took a huge glug of it. She nearly passed out in her chair if it wasn't for her scream, 'What on earth is in that!!' I told her it was just a bit of medicine! As a result she now won't take anything from me to drink unless it has been thoroughly checked beforehand!

I was absolutely delighted when she received her damehood in 2005, and I can think of no more deserving recipient, not just because of her athletic achievements which put her out on her own, nor because of the tireless work she does off the field for charity and helping the likes of me, but also for what she has done for disability sport and for those less fortunate than us around the world.

She was elected to the Laureus World Sport Academy in 2006 and is now the vice-chairman which tells you something about her passion for whatever she gets involved in. The work we do at Laureus is very dear to my heart and to see her so heavily involved makes me feel very proud of her and also reassures me that our future work is in a safe pair of hands.

DAME TANNI GREY-THOMPSON

It was only halfway through university that I thought I could be really good at wheelchair racing. I had gone to Loughborough for the sport and I had shown a little bit of promise beforehand, but it took me until then to really make my mark, but it was always something that I wanted to do. I had so much enthusiasm for what I was doing that it seemed like the most natural thing in the world for me to do. I suppose that is what youth does for you.

The back surgery I had in 1989 actually happened at a good time for me because I was able to come back strong for 1992, but it took a lot of hard work to get there. I was training twice a day, six days a week, fifty weeks of the year, which was just physically hard especially when a lot of the time you're training on your own. But the important thing is that I loved doing it, and no one was making me do it. People often ask me whether I was lonely doing it and the answer is no!

Once I started winning the hard thing to deal with was public expectation. People just thought, after Barcelona, that I just turned up and won and that was it.

I was hugely self-critical and that made me train harder because I just never felt like I'd done enough. I'm incredibly stubborn and I had an internal drive that made me just want to keep going and going, and it is actually quite hard to explain. Even after the Sydney and Athens Games, I still didn't think I'd done enough nor was I good enough. I had a fear of failure and a fear of all sorts of things and together they all kept me going. It is only at the end of my career and when I look back on it that I can say, 'Yeah, I did enough and my career was alright.'

Paralympic sport is now a million miles away from what it was like when I started. We didn't have an institute of sport, we didn't have lottery funding, we just didn't have anything really, it was just what you did on your own. When I was racing it was up to me to be successful because it was my money I was spending, which I think was really good for me and it made me realise that it was what I wanted to do.

When I started people used to say, 'Ah bless, isn't that lovely that you can do the marathon!' in a really patronising tone, but thankfully you don't get that too much any more.

At least they certainly wouldn't be saying that following a leg of Ian's charity walks which really are hard work. The marathon might be over in an hour and a half, but this is four or five hours' worth of toil including on the steep slopes where I've got to pull myself up backwards to stop flipping over. I hurt for days and days after that!

It is great being involved with Laureus along with Ian because we both get to see how sport changes lives for people all over the world, and I quite enjoy being involved as a trustee on the board where you're dealing with budgets and things like that.

A trip to Rwanda put things into perspective for me especially when a Paralympic athlete from the squad phoned me up to moan about their lottery funding and I had to put the phone down knowing that a school I'd visited had just $3 per week to feed the kids there. It was really humbling and a lesson for us all that no matter what your circumstances are in the UK there are those much worse off than you.

TONY JACKLIN
LEADERSHIP

When you're a top-level sportsman or woman, your only concern really is how well you can do, or how well you can play to help your team win. Those are the only real considerations you need to have. If you can entertain and be stylish with it then that's even better, or if you can do something new and different to take your sport to a new level then that certainly gets a tick in my book. What I don't think you can do is go out and play with the thought of what you might be leaving behind when you're done, yet that is perhaps the greatest achievement a sportsperson can have – an enduring legacy.

When it comes to golf, Tony Jacklin's legacy is in a league of its own, not so much for his performances on the golf course but for what he did off it. Don't get me wrong, his golfing career in which he won two Majors in the shape of the British Open in 1969 and the US Open in 1970 is enough to qualify him as anyone's sporting hero, but for me it is what he did for the Ryder Cup that makes him a legend.

Tony took a competition that was dying on its backside thanks to American dominance and European laziness and turned it into the most hotly contested match-play golfing tournament in the world. He is without question the European godfather of the Ryder Cup and without him one of the greatest sporting contests would never have survived.

MY SPORTING HEROES

Looking back over his career though, it would be remiss of me to acknowledge just how special a golfer Tony was in his prime. And his prime came relatively early in his career. By the time he was twenty-six he had already won two Major championships and had set the new standard for British golf. At the time British golf was going nowhere fast. There hadn't been a British champion in a Major for 18 years before Tony came along and after his twin successes there wasn't another British winner for 15 years until Sandy Lyle claimed the Open in 1985.

Tony literally stood alone as the man carrying the flag for British golf and I shudder to think what the game might have become on our shores if it wasn't for him. As we've seen in so many sports, success breeds success and without people like Tony, you wouldn't then get the Sandys or Nick Faldos or Ian Woosnams of this world. The more I think about Tony's golf career the more it impresses me, and the greater debt of gratitude I think we owe him.

If I'm honest my ability to play golf hadn't fully developed by the time Tony won his Majors because I was busy trying to forge my way in the cricket world, but as I've got older and more adept at handling a golf club it has become one of the biggest passions in my life. I've always loved the game and secretly would have loved to have been a successful golfer if I hadn't been a cricketer, but that wasn't to be.

Since Tony won the US Open back in 1970 no Briton has ever claimed the prize, which tells me a couple of things about his triumph. Firstly that he must have played some sensational golf to win it, and judging by the reports I read at the time the course at Hazeltine Golf Club was playing particularly tough due to high winds. He was the only player to break par for that tournament, leading from start to finish, and his seven-stroke final winning margin was the biggest in nearly fifty years. It was an amazing victory, no make that procession,from him and it has yet to be matched by anyone from these shores.

Secondly, it also tells me that the mental strength and toughness you need to succeed away from home, which a lot of sportsmen don't have, was there in abundance. It shows that when he got taken out of his comfort zone and into the American bear pit he was able to shine.

TONY JACKLIN

You have to remember that the 1960s and '70s were all about the American golfers like Arnold Palmer, Jack Nicklaus and Lee Trevino, so for Tony to upset their apple cart was magnificent. After his two Major successes Tony struggled to live up to the same standards. He might have had another Open victory in 1972 had it not been for Trevino's chip in on the 17th green in the final round that gave him a one-stroke lead. From there though Tony's golfing career refused to reach the dizzy heights he once had and it was to be his work with the Ryder Cup that cemented his place in history and in my heart as one of my heroes.

He had already enjoyed some memorable moments with the Ryder Cup such as the greatest show of sportsmanship from Nicklaus in 1969 where with Tony needing a five-foot putt to share the Cup, Jack conceded the shot to make sure that his foe didn't have to go through the possible embarrassment of missing it. It was a wonderful gesture that is as much a part of British sporting folklore as Andrew Flintoff's heartfelt handshake with Brett Lee in the 2005 Ashes win at Edgbaston.

It was the only time in seven attempts that Tony didn't finish up on the losing side during his time as a player as the Americans dominated. Even when the British team was opened up to include Ireland in 1973 and then mainland Europe in 1979 nothing changed. America won and the Europeans floundered. In truth the European operation was being run in such an amateurish way that it was hardly surprising. They had shoddy equipment, shoddy clothes, shoddy management and shoddy behaviour.

That was until Tony took charge. He had experienced the rough side of the Ryder Cup as a player and so when he was asked to be captain in 1983 he made it clear that things had to change. It was a brave move from him, and one that could have backfired spectacularly. He demanded that the team travel not just first class, but by Concorde, he wanted caddies to be allowed on board, he wanted a team-room at the players' hotel, separate food and drink for the team and he wanted the best threads they could get.

After such a humiliation in 1981 when Europe lost 18.5 to 9.5 he got his wishes, but his biggest request of all was to get Seve Ballesteros back in the fold. Incredibly, Seve was left out of the side in 1981 despite being one of the best golfers in the world. His flamboyant and thrilling personality didn't sit well with some of the 'stuffed shirts' running the team, and so Tony had to fight to get him back in 1983. It oh so nearly paid off as a strong American side were taken to the wire, only just edging it 14.5 to 13.5 in Florida. Seve was to be Tony's general out on the course and it worked brilliantly; the Ryder Cup had been energised by the close fight and Tony rightly got another shot at glory.

The 1985 Ryder Cup is a tournament I will never forget because it was the first European victory for 28 bloody long years, and my old mate Sam Torrance was the lucky man to drain the winning putt. The success of that team though came from some brilliant captaincy from Tony who again had to be brave to get the right result.

Because of Tony's dedication to the team philosophy Europe began to dominate the four-balls and foursomes as they worked together in tandem. With Seve playing brilliantly alongside his countryman Manuel Pinero, the tone was set in the pairings. However, with only a two-point lead going into the final day singles, Tony's men had their work cut out. His stroke of genius was to change a long-held tradition where your best players go out at the end to bring home the points when they're supposedly needed. Tony worked out though that with 14.5 points required to win the Cup, what was the point of having your best players coming into the final holes if the Cup has already been lost? He stuck his main man Seve in at number four in the list followed by Sandy, and Bernhard Langer. It worked a treat as Sam wrapped things up by the seventh match. Europe actually lost three out of the last four matches, but it didn't matter; they were the champions!

From there the Europeans became an unstoppable force as they claimed their first ever success on American soil in 1987 before retaining the Cup in 1989 under Tony's expert tutelage. In the blink of an eye, the Ryder Cup had gone from being a dud event to being a must-watch, must-win, must-attend competition.

The credit for the success that Europe now has in the Ryder Cup by winning eight out of the last twelve can be laid squarely at the feet of Tony, and I know for a fact that the likes of Seve, Bernhard, Sam and Ian Woosnam, who have all captained winning sides, respect the godfather of the Cup for his amazing work. He was the man that said enough was enough and injected some much-needed razzmatazz. As a result it is the Americans who get excited if they win one now and until their win in 2008 I was beginning to get worried that the Americans would actually pull out of the Ryder Cup and stop it because they were getting beaten so often!

I've said it throughout this book and about a number of the great sportsmen and women that appear within these pages, but the plain fact remains the same that the greatest victories often occur in the aftermath of the worst defeats. It is how you deal with these tough times that define you as a person as much as anything else.

In Tony's case the private and then public turmoil he went through when he lost his wife Viv to a brain haemorrhage in 1988 was just about the hardest thing anyone can go through. His life was turned upside down and from the joyous scenes he would have been a part of in Florida to the devastation of losing his wife I just can't imagine how tough it would have been.

He then had to suffer at the hands of the British press who can be quite cruel sometimes in the way they report the private lives of people in the public eye. I've been there and so too was Tony, even though he was just trying to get his life back into some kind of order. Sometimes we don't treat the people we should be proudest of particularly well. Even so, through that difficult period he managed to get to the other side thanks to his second wife Astrid and I'm pleased that things worked out better for him than they might have done.

Incredibly, he was able to focus on the job in hand with the Ryder Cup at the Belfry in 1989 and after he'd triumphed once again there is a famous photo of him hugging the Cup which I think revealed just how much the success meant to him at that time.

Tony has achieved an awful lot in golf apart from these successes, but it is for these reasons that I admire him so much. I've met him a couple of times and have got on well with him when we've had a brief chat. He has always struck me as a very determined man who is confident about what he is trying to achieve, whatever it might be.

MY SPORTING HEROES

I've been lucky enough to get a ringside view of the Ryder Cup over the years thanks to 'Woosie' and Sam. The hype and the expectation around it is like nothing else, and it reminds me a little bit of an Ashes series when it comes to the level of competition and the amount of national pride riding on it. For that I thank Tony Jacklin, our godfather of the Ryder Cup.

WILLIE CARSON
PASSION

The world of horse racing is a world like no other. It has its own rules and regulations, its own language and customs, and to the uninitiated it can be hard to fathom. What is clear though is that the better the rider the better the horses he gets and the more of them too. It is why the champion jockey often wins that accolade more than once, but it still takes a lot of hard work and effort to get the wins you need to be triumphant.

It is incredibly tough to get the consistent performances you need to get the good rides in the first place. It can be a bit of a vicious circle in that bad horses can make even the best jockeys look poor, so if you're not winning on poor horses it can be hard to show that you deserve better ones and even then just because you've got a half-decent horse it doesn't necessarily mean you are going to win.

I think the one good thing about this system is that there can be a lot of opportunities to ride full stop, so if you're good enough you can get unexpected results out of the bad nags and then as long as you don't make silly mistakes with the good ones you should get spotted – although as we all know sport doesn't necessarily work like that.

Much like Nigel Mansell in motor sport or Ian Wright in football, Willie had to pay his dues to get to the exalted position he ended up in and it wasn't a walk in the park. Having been an apprentice at Middleham he then moved to Newmarket under Sam Armstrong and it was there that he first made a real impact on the racing world, winning fifty-eight races in four seasons, but it took him twenty-two rides before he got that first winner.

Some champions know they are champions from the moment they can walk, while others take a little bit longer to convince not only the wider world how good they are but also themselves, and I think Willie is a case in point. He has said that in the early days he didn't feel that he was getting better quickly enough and deep down he didn't think he was very good because he couldn't handle the horses he wanted to. That all changed soon enough.

As a working-class lad from Stirling, Willie was soon hobnobbing it with the upper echelons of the racing society and his big break came when Lord Derby decided to take him on at his yard under trainer Bernard van Cutsem. It was there that he won his first classic – the 2000 Guineas Stakes on High Top. It showed that he really could mix it with the big boys and all this after quite a serious accident, not from the track mind, from a car crash that left him with a broken leg and a broken jaw, and needing 27 stitches in his head.

That was long behind him in 1972 when he not only claimed that first Classic winner, but also became Champion Jockey for the first time. If anything would have convinced him just how good a rider he was, this was it. He was getting the good horses and doing the business with them, leaving some of the greats of the racing world in his wake. One in particular that cast a huge shadow over Willie and the rest of the jockeys at that time was of course Lester Piggott. He was the man to beat throughout the 1960s and '70s and after winning eight consecutive Champion Jockey titles that is exactly what Willie did.

In 1972–73 Willie took that coveted title away from Lester and that was a sign of the fierce rivalry the pair were to have throughout their careers. Willie was growing in stature if not in height all the time! He was riding winner after winner and the 1970s were being very good to him.

A couple of changes of yard had him under the legendary Major Dick Hern, who looked after royal horses at West Isley, and it was there that he really found a place for himself in the hearts of the British public.

I was busy making my Test debut in 1977 and as the Queen's Jubilee year it was a very special one. Virginia Wade was busy winning Wimbledon and on the track Willie was doing Her Majesty proud by winning the Oaks on Dunfermline – her horse. We're both incredibly proud of our country's Royal Family and I know that winning for the Queen in such a special year ranks right up there for him. Once he had done that it was only a matter of time before he won the biggest flat race of them all – the Epsom Derby.

In 1979 he smuggled home his first Derby winner on a horse aptly named Troy and it was a sneaky victory because he had been so far back in the field. Coming round Tattenham Corner he was seriously lagging, but the horse was a supreme specimen and sprinted home to give Willie the win every flat jockey craves.

When he grabbed his second win the following year, Willie had officially become English horse racing's latest superstar and he did something that only superstars can do by winning three classics in five days in the Derby, the Oaks and the French Derby.

I was only taking a passing interest in horse racing then, but it is fair to say that my love of horse racing and those grand days grew with my international cricket career, and I've been lucky enough to watch races all over the world as a result. I was first introduced to the horses by my mentor at Somerset, Brian Close, who would have a transistor radio strapped to one hand and a copy of *Sporting Life* in the other. He tried to show me the way, but my knowledge of horses was very limited then and as a young player it wasn't really the focus for me.

I got into horse racing quite a bit more when I started owning horses in the mid-1980s and it was during that time that I began to understand the racing world a bit more and could appreciate just how good someone like Willie Carson was as a jockey.

All my horses operated on the flat and I would have loved to get Willie on board one of them, but I didn't really operate at his level – I think the Queen was always going to get first dibs on a jockey like Willie over me!

MY SPORTING HEROES

I really first got to know Willie when he was on *A Question of Sport* as a team captain, and then of course in subsequent years when I was a captain he came on a few times. We both had a love for horse racing and there was always a lot of banter and flying about.

I can remember during the picture round once, Willie got this picture up of a jockey and his face was obscured by his goggles and some mud down the side of his face. I turned to Willie and said, 'Come on little man, you can get that one for me no trouble.' He said, 'Oh Beefy. I'm not so sure about that one, it's a bit distorted with the mud and the goggles. I can't quite make it out. I think I know who it is, but I'm really not sure.'

Anyway, after lots of 'oohing' and 'ahhing', and scratching of heads and chins – Willie loved to make a bit of drama out of an answer – he eventually said, 'It's Pat Eddery!' David Coleman chuckled in that way of his and told him he was wrong, it was in fact Lester Piggott. Willie was crestfallen and held his head in his hands. I just tapped him on the shoulder and said, 'Don't worry Willie, I shouldn't have expected you to get that, after all I supposed you're only used to seeing his backside!'

Willie does make me laugh though; he has a great sense of humour and he can laugh at himself, which I think is essential in this life. He was one serious competitor when it came to racing but out of the saddle he is a lot of fun and I suppose when you're standing as small as he does you've got to be able to laugh. I think he carries a cushion everywhere he goes! He did so well as a jockey in an era that included three of the greatest jockeys the horse racing world has ever seen in Willie, Lester and Pat.

The only thing that surprised me was that he never went into training when he finished. I know he took on a stud farm and breeds horses, but that actual bread-and-butter work of training a horse from start to finish I thought would be right up his street. He has such a passion and love for horses and for racing horses I thought that he would make a fine trainer. He really does live and breathe horse racing – it is in his blood. You can see the enthusiasm and the passion he has for it when he co-presents the BBC's coverage alongside Clare Balding – and he really does need a step box for those moments on camera. He loves being around

WILLIE CARSON

racecourses and he loves the whole atmosphere of a big race day. It is a wonder he ever leaves.

I saw Willie race many a time and what I liked about him and his style was that he always seemed to give the horse a good run rather than ease around a course. He always thought he could win on a horse even if the punters and the bookies didn't. And in a sport that has got its fair share of detractors who suspect that all is not as kosher as it should be, Willie stood out as a man who always went out to win. I guess it is ingrained in a champion's psyche that you compete to the best of your ability and if you can't do that then you're better off out of it.

I used to watch Willie race all over the place and he was one of the few jockeys that I would back regardless of what anyone told me. I thought if Willie was riding then that horse has got a chance – and thankfully he brought home the bacon a few times for me which pushes him up a notch in my estimation!

He is just a lovely little bloke who always seemed to be there or thereabouts when it came to flat racing. He went on to be Champion Jockey five times no less, although he actually came second in his biggest year of winners. In 1990 he managed to cross the line first a whopping one hundred and eighty-seven times including six at one meeting in Newcastle, but was still beaten to the title by Pat Eddery who claimed two hundred and nine.

It didn't matter too much though because Willie's position in horse racing had long since been secured. When he retired in 1996 he had ridden 3,828 winners and was the fourth most successful British jockey of all time, and that is a remarkable achievement.

To me the name Willie Carson is synonymous with success and fun. He has always been great to be around unless you're riding against him – at which point he casts an awfully big shadow for one so small.

WILLIE JOHN McBRIDE
LEADERSHIP

Quite simply Willie John McBride is a legend of British and Irish rugby, thanks to his incomparable deeds for the Lions, and to me he epitomised everything that is good about the game of rugby union.

There is something about the British and Irish Lions that stirs the heart. The idea that the cream of our four nations can knock lumps out of each other throughout the Six Nations and then come together with a common goal to take on the might of Australia, South Africa or New Zealand is such a fanciful one that it somehow works.

You'll not find a more intense rivalry than that between England and Scotland, yet on a Lions tour they stand together side by side as team-mates and they have to be prepared to treat each other as brothers. Only under a captain of the stature of a Willie John McBride will you get that genuine bond. Only under a man like Willie do you find some kind of common goal to put your differences aside and put your body on the line.

Unlike in cricket where individuals can still succeed without much help from their team-mates, rugby sides will be horribly exposed if there is a chink of weakness in the link and from that sort of starting point you get something like the '99' call on the 1974 tour to South Africa. The '99' call has gone down in the folklore of Lions rugby and essentially meant that no Lion would be left to fight on his own if things got ugly; instead the shout '99!!' would go up and everyone in a red jersey would pile in for all they were worth. Strict disciplinary structures and television cameras everywhere means that we're unlikely to see something similar now, but in 1974 it was needed and it worked a treat.

In cricket you make your point with a thunderous shot or a wickedly fast bouncer. There might be a stare and a few choice words, but physically there is nothing you can do. On a rugby field in the mid-'70s there was plenty you could do and the '99' call in the violent third Test was a brutal example. The Lions decided they would not take a backward step against the Springboks, who were regarded as the most aggressive rugby nation, and after two defeats in the first two Tests it was inevitable things would kick off at some point. Rather than sit back and let the South Africans beat them by fair means or foul, Willie's side took matters into their own hands and fought their way to a historic win that sowed a seed for the Lions organisation that remains today.

I've known Willie for quite a few years now and when I think of him I'm reminded of when he turned up on one of my charity walks on the leg from Belfast to Dublin, and he presented me with a huge bottle before we set off. It was just about the biggest medicine bottle you had ever seen and he simply said, 'Beefy, this part of the walk could be a bit of a test for you. Ireland is a beautiful country but it might wear a little heavy on those legs of yours so I've brought you some medicine to get you through it.' As many people will know I already had a little concoction that I used to help me through the walks – a mixture of tequila and orange which doubles up as either a painkiller or rocket fuel depending on the stage of the walk. This was something altogether different.

'It is a brew of my homemade poitín!' exclaimed Willie. Well, I always like to try new things and the best way to describe this particular drop was that it tasted like 120 per cent proof Benylin cough syrup. It was stunning stuff and I can promise you it got me through that leg in better shape than I could have imagined.

It was a typical gesture of the guy who is as gentle a giant as you will ever meet. I bumped into him not long ago and despite being a little greyer and carrying a few more laughter lines, he was exactly the same man I met back in Ireland after a Six Nations match when England were captained by Bill Beaumont. I had just rocked up as a punter to watch the game and to see Bill, and he introduced me to Willie with a touch of reverence and respect, which I thought was a sign I was meeting someone special – and with five Lions tours to his name I clearly was. I'd watched him play for the Lions and I'd heard about him in rugby circles, so I wanted to know what all the fuss was about and it was a pleasure. He treated me and all the people with us just the same. He's got a dry wit and knowledge of the game that is second to none; I actually just enjoyed listening to him and to his stories about Lions tours of years gone by.

I know it is a well-known anecdote these days, but I thoroughly enjoyed listening to him as he told me the famous story about him on the same 1974 Lions tour to South Africa when after a Test match victory his players got a little raucous with their celebrations and caused a bit of a mess and a bit of damage to the hotel they were staying in. The way Willie was telling the tale I could almost have been there myself – and I'm sure I'd have enjoyed it too!

As a result the hotel manager turned to him and said, 'I'm sorry, Mr McBride, but we've had to call the police because your players are out of control.'

Willie serenely took a drag on his pipe and asked, 'Will there be many of them?'

He was a calm, unflustered leader of men who knew what being a sportsman was all about both on and off the field. He was as fierce a competitor as any and he wouldn't yield an inch to the opposition if he could help it. I love that tough, in-your-face approach in sport and I was always up for the confrontation that international sport provides.

With the Lions concept whatever you gain in quality, you lose in organisation, team spirit and understanding. All the features that often take years to gel together for clubs or national sides have to be found in the space of weeks and that is what makes the challenge so hard.

WILLIE JOHN McBRIDE

For Willie John McBride to have played a key role in the one and only win in New Zealand as the pack leader, and then to skipper the first ever win in South Africa speaks volumes for him as a player and a leader and it is why he has made my list.

He had an ability to get people around him to gel into a tight unit and to play as one, which is absolutely vital for any sports team let alone a Lions side. And I am convinced that the reverence held for the Lions to this day is a result of Willie's sides in the 1970s. Before that 1971 tour to New Zealand the Lions had been in the doldrums and Willie had been through the tough times with them, losing almost every match they played in the 1960s, so when they set off for New Zealand, a place where rugby is more important than breathing, no one gave them a hope. But with the Welsh producing some of the greatest rugby players ever to walk the earth, the Lions not only gave a good account of themselves but they became the first and still only side to win a Test series in the land of the long white cloud.

That win gave the British and Irish Lions a much-needed shot in the arm and it restored the faith in the idea that the best of British could compete and overcome the rest of the world.

I don't think it says enough to suggest these players would have run through a brick wall for him; they became brothers in arms and the bond ran much deeper than just being team-mates on a pitch. They became friends for life through high jinks off the field and passionate rugby on it, and to foster those kinds of relationships takes special leadership. Not many sportsmen have it, but the best cricket teams I ever played in were ones where the captain took control and every other player was prepared to put their ego aside and do their bit. Willie earned that kind of respect.

Recently the England and Wales cricket board have come up with a nice idea regarding new Test players. Whenever a player makes his debut for England he now gets his cap officially presented by a notable former England cricketer. It adds a bit of ceremony to a very special occasion in their career and I think it is a nice touch. I've been lucky to be asked to do the job a couple of times for Stuart Broad and for Graeme Swann and I don't think they had their tongues in their cheeks when they told me it gave them a buzz to get their cap from an old timer like

MY SPORTING HEROES

me. Even though I spend a fair bit of time around the England team through my television work, it is nice to have the chance to share a few quiet words with a young player about playing for England and hopefully passing on a few traditions and thoughts that might help them. My time is most certainly over and it is about getting the best out of the guys doing the job now, so it came as no surprise to me that Willie John McBride was chosen as the man to hand out the Lions jerseys of the 2001 vintage for their battle with Australia. It had been fully 27 years since he last wore the jersey in anger, but his standing in the game remained and when you hear of great players such as Jason Robinson and Brian O'Driscoll describe what it meant to them to have Willie do the honours you can understand just what a mark he has left on the game. They spoke of him in awe and O'Driscoll called him an inspiration to the Irish players that followed him into Lions folklore – spot on in my book.

There are lots of ways of thrilling a crowd on the sports field and I'm a huge fan of anyone who plays their game with style, verve and charisma, but in a game like rugby union you rarely get a chance to see the jinking feet of a winger or the shimmying hips of a centre if the grunt work hasn't been done by the forward pack. As a towering second row Willie was one of the men who got on with plenty of that grunt work and it is why he failed to get his name on the scoresheet for Ireland for all bar one of his sixty-three internationals. That his one and only try came in his final match to win a tight game over the French (and you've got to love that) was a wonderful way to cap a truly great career. Willie John McBride is my ultimate rugby hero.

ACKNOWLEDGEMENTS

Putting this book together has been a labour of love because it has forced me to think long and hard about the people I rate in sport and what it takes for them to achieve what they have won. However I couldn't have done it without the help and support of a few people.

Firstly I'd like to offer a big thank you to the sportsmen and women within these pages for providing me – and the general public – with such wonderful entertainment and memorable moments over the years. Through your achievements on and off the sports field you have demonstrated all the necessary qualities that go into making athletes truly great and this book is a small nod to that.

In addition I'd like to offer special thanks to those in the book that helped me by collaborating and offering some insights into their careers. I've been lucky enough to meet a lot of the people mentioned in this book, but that doesn't mean they will automatically drop everything and spend a bit of time chatting about their lives. They are all tremendously busy people so the fact they did contribute means an awful lot and I hope you will find that their comments make the book an even better read.

When I first discussed the idea for this book with my agent, and friend, Adam Wheatley (of Mission Sports Management) we came up with a few ideas of how it could work and just how it could all come together with a publisher who might share our vision and in Iain MacGregor of Mainstream publishing we found that man. With Adam driving the project together alongside Iain we found a working blend that isn't always possible, but when it comes together like it has is a real joy to be a part of. The team at Mainstream have been a vital source of support and ideas to help this book come to fruition and I can't thank them enough.

This book has been worked on for some time in some of the deepest corners of the world from India to Guyana, so I would also like to that the various hotels and cricket grounds that provided me with a quiet spot to work in when I've needed it. My boating chum Rod Bransgrove also has to fall into that list and his generosity in providing the perfect working environment is much appreciated.

Finally I'd like to thank 'the Ghost' Dean Wilson for his efforts in pulling the book together and helping me craft some decent anecdotes about some of the world's greatest sports stars into a coherent narrative. It has been great to have a guy like him alongside me that I can trust, and who shares my passion for decent wine although his lessons have only just started!